MICHAEL
BETWEEN THE LINES
CARRICK

MICHAEL
BETWEEN THE LINES
CARRICK

MY AUTOBIOGRAPHY

BLINK
bringing you closer

Published by Blink Publishing
2.25, The Plaza,
535 Kings Road,
Chelsea Harbour,
London, SW10 0SZ

www.blinkpublishing.co.uk

facebook.com/blinkpublishing
twitter.com/blinkpublishing

Hardback – 978-1-788700-49-8
Trade Paperback – 978-1-788700-50-4
Ebook – 978-1-788700-51-1

A CIP catalogue of this book is available from the British Library.

Printed and bound by Great Britain by Clays Ltd, Elcograf S.p.A

1 3 5 7 9 10 8 6 4 2

Every reasonable effort has been made to trace copyright holders of material
reproduced in this book, but if any have been inadvertently overlooked the
publishers would be glad to hear from them.

Blink Publishing is an imprint of Bonnier Books UK
www.bonnierbooks.co.uk

To Lisa, Louise and Jacey

CONTENTS

1

RED

I didn't just play for Manchester United. I lived for them. My whole life is wrapped around the place. Whatever I do and wherever I go, Manchester United are always in my mind and in my heart. I love and grasp the challenge Manchester United set me. You see, there's no escape when you play for this great club. Pressure and expectation levels are off the scale here. Some players can handle it and enjoy it, others can't. It's relentless.

I thought I was dedicated before I arrived at United but I was nowhere near. Monday 31 July 2006 was the day my life changed forever when I joined a club famous throughout the world. The Manchester United story is the stuff of legends – the Busby Babes, the Munich Air Disaster, George Best, Sir Bobby Charlton, Bryan Robson, the Class of '92, Sir Alex Ferguson, the '99 Treble, and on it goes. The history, tradition and culture make Old Trafford such a special place. When I arrived from Tottenham Hotspur, I was immediately swept away by the power and romance of Manchester United and went on an adventure I could never have dreamed of. I've been one of the lucky few to represent this incredible football club and never once have I taken this privilege for granted. I made sacrifice after sacrifice to be the best I could and I carry that responsibility with great pride.

I'm just a normal lad from Wallsend in the north-east, nothing special, no better or worse than anybody else, and I feel unbelievably fortunate to be at a club that lifts the lives of so many people from so many backgrounds. The emotion United brings into people's lives is something quite beautiful. I love to see United fans celebrating and sharing their passion as if their lives depend on it. At Old Trafford, the sight and sounds of 75,000 people coming to support us every single week is magical. It's not them and us. It's us. From the beginning I've been a fan, just one with his boots on and carrying more responsibility and pressure. From the start, I learned all the United songs, educated myself in the club's history and became so passionate about United that I promised myself that one day I'd stand shoulder to shoulder with our fantastic away support at a match. I heard our supporters at every away game, always loud and proud, and I craved the chance to join in with that party. The opportunity presented itself on 17 January 2016 when I was injured for the game at Liverpool, our most bitter rival. At first the club were concerned for safety reasons about me going in with the fans. They wanted me to be in the directors' box instead.

'Thanks, but no chance,' I replied. 'I'm going in with the fans.'

Phil Jones was also injured and heard what I was up to. 'Are you going in with the fans, Carras?!'

'Yes, 100 per cent, I'm going, Jona.'

'All right then! I'll go as well!'

So Jona went with his mates and I travelled across with my brother Graeme and my close friend Alex Bruce. We left our car in Stanley Park and walked up, stepping into enemy territory. I'd been to Anfield so many times but always on the team bus and always with heavy security. 'This could be a bit lively,' I whispered to Graeme as we hurried towards the away entrance in the Anfield Road end. I didn't want fighting or anything like that but I hoped for some edge, and a feel for what United fans went through at Anfield. I was genuinely excited as we entered. I wore a bobble hat and a scarf so people couldn't really see me but I could see everything. I took in every detail. Inside the concourse, underneath the stand, it was rammed. I got a few double takes from United fans and it was funny to see some of them tapping their mates on the shoulder looking baffled. Is it Carrick?!

Yes! I wanted this experience. Outside, I looked at my ticket with its seat number and looked at the fans, and laughed. Standing only! Just grab a space and stay there! Brilliant! Before kick-off, the singing from United fans was absolute class and it kicked on again even more when the match began. It was mad in there, better than I'd ever hoped for! It went even more mental when Wayne Rooney scored and people came from 20 rows back to jump on me! Carnage! This is what I came for – the explosion of emotion that only football brings.

I loved being in with the Manchester United fans at Anfield. Standing together, behind the team, willing them to win. One of the best compliments anyone's ever paid me in my life came from Gary Neville in the programme to my testimonial in 2017 when he wrote: 'People might not know it, but Michael's totally bought into it. He's always there, whenever we win things and we have a party, he's always there, the loudest having a sing-song and he's always the last to leave. He enjoys it the most.'

My kids, Louise and Jacey, are just as obsessed with United as I am. Louise has grown slowly into it as she's got older. She now plays football herself and knows more about the players than I do. She's really knowledgeable and talks tactics. Lou's love for United and football has come as she's gone through school and had to learn how to deal with being my daughter; unfortunately there is no hiding place and she has to face the playground battle, fighting my corner. She has my back. Jacey has been into football since day dot just like me, kicking a ball around as soon as he could walk.

Old Trafford is like home to them and they've been to Wembley but Jacey kept nagging me to take him to watch United away, so I drove him to Burnley on 20 January 2018. We pulled up at Turf Moor and Jacey went, 'Dad, is this it!?' Not in a bad way, Jacey wasn't looking down on it, he was simply fascinated by the place. Curious, like.

'Yes, Jace. This is right up your street. Proper old school.'

'Oh, right!' He replied, and quickened his pace towards Turf Moor. To reach our seats Jacey and I had to go through the tunnel as our lads went out to warm up, so Jacey gave them all high-fives. He thinks they're all his mates as he's seen them around the training ground at Carrington a couple of times. We had to walk past the changing room and as it was empty of players I took him in. José Mourinho came over and made a real fuss of him. Jacey sat in David de Gea's seat, looking through the programme and having his usual sing-song with the kit men. Jacey belted out, 'From the banks of the Irwell to Sicily, we will fight, fight, fight for United FC'. He loves it. Bucks the kit man also loves a sing-song and he's always getting Jace to sing. Louise and Jacey especially love the Cantona song, 'We'll drink a drink, a drink, a drink; to Eric the king, the king, the king…'

They know all the songs, and so many of the old United players. Often, I think, *How do you know that?* They must've got it from me, because I loved that when I was a kid, the songs and that sense of togetherness. When I see them with their mates sometimes, and they're leading a United sing-song, I'm thinking, *Go on!* They share my love for Manchester United. It makes me laugh when they sing the fans' song about me. They'll follow Manchester United the rest of their lives.

Back at Turf Moor, I'm not sure Jacey realised quite how lucky he was. All the time I've been at United, I've never seen a kid allowed in the changing room before a game. I was conscious of getting out of the way when the lads returned from their warm-up. I left Jacey outside while I saw the lads. It's a really tight corridor at Turf Moor, so Jacey and I squeezed against the wall when they came back out. Every one of the players gave Jacey a high-five again and his little face was just a picture. That's my club, caring.

We went outside and at Turf Moor, there's a section in the middle of the away end that Burnley reserve for their staff and visiting staff because the changing rooms are right behind it, so you can nip back there quickly at half-time. Jacey and I went there and it was great as the United fans were only five or six seats away so Jacey sang his heart out. They soon spotted me and started demanding, 'Carrick, Carrick, give us a song.' Even now, in my thirties, I'm still quite reserved so I hesitated until Jacey nudged me in the ribs. 'Go on, Dad. Sing a song.' Proper banging me in the ribs. 'Go on, Dad! You've got to sing a song.'

'You start it off, Jacey, and I'll sing.'

'No, no, no, Dad. You do it. Now.'

So I got up and began, 'U-N-I-T-E-D, UNITED ARE THE TEAM FOR ME…' Then I stopped and sat down. The United fans took it on and the place was absolutely bouncing! I loved it! At half-time we went back down to the changing rooms and Jacey waited in the corridor with a bag of sweets. Marouane Fellaini came past and nicked a couple of Jacey's sweets. Jacey carried on singing throughout the second half and when Anthony Martial scored, he wanted lifting up so he could see the United fans going mad. What a day!

In the car on the way home, I asked Jacey, 'Did you have a good day?'

'Yes! Do you know what the best bit was, Dad? When you stood up to sing!'

Bearing in mind all he'd seen, being in the changing room, high-fiving the players, meeting José, I had a little smile to myself. The simple things, eh?! When we got home, Jacey flew into the house singing at the top of his voice his new song, 'Rom, Rom, Romelu, Romelu Lukaku, Man United's No 9, Romelu Lukaku.' Seeing Jacey like that after the trip to Burnley, eyes wide with excitement, carried me back to my own childhood, when my dad would take me to St James' Park to watch Newcastle United. I felt like I was passing on the baton of that passion for football.

2
THE BOYZA

Football might never have been an option for me. I could have ended up in a wheelchair. As a toddler, my knees knocked together and I had flat feet. Doctors in Wallsend, where I grew up, feared that when I started growing I wouldn't be able to walk or run properly so they were keen to operate. Poor Mam and Dad sat in the surgeon's office confronted with this massive decision – operate, or stick with how I was and hope I wasn't restricted when I grew? Such a tough call. Once the surgeon talked about a 50/50 chance of success or me ending up in a wheelchair, my parents said, 'No chance, it's not worth the risk.' Then, they marched me out the clinic.

Thank God Mam and Dad stopped the op. As I grew, my knees still went in a little and I still had dropped arches, but I ran without any trouble. Believe it or not, I could really shift back then! I went to see a foot specialist a few years back for some orthotics for my boots and he examined me, commenting on my unusually narrow hips. Being knock-kneed gave me some issues over the years, bad Achilles and the like, but never stopped me playing. Football has always been my life. When I was a toddler I always had a ball at my feet or I'd want to carry one around. Even when I was taken to a toy shop, I'd come back with some kind of ball.

My first vivid memory of playing football was on a Saturday evening at Wallsend Boys Club – the 'Boyza'. It was early 1986, I was only four and a half. The club was a 15-minute drive from home and Dad took me and Granddad in his old Austin Princess. That was a big deal for them, you know, taking their boy for his first proper football session. I watch Dad now when he takes Jacey to football, and it's so special to see how much he loves it. It's family heritage, in a way. Granddad took Dad to football, then they took me to Wallsend, and I took Jacey to Turf Moor with the Manchester United fans. This love of football has been passed down from generation to generation.

Back then, Wallsend Boys Club ran an all-comers' night for kids up to nine years old at 5pm on a Saturday for a couple of hours when you could turn up and play anyone else. You didn't need to be a certain standard, it was just come and have a kickabout, have fun, really. For a little kid like me at the time, it was an incredible adventure. I immediately fell in love with the Boyza – it was a completely rundown building with a unique smell that was utterly magical to me. Going through a tiny entrance, you paid your subs at a small desk and then hurried on into what seemed to me to be a huge space. It just opened up and I was drawn in. A large board displayed the week's fixtures and kick-off times for the leagues they ran. Kids and their parents huddled around the board to see who was playing who, what the league table looked like and who you had to beat to move up a place. A couple of pool tables close-by were surrounded by loads of kids watching their mates play or waiting their turn after putting down a 20p piece on the side. Arcade games flashed away and people rushed past, some heading up the stairs to the canteen where you could buy a hot dog or an ice pop.

The centrepiece, the heart and soul of the place, was the pitch where dreams began. There were six or seven steps down to it. You had what seemed to us kids this huge viewing gallery, about five feet up, right on the edge of the pitch. Above that, you had a balcony where people would stand and watch. Mams and dads came along with their kids, and sisters and brothers with their siblings. The place was packed.

On that first night, I raced towards these steps and gazed down at this amazing maple-wood floor, a trainers-only hallowed ground. Football started for me right here. I was one of the youngest of the 30 or so kids there. We all lined up at one end of the hall in fives and sixes, like relays, and raced to the other end, touched the wall, and dashed back. That was our warm-up. The five-a-sides were run at the time by a guy called Bob Slone. He wasn't a coach at all, more a youth worker, a volunteer who just wanted to get kids off the street and give them a game of football. He was one of those good people who just wanted to help others. Bob had a kit bag with these strips in and you'd see him down Wallsend High Street during the day sometimes, carrying his kit bag. That evening at the club, we would sit there, buzzing with excitement, and Bob would go down the row handing the kits out and then write the teams down on a big blackboard. 'You're Brazil.' 'You're Germany.' 'You're Newcastle.' 'You're Dundee.' Bob had been a goalkeeper up in Scotland, so he'd always have a few Scottish teams in. You'd get a team complete, and you'd all cheer. Then Bob would say, 'Right, Newcastle versus Aberdeen, on now.'

I can't remember what my team was that first night, but I'll never forget the emotion of going on to a pitch for the first time. There were two sets of steps going down to the pitch from each end of the viewing gallery. These steps were full of the kids playing next, one team on one of the entrance steps and the other team standing on the other, and you never mixed, you were either too nervous or too fired up to be stood next to them so close to kick-off. I remember getting to the steps, looking down and pausing before picking up courage and reaching the bottom. Then I started crying my eyes out. It was just too much for me. I wanted to be on there, but I was scared. I could see big kids of seven, eight years old out there, and they looked like giants to me. I was desperate to get on as well, to be part of this magical game, and I suppose it was simply that first step into something new that unnerved me. Dad came down to reassure me and Granddad gave me a little bit of encouragement. They bolstered my confidence, I stepped on to the pitch, and instantly settled. Once I was out there, all my shyness disappeared. I felt different, more at ease. I felt at home. I never looked back.

I soon learned the routine – you'd race to get the ball first so you had about 30 seconds' kickabout before the game and more importantly, you'd get the kick-off. As I got older, it was quick, high-tempo stuff as the playing area was tiny. There were no high balls, so the game was played on the deck with lots of intricate 1–2s with my teammates or off the walls. Games lasted 10 minutes, there were no half-time team talks and substitutions were made only at the break unless there was an injury. The substitute stood on the stairs for the whole first half as a reminder that somebody was coming off and their fun was ending in a few minutes, so you'd go 100mph because you didn't want to come off at half-time. If you did, you'd go trudging off. Coming off at half-time was soul-destroying.

There was a 20-foot cargo net in-between the viewing gallery and the pitch that acted as a barrier to stop the ball going off. Parents shouted encouragement through it, kids pushed their faces through the holes in it and some even gnawed on the rope in nervous excitement. This was my new home. I remember my delight when Bob decided to put a team of five-year-olds in the Under-8s league and I was asked to play. He called us 'Scotland'. Our first game we got beat 7–0. Bob said, 'Forget about the score, just go out and enjoy and learn how to play.' Such wise words.

Granddad watched me play for a few years at the Boyza before he died. I knew he'd been a war hero and played a bit of football, and I was proud of all that. But I was so young, I didn't really ask him about the war or football, and that generation never talked about what they'd done, did they? Granddad was there at the very start though and I owe him so much. Dad was often at the club too. He'd volunteered there before I came along, helping to run leagues and referee. Now, his time was taken up supporting me. During my time at school, which was spent first at Stephenson Memorial Primary in Howdon, then Western Middle School in Wallsend before finishing up at Burnside Community High School, I kept going to the Boyza. I did so until I was 16, and those five-a-side leagues had a massive impact on my development. Different ages played on different nights, so, say, our league was on a Wednesday night, that was all I thought about at school that day. The day dragged because I just wanted to get to the Boyza. Sometimes I actually got to play two games in one night if there was an uneven number of teams in the league – those nights were like Christmas.

Thankfully, for me, there were five-a-side leagues pretty much every night of the week, from Under-9s to Under-16s, five minutes each way. Bob had teams in almost every league, and his No. 1 team was 'Brazil'. When I turned eight, I felt like I was in the best team in the world if I got a game for Bob's Brazil. It wasn't even the proper yellow kit, it was the green one, but we didn't care, as far as we were concerned we were Brazil! Mr and Mrs Sweeney ran a team at the club called Ardieonians and it was like a big Derby with Bob's Brazil. It was quite famous around Wallsend – Brazil and Ardieonians. It was like, 'Playing for Ardies tonight! Yes!' 'Playing for Brazil! Yes!' I played for Brazil and Bob for a couple of years, then moved over to Ardies for a couple of years. It was like going from United to City! Bob was totally devoted to the Boys

Club for 35 years, and when he passed away in 2013, I put a tribute on social media which ended '#Brazil', and I got replies from people who knew what that meant, and basically what Bob meant to us.

Essentially, everyone gathered at the Boyza. The club had been born out of the Swan Hunter shipyards and was famous for producing players who turned pro. I remember watching TV when Alan Shearer scored for Blackburn Rovers at St James' Park after returning from being out with a knee injury, and the commentator talked about him being a Wallsend lad. I knew I was following players like Alan, Peter Beardsley, Steve Watson, Alan Thompson and Lee Clark. Steve Bruce was there, and, more recently, Steven Taylor and Fraser Forster. Wallsend Boys Club was a breeding ground for talent, and more than 60 professionals started out there. On presentation night, I'd get excited to see close-up the local lads who'd gone on to play for Newcastle come back and, sometimes, I even got to shake their hand! I'll never forget being in the Wallsend Parade in 1992 – 12 of us boys singing our hearts out all the way through town on the back of a red lorry with a banner stating 'Wallsend Boys' Club, suppliers to the football industry'. The Boyza was just huge on the north-east footballing landscape. We almost took it for granted that us lads from Wallsend would become footballers. Even quite early on, that opportunity seemed quite real, and I desperately wanted it.

3
GROWING UP

Looking back, I realise how lucky I was. I'm fortunate to have had a stable upbringing in a calm household where Mam and Dad never argued or fought. To have parents that made Graeme and I feel so happy and protected but at the same time who allowed us to follow our dreams in the big world is something I have always appreciated.

Home was Howdon, an area of Wallsend about six miles from St James' Park. We lived in the upstairs flat of a semi, me and Graeme in bunk-beds, and being older I had the top bunk. Howdon was classified as a deprived area at the time but we never went without. Dad worked hard as a manager in nuclear power stations all over the country, controlling what equipment went in different reactors. There were periods when Dad would be working away, ranging from three weeks away to one week home, or Monday to Friday away and the weekend at home when he'd spend hours playing football in the garden with us. It must have been hard for Mam when Dad was away and she had to hold the fort. Dad would come back and us boys would be all over him, showing him our new tricks. Mam, bless her, would have to wait hours to finally spend some time with him. Dad working away and missing out on things must have killed him at times and Mam must have suffered on her own, juggling two sports-mad boys alongside also her own work in a school.

As the house our flat was in was on the corner plot, we had the slightly bigger garden, which we thought was amazing. We used cricket stumps as posts, a hedge as the net and that was our Wembley. Graeme and I played for hours together, making up moves and 1–2s with no goalkeeper while commentating on the whole thing. In our imaginations we were replaying all the games we'd been watching on TV. Graeme was a very good footballer from a young age and soon played along with me and my mates, who were four or five years older. I was always proud when Graeme joined in. The lads all accepted him as he wasn't out of his depth. We'd play together as a team against three or four of our mates, sometimes Graeme in goal and me against the rest to make it harder so I could practise my dribbling and test myself. We'd be out for three or more hours, and during that time, I'd think, *I might try with my left foot a bit today*. I self-coached a lot. I'd cross with my right, then left, trying to get the technique the same with both feet. I wanted to perfect it either way, pass or chip, telling myself, 'If I do this, I'll be a player or win a trophy.' I constantly challenged myself.

I had a little sponge ball in the house and kicked it against the sofa – two bounces, half-volley, repeat. I'd try to hit a cupboard door or chip it on to a certain cushion, setting myself challenges, 'If you do this, you'll play for England' or 'If you do this, you'll score at St James'.' I'd only ever give myself one shot, as if it were real.

I noticed I kept kicking the floor with my left foot, so I adjusted my technique and practised some more. Now I see Jacey going around the house with a ball and I think, *Yes, that's what I was like*. I was always conscious of improving my technique. I'd be like, *Why am I not getting that little bit of spin on the ball?* So I might have two or three goes at it, working on the spin. Coming back from school, I'd play 1–2s around lamp posts. I loved passing, just feeling the ball against my foot, almost part of it, and thinking what I could do with it. If the ball didn't come off my foot quite as I wanted it, well, that really frustrated me. It had to look clean. The technique had to be right and I became obsessive about it. Mam went mad because Graeme and I wore the grass out and the lawn soon transformed into this patch of mud where the goal was. When it rained, we played in the street because the garden was ruined.

Graeme and I have always been very close, even though we're very different characters. I'm a little cold, a bit more clinical and objective. Whereas, sometimes the red mist would descend for Graeme when we played football or if I nicked his ball. Then, I'd put my hand on his forehead and because my arms were longer, he'd start throwing wind-mills but hit thin air in front of my face, which wound him up even more. Dad and I would be laughing, which just made him even angrier. It never lasted very long. Mam took Graeme's side, her little baby. 'Leave him alone, stop winding him up,' she'd say. One day, we were playing at the local sports centre in Wallsend and one of the older lads, a boy called Skiv, pushed Graeme against the boards. Graeme jumped up, crying and wanting to fight Skiv, who was almost twice his size, and we all just laughed at him for even trying. I would never have tried that. I was too soft.

Graeme was fiery, but nothing really angered me. It was very rare for me to lose my cool. As a kid, what wound me up most was we had to be home earliest of all the lads out playing football. Why? Some of my mates were allowed out until 9pm. That's probably too late, I know. Mam was like, 'No, you're coming in at 7.30. I don't care what the other boys are doing, this is what you're doing.' If it had been up to us, we'd have been out all night. I loved being with the lads.

Aged nine, I started playing 11-a-side for the Boyza. The football was a decent standard but some games were a real fight on some horrible pitches in minging weather. Ken Richardson and Alan Train, who were volunteers like Bob, took me for two or three years and that was when I received my first real coaching. Ken and Alan were brilliant. Ken worked part-time at Newcastle United and was also a milkman with an open-sided van, so he could load the milk on and off. He'd clear all the milk out on a Sunday, and we'd all climb in the back. I remember us all bunched up in the van, sometimes as many as 12 kids with one sitting on the wheel arch, rattling about as we set off to play Cramlington Juniors or whoever. Looking back now, it was madness safety-wise but what a great time it was, when we were all together as a team. There was a real pride about representing Wallsend Boys Club. We even had to pay a 10p fine if our boots were dirty. I remember playing Ponteland away. It was raining hailstones with occasional snow, windy and freezing, disgusting weather, but we were leading 3–0 and I was meant to be coming off. I was desperate to get some layers on and to feel my hands and feet again until one of the other lads started crying. So, he came off because he was so cold. I was gutted. We didn't wear 'skins' in those days!

Ken was the good cop. He taught me tactical discipline, and the structure of a team, even at nine. Alan was the bad cop. 'Michael, you'll not make a footballer until you clatter the goalkeeper,' Alan said to me over and over. I was a centre forward at the time and was like, 'What have I got to clatter the keeper for?' I'd hear Alan say to Mam and Dad, 'Michael's too nice, he'll never be a footballer until he smashes the keeper…' 'He's never going to do that,' Dad replied. Mam was like, 'No chance.' She got quite angry, 'I'm not telling Michael to do that. He won't do it.' I was never physical. Alan wasn't on about injuring the keeper, just questioning my inner aggression. Other lads at the Boys Club were flying in here, there and everywhere. Not me. I enjoy watching Jacey when he plays now and he's the same as I was. If the goalkeeper comes sliding out, Jacey always tries to nick it past him too. Jacey plays like my dad, left-footed, playing one touch or touch and pass. In a way, I feel there's a Carrick style of playing. Granddad was always on to me about 'pass it' and 'switch it'. It's what he taught Dad, and he was really keen to pass that on to me. Like Granddad, Dad always told me to 'pass, pass, pass to someone else who's in a better position'. 'Play for the team' was massive for Dad, too. He couldn't abide selfish players. It was always about the team for him. We played Staff v. Guests in a hotel in Dubai recently, with Dad, me, Graeme and Jacey. Dad was the best player at 66!

Even as a kid, I knew how much Dad loved watching me play, he was always encouraging me, but not wanting to show much emotion. I had the most loving and supportive parents. They never missed watching both me and my brother Graeme. We came first. Just seeing them being there, knowing what sacrifices they made, was great for us and they never put any pressure on us. Dad would just say, 'Enjoy it. Work hard. Get stuck in. Try your best. Well done.' Even now, Dad's the same. If Manchester United lose, Dad says, 'Oh, well, do better next time.' Dad's not competitive, really, he's too nice for that. I look at myself and think, yes, I have two sides: in football when I'm ultra-competitive and desperate to win and away from that I'm quite easy-going. If I lose at golf but know I've played well, then it's no big deal. I guess that's the laid-back part of me but then there was another side, and when it really counted in games, I absolutely had to win. I just never felt the need to shout and scream.

My childhood was a wonderfully happy blur of either playing football or watching football. I'll never forget my first experience of a football crowd, when I was six years old. I can still feel the excitement of rushing out of the Metro station and gazing up in awe at St James' Park for the first time. Newcastle United's home up on the hill felt like the best place in the world and I fell in love with life on the terraces instantly. We arrived nice and early. Dad's always early. It was just me and Dad to start with, as Graeme was only two at the time. So, the two of us queued at the tiny, narrow hole in the wall. You didn't need a ticket in those days, I just handed over my £3, pushed hard on the heavy black turnstile, and entered this paradise called the Gallowgate. That exhilaration of climbing the steps inside the Gallowgate will never leave me. I was impatient to see the pitch, and join all the people I could hear singing on the terraces. Reaching the top of the steps, I came out in to the stand, looked down and there was this unbelievable sight – this huge pitch. It took my breath away, it was so large that I couldn't speak for a minute or two. 'This is incredible!' I whispered to myself. 'This is it! The best stadium in the world!' Dad perched me on a concrete barrier, so I could see the Newcastle players. Mirandinha made a lasting impression on me because he was so different. I don't know if he was that good, actually, but there was a genuine excitement from the Gallowgate hoping for something special. A Brazilian in Newcastle! As a six-year-old lad, the noise captivated me. I'd never been anywhere so loud. I wasn't scared or intimidated, I just loved it, I felt at home with the camaraderie, singing 'Blaydon Races' and seeing just how much it meant to Newcastle fans. I sang away as I sat on the uncomfortable, concrete barrier towards the back. I always felt safe because I knew Dad stood behind me, ready to catch me if the crowd surged. I remember it was always the same barrier in front of the scoreboard. The buzz was unreal and I was hooked.

I have many intense memories of St James' Park, little details like they used to throw nuts up from pitch-side over the fence, and also huge historic events. When Kevin Keegan came back as manager in 1992 I was 10 and St James' just went mental. Everywhere and everyone was buzzing. He could sell a dream, couldn't he? He saved the club from relegation to the old third division, Rob Lee signed, Steve Watson and Lee Clark were there, and Peter Beardsley soon returned. It really was a special time. It was the best football, that Football League Division One, because we were winning all the time and scoring loads of goals – Andy Cole was on fire. We flew up into the Premier League, the good times were back. It lifted the whole city. The difference in the place if Newcastle are doing well or not is incredible. For those three to four years, the city was bouncing.

Dad worshipped Newcastle. He's now part of the Fairs Club where Newcastle fans talk about old games and meet up with the old players. I know it sounds odd to say but Dad never fully grasped me playing for Manchester United. He doesn't go along with all the glamour. It doesn't interest him one bit. Whether it's Coventry or Barcelona, Dad's just happy watching football, going to the game or sitting at home in front of the TV.

Growing up, we had one TV, no remote, only four channels. One day, Dad came back from working away with a new TV he'd bought, a big square thing, which we stared at in amazement. The back of it was as deep as it was wide and wood surrounded the screen. We'd plug our Spectrum into it and play that tennis game with two lines up and down the side and a dot going from one side to the other. I spent many hours with Dad and Graeme watching Dad's collection of VHS videos of George Best – Dad's all-time favourite player. He'd also often put on the video of his favourite Newcastle player, Malcolm 'Supermac' Macdonald! We had videos of Best, Law and Charlton, Brazil videos, Maradona videos, 'European Top 500 Goals', the lot. Dad liked Celtic so there were a few of their videos, Lisbon Lions and all that, and he bought me a few Celtic shirts. I used to look at the cabinet where Dad kept his videos as if it were a treasure chest. He had FA Cup finals on tape, which we watched over and over like the 3–2 Liverpool v. Everton in 1989. Graeme and I would then go into the garden and practise the

Beardsley shuffle. Beardsley, John Barnes – all the names that went with Liverpool, I remember them all. I began following Liverpool because my cousin Gary was a big fan. I wore the Liverpool kit, the one with Crown Paints on the front, and then Candy from '88. I loved watching John Barnes. He was smooth, wasn't he? Clean and neat. Beardsley was a big hero of mine. Jan Mølby was special too. I wish there was more footage of Mølby, really, as I see a similarity in our game. Unhurried, definitely, although Mølby scored more than me. We'd watch *The Big Match* on a Sunday, all crowding round the telly, taking in the live action. I'll never forget watching Liverpool v. Arsenal on the Friday night, the title decider in 1989. I sat there and watched it with Dad. He didn't say much. He's not a big talker anyway, not even now.

But Italia '90 was the first tournament I really remember and the images are still fresh in my eye. I was nearly nine and I almost couldn't move from in front of the TV that magical summer. When me and Graeme went round to my grandma's house for tea one day, we asked if we could watch Argentina's quarter final with Yugoslavia. I'll never forget Diego Maradona rolling in his penalty against Italy in the semi-final shoot-out. I watched every moment of that World Cup and all these wonderful foreign players with their exotic names which I kept saying over and over: Schillaci! Baggio! Völler! Klinsmann! Matthäus! Careca! Of course, England were my passion. I was Gazza, always Gazza, England No. 19, in the garden and in my dreams. I even had the England tracksuit – more a shell suit, really – which I wore like a lucky charm as England marched through Italy. I was convinced England would do it, and we'd actually become world champions. We had GAZZA!! The West Germany semi in Turin, and that defeat on penalties, was total devastation for me. Football, England and Gazza meant everything to me and it broke my heart that we were out.

In 1988, Dad even got tickets to Wembley to watch Liverpool play Wimbledon in the Charity Shield. Tickets to Wembley! Just like going to the Boys Club and then St James', my first visit to Wembley was going to be special – it had to be. We planned to stay down, us two boys, Mam and Dad. So, we booked into a bed and breakfast in north London and me and Dad headed off to the game, while Mam took Graeme in the pram for a bit of shopping in London. Dad wanted to do it the proper way. 'Come on, son, let's go on the Tube and then walk up Wembley Way.' It was a big deal for Dad, he's massive on tradition, real old school, and I love the fact that he's like that.

I thought St James' was big. Wow, Wembley was a monster! We sat in line with the 18-yard box opposite the Royal Box. I still recall the thrill as the players came out of the tunnel, the noise, and John Aldridge scoring twice. Liverpool beat Wimbledon so it was revenge for the FA Cup final, I guess. My first experience of Wembley ended badly, though. When we got back to the B&B, Mam was crying. She'd been there for ages, bless her, waiting for us. 'I can't stay here,' Mam said. The room was really horrendous, a dirty basement with black bin bags outside our door, and Mam wouldn't touch anything. 'Come on,' Dad said. 'We're going home.' So, we got in his Princess, with its massive long bonnet, and drove home. It took seven hours, but it was worth it. We couldn't have stayed there. It was a disaster of a place and we always loved being at home.

From a very young age, every weekend on a Sunday we were taken to church with the Salvation Army. We've always been brought up with strong Christian values. It's been important to Mam and Dad. Mam has nearly always been in the Salvation Army. So, on a Sunday we would go off to church and Sunday school. When we arrived, me, Graeme and our cousin Garry would go straight into the community hall before and even after the service and start playing footie.

We always had our sponge ball and we'd kick it around, using chairs for goals. Eventually, I started to realise that none of my mates from the Boyza went to Sunday school and I was quite sensitive about it. In the end, I spoke to Mam about it. I just explained none of the boys attended Sunday schools, so why did we? I went for a little while longer but at the age of 11 I stopped going every week, although we would all go as a family on special occasions. Mam was fine with it. She's always encouraged us but has never imposed her beliefs on us. I was actually christened a Catholic because Dad came from a staunch Catholic family and Granddad was caretaker of a Catholic school. When my kids go back to Wallsend, they enjoy going to church and Sunday school with Mam and they love listening to her stories about when she was a Youth Club leader, and Brown Owl and Guider in the Girlguiding movement. Mam always planned great day trips and lovely holidays to places like Scarborough, Skegness, Butlin's and even Corfu. But poor Mam, the moment we'd arrive anywhere and we saw a patch of grass, the shout would be, 'Let's get the ball out.' Mam would smile and say, 'That's my boys.' I now wonder whether, being in a house full of boys, Mam ever craved a girl.

I love and admire Mam so much. She's an incredible woman, always doing good, always organising. She loves sending cards to everyone, birthdays, anniversaries, thank yous, congratulations – she must have a book full of dates and addresses. The community is her team and she contributes so much. She never thinks of herself, it's always others. When I was at the Boyza, Mam was the one who brought all the biscuits and the tea for the lads. She was the one making the packed-lunch picnic for everyone. It wound her up because people turned up with nothing and then went, 'Oh, Lynn has something.' To be fair, she always did. Mam had this industrial-type flask with coffee, enough for an army. We'd turn up with all sorts of coats, hats, gloves, bags, the lot, just in case anybody was short.

Mam loved it because Graeme and I were so happy at the Boyza. She'd come with us, sometimes taking four buses to wherever the match was, especially when Dad was working away. She never said, 'Oh, I can't be bothered taking you tonight.' Mam's never driven a car. But she made sure we always got to games, taking us there on the bus. I can never thank Mam enough for all the sacrifices she made. She taught me sound principles and to be responsible with money. I remember she came to me one day and told me she'd sorted me a little savings book which I put money in and took to the bank. 'Your dinner money's going into the bank and a bit of pocket money every month, and you've got to learn to handle that,' Mam told me. 'If you can save any money in that month, that's all yours. Mind, by Friday, if you haven't got money for your dinner, you'll go without.'

One of my favourite childhood memories was going with Wallsend Boys Club Under-12s to Holland and being mesmerised by all these Dutch kids passing up from the back. I can't remember who we played, but I do remember Mam threatening the ref with her handbag. It's not the type of thing you forget! Long story short, the place we stayed in had a lake and a slide, and I slashed my knee open going in the water. Good old butterfly stitches were put in, a big bandage stuck on my knee, and because you're on tour, you play. Wallsend were up against this Dutch side with a few ringers because they definitely weren't 11-year-olds like us, no way, anyway this big lad pushed me over and I went down holding my knee. Mam shouted at the ref, and started to come on the pitch wielding her handbag. She realised halfway on what she was doing and started slowly to backtrack. She's never lived it down. She got hammered for it!

Graeme's like Mam, whereas I'm more like Dad. When I was younger, I was shy and maybe naïve. I'd see other lads messing around, getting into trouble, ending up in fights, or knocking on people's doors and running off, stupid stuff, but not for me – I was too worried about getting caught. I was never scared of Dad but I was frightened of Mam, mind. She's a strong woman, and can be very stubborn (a trait I share), but is so loving and caring. Every few months, Mam would have a blow-out and totally lose the plot, especially when our football took over family life. She'd shout, 'There's too much football in this house. I've had enough.' Then, she'd slam the door and storm out. Dad and I would look at each other, half-smiling, 'There she goes again!' And if my homework wasn't done, Mam wouldn't let me go to the Boyza. 'School first, football second,' she'd say. Mam and Dad were strong on education. Once I had to miss training because I hadn't done my schoolwork and I was so embarrassed when I had to tell to Ken why I wasn't there. Never again.

At my first school, Stephenson, I wasn't really involved in football. Mr Dobson was quite an old-school, strict PE teacher. We were awful as a team at Stephenson, and didn't have any real footballers, so I played for the year above and because I had an idea how to play, Mr Dobson used me as a sweeper. I played there one afternoon against Western, where they had a teacher called Colin Mackay. Mr Mackay saw me play and invited me to trials for Wallsend Town, which was a big deal. Quite soon after that, I moved to Western, and was playing for Mr Mackay which was brilliant, just the best. Western were far more into football than Stephenson. At Western, there were a group of six or seven of us sports-mad kids, including my best mates Chris Hood, Steven Bradley and Stephen Rutherford. Hoody was at Newcastle's Centre of Excellence, Paul Docherty and Kevin Urwin were at Middlesbrough with me when I trained there for a while, Phil Walton went to Hartlepool as an apprentice, Chris Thorman went into rugby league, then played Super League, captained England and is now assistant coach at Huddersfield Giants. Steven Bradley and Stephen Rutherford signed for Hull at rugby league as well as Gateshead Thunder. We were decent! Western even played in the national schools five-a-side finals at the Aston Villa Sports Centre in 1992. We all pushed each other on with Mr Mackay guiding us. When I made it as a professional, I realised how fortunate I'd been to have such a great sports teacher as Mr Mackay who encouraged me so much in my early years. He was from Aberdeen and was really enthusiastic, and when I think about how much he helped me, well, my gratitude runs so deep. I've never lost touch with Mr Mackay because he shaped my career really. Weeknights and Saturday mornings, he gave up so much of his time for us.

Mr Mackay even entered me for the Northumberland county athletics championships in 1991. 'We need somebody for the Under-12s' 60m hurdles,' he said. 'Oh, I'll have a go,' I replied. I was nine, racing 11-year-olds and hadn't had any training. It was madness, really, as I didn't know anything, not even how many strides to take between each hurdle. I was also hardly dressed for the part. I remember wearing some random baggy Reebok kit and massive trainers, standing there, not knowing what I was doing. The guy in the lane next to me had spikes and starting blocks, and I stood there thinking, *What am I doing with some big baggy shorts on?* Anyway, I set off and all I could hear was Mam shouting, 'Come on, Michael!' I got through a couple of heats and then won the final. Northumberland county champion! The next year, Mr Mackay entered me again, but I finished second so athletics got binned.

One day, Mr Mackay said, 'There are county cricket trials, you're all decent cricketers, do you want to go?' We weren't sure. 'It's at Jesmond Cricket Club, 2pm. You'll have to leave school early.' Get out of lessons early? Yes, count us in! We rocked up at Jesmond and immediately realised we were so out of place. We were scruffy, had just turned up off the street and didn't have bats – we didn't have a clue, really. All the other kids were from private schools and wearing whites and I could see them thinking, 'Who on earth are this lot?' Me, Hoody and the lads stuck the pads on, borrowed a bat and gave it a go. I'll never forget how Hoody started smashing this ball all around. He leathered these smart bowlers everywhere. Thorman was a quick bowler. We didn't get asked back, though. Play for the county?! They wouldn't have let us. Wallsend boys weren't their type. I knew I could play cricket, but I didn't really know anything about it. I felt out of my depth and out of my comfort zone. It felt like a different world that I shouldn't be part of. And I still recall the first ball I faced, coming at me much faster than any I'd ever faced, too fast. There and then I decided, *No, it's not for me, this.*

Under Mr Mackay, we all played rugby union at school and some of the lads played league on a Saturday. Graeme was good enough to play league at Wembley for north-east schools before the 1995 World Cup final. He didn't really take it that seriously. 'Fancy a game of rugby?' Rock up, 'What's the rules?' Score a few tries and take a few tackles. Not my scene, really, and I still have the scars. One day, we were playing rugby on the beach at Whitley Bay, about seven miles from Wallsend, it was a pretty full-on game and my nose got smashed. When the lads saw all this blood, they sent for an ambulance. We were down the bottom of the small cliff, and they left me there. The ambulance man had to hike all the way to the bottom and found only a 14-year-old with a bust nose. 'You could have walked up,' he said. Anyway, he took me to North Tyneside General and they called Mam. I didn't want my nose fixed but Mam arrived and insisted they re-set it. 'Well, your son has the final say,' the doctor told her. Mam went, 'Pardon me, I'm his next of kin. That's my son. He's 14 and I'm responsible for him.' The doctor was adamant: 'Michael's chosen not to have anything done and, if we're talking responsibility, you weren't there when the accident happened.' Mam still has the letter North Tyneside General sent to Western, saying I was out by myself with friends.

By that stage, football was a complete obsession and I was moving away from playing a range of sports with my mates to focusing fully on football. Hoody was at Newcastle's Centre of Excellence but Hoody, Bradley and Rutherford weren't football-mad like me. They're more rugby lads. Rutherford rang me once when I was abroad with Manchester United on the coach going to a game. 'Where are you?'

'The Bernabéu!'

'What's happening there?'

'Playing Real Madrid. Just a Champions League knockout first leg!'

'Ah, OK, good luck then! I'll speak to you tomorrow.'

It was harder to not know about it! One of the biggest games in the world! That's what I love about Rutherford. I think it's great. After all, there's more to life than football.

School got in the way of football, but I knew I had to study and I did work hard. I find it fascinating reading back through my sports reports at Burnside, to see how I grasped the essentials of the game early. 'Michael demonstrates a good understanding of tactics in games… although he competes aggressively, he does so with a sense of fair play,' read my PE report in 1993. Twenty-five years later, I hope I've not changed.

I didn't waste my time at school, but my ambition was always to be a footballer. Scouts were always watching me and inviting me to train at clubs. I went to Middlesbrough when I was nine, only because a couple of the other lads at the Boyza went, Kev Urwin and Paul Docherty, who was a great little player. Docherty had all the turns in the bag – right foot, left foot, Cruyff turns, step-overs, the lot. I only played once for Boro, at centre forward, and when my friends got released, I left a year later when I was 12. I've still kept a picture of me standing next to Gary Pallister outside the players' entrance at Ayresome Park in 1992. I looked round other clubs and guested for Stoke City at the Ayr tournament when I was 13. I also started spending some holidays down at West Ham United, training and getting to know the staff and set-up there, and was soon going down once a month. I kept playing for other clubs and Newcastle wanted me to sign. It was pretty exciting for me as a Newcastle fan when the director of their Centre of Excellence, John Carver, invited me to join their Under-14s in the Milk Cup in Northern Ireland, a year young. When I agreed, John went into the club shop at St James', got a tracksuit off the peg and handed it to me. 'Here,' John said. 'You're ready to go.' I still laugh about it with Mam now. The trousers were ridiculous, far too long, and it cost Mam a fortune to get them altered in Wallsend. Anyway, with me in my tailored tracksuit, I reported to St James' on my thirteenth birthday, 28 July 1994, and Peter Beardsley came down and gave me a cake. I appreciated that gesture, but I hated the trip. It was a good tournament, full of classy players, but it was tough off the pitch. One night in Portrush, the Newcastle coaches gave us some money to go and play the slot machines and a few of the players went out and borrowed a Mini off a girl they'd just met and drove it round a car park. It was that sort of trip and as much as I loved Newcastle United I knew I couldn't sign for them. The atmosphere couldn't compare with West Ham, really.

'I like Newcastle but I'm not going there,' I told Mam when I got back. My heart was never in Newcastle. They didn't have reserves, so it was difficult to see what route there was into the first team. That's the one thing every kid going into a club wants. A chance. Despite my huge love for the club and the joy I felt on the Gallowgate, I just didn't feel at home at Newcastle. My thoughts were more and more on West Ham.

A year later, I went back to the Milk Cup with West Ham alongside Mark Maley and Steven Watson from the Boyza and I shared a room with Shaun Byrne. Byrney and I became so close over the years. We got drawn against Newcastle, and our coach made sure we were all up for it. 'Right, we've got three Geordies here and we're playing against Newcastle so you better pull your fingers out and win for these three lads,' he told the team. We beat Newcastle 5–1.

It was always fun. For most of my childhood, football was fun, playing was trial and error, practising, learning but always loving it. I never said, 'Do I have to go to training tonight?' I couldn't wait to get to the Boyza with my mates. We'd talk about it in break at Western, 'Who are you playing? What time are you on? I'll come and watch you.' Playing for the love of it was probably why the FA's School of Excellence at Lilleshall didn't feel right to me either. It was a hothouse for the best kids, supposedly. At 14 I was selected for a trial at Doncaster that gave us a chance at the last two trials for Lilleshall. After Mam and Dad dropped me at this remote place in the Shrop-shire countryside, I saw all these hyper-keen kids, and just felt out of my depth. The other lads seemed so much more streetwise about how the world worked, how the game worked and how the system worked. I was naïve, basically not grown up enough. I was a July kid, a late birthday, always the youngest in my age group, too young really. We stayed at Lilleshall, and I lay in bed, anguished, just thinking, *Do*

I want to spend two years here, away from Mam, Dad and Graeme, away from my mates?

I desperately wanted to be a footballer but I needed to feel comfortable, looked after, safe. So, I didn't play well in the trial, my heart wasn't in it. I let the game go past me. Mam and Dad were watching, and Dad knew straightaway. Mam told me a year or two later that Dad said, 'What's wrong with Michael? I don't think he wants to be here.' In the car on the way home, I told them, 'Oh, Dad. I don't want to stay at Lilleshall. I can't leave home. I don't want to be here for two years. I'll never play, Dad.' All Dad and Mam cared about, really, was me being happy. 'If you don't want to go, son, you don't have to go,' Dad said. 'Mam, I don't want to leave home.' 'Well, you don't have to,' she replied.

After those two trial games, the FA was down to 30 lads and wanted only 20. Two weeks later I got a letter from the FA, saying I was on standby, first reserve in case anybody dropped out. Yes! I must have been the first kid in Lilleshall history to celebrate not getting in. It was a lucky escape, actually. If I'd gone to Lilleshall, I know I wouldn't have lasted long. Mam and Dad had conversations on the touchline at Lilleshall with other parents who were so set on their boy making it to the school. Some of the lads seemed like ready-made footballers, almost designed for that hothouse environment. I just wasn't ready at all. At Lilleshall, I felt vulnerable. They made a programme on Lilleshall, and Alan Smith was in it. Alan and I later became teammates at Manchester United, but at the same time were both at Doncaster College building up to the Lilleshall trials, so I knew him well and I'd always thought, *Wow. Smudger's ready for Lilleshall, he knows the game.* Yet he left after a few months. Hearing that, I felt even more certain that I dodged a bullet.

Seeing the photographs of all the successful professional players on the wall at the Boyza made the dream seem possible despite passing on Lilleshall. Deep down, I always thought I'd make it as a player. I've always had that stubbornness, that inner strength. I'd never say I was better than another player, but I'd think it. I looked at the players going to Lilleshall, and told myself, *I'll outlast them.*

So, I was happy going to the clubs, training and having a look, and just staying on that pathway. West Ham were in there early, and I had an immediate connection with them. But soon there were other scouts knocking on the door at our new home in Wallsend, where we'd moved when I was 11. In the end, there were up to 12 clubs, who all wanted to sign me. 'It's up to you, son,' Dad said. 'It's your environment, it's your job. Pick a club that you feel comfortable with.' So, I spent every school holiday when I was 13 and 14 going round clubs. In the summer when I turned 14, I spent six weeks in eight different places. I went to Arsenal, who put me in a big hostel and I didn't like that. Although, I did get to see Ian Wright at the training ground. That was a 'wow' moment for me. I went to Crystal Palace, then Mam took me down to Chelsea on the train. They picked us up in a minibus and drove us to Harlington, Chelsea's training ground at the time near Heathrow. I got out and went off to play, but they left Mam sitting in the minibus for ages. They forgot about her, I think. Gwyn Williams, who looked after the kids at Chelsea, did let her get out. Mam said, 'I've come all this way…' When I came back into the changing rooms, my watch was gone. Well, I couldn't wait to leave. 'They wouldn't pass me the ball,' I told Dad when I got home. I felt like an outsider. First impressions go a long way and I just didn't feel comfortable at Chelsea. 'I was shouting for the ball and I wasn't getting it.' Chelsea was a no-go.

Eventually, I chose West Ham. They were the ones who made me feel most welcome and relaxed, and they played the game the right way

– the West Ham Way, as they called it. 'They play two-touch football, Dad, they don't launch it. It's two touch, 1–2, pass and move.' I compared everywhere to West Ham because I enjoyed it so much. I also went to Oldham, Swindon, Forest, Everton, Sunderland, Wimbledon and after I played in a trial for Coventry's Under-14s in April 1995, I told Dad, 'I've had enough of this now, it's too much.' My heart was set on West Ham and an apprenticeship. At 14, I still trained in the north-east and from 14–16, I was at the independent Centre of Excellence, Chester-le-Street for players who signed for clubs too far away to go every week. The coaches were Kenny Wharton, who had played for Newcastle and coached at their academy, and Vince Hutton, who was to become a big influence on me and who used to pick me up and drive me to Boro every week. They were good coaches, and I learned a lot. I played all types of football growing up, under serious coaches like Wharton and Hutton – 11-a-side, five-a-side, league as well as continuing my regular kickabouts in the street with my mates. This variety was important for my development. There was fun in experimenting and exploring without the fear of being judged. Back then, it was about getting into the habits of a specific skill or movement. It was like learning a language I wanted to be fluent in. *Can this work?* I'd ask myself and try it. I had the confidence to attempt tricks and moves because I was messing around with my mates. In the schoolyard, I'd try and be on the team with the fewest players or the worst players to make it more of a challenge for me. I enjoyed it more this way.

But West Ham were my main focus now. My careers adviser at Tyneside Careers, Mr Allott, recommended some local colleges in Redbridge and Barking for when I went south. I appreciated the advice, but university was never in my thoughts, all I could think about was the Academy of Football, West Ham.

4

THE ACADEMY

I can't help but smile as I remember my naïve, gawky 14-year-old self climbing on the train at Central Station, clutching his boots, full of dreams and heading down to West Ham in the holidays for a couple of days here or a week there. I always had the same routine on the train: head straight for the buffet bar for a packet of crisps and a Dairy Milk and then back to the group I was travelling with. To start with there were six or seven of us lads on the train with north-east scouts – Dave Mooney and Bill Gibbs. Looking back, I think about all those lads on the train with all their hopes and how it sadly didn't work out for some. West Ham also wanted to sign Mark Maley who was from the Boyza and England Schoolboys captain. Mark came down a few times and ended up choosing Sunderland. He played a few games in the first team but unfortunately his career was cut short by an accident. I remember what a good defender he was and shudder at the memory of hearing the tragic news that his career had ended when he was accidentally shot in the eye with an air rifle by his teammate John Oster. Mark and I had so many great times together. It was a cruel blow.

When the train pulled into King's Cross, a wonderful man called Jimmy Hampson was always there to greet us. Hampson's job title at West Ham was director of youth development but really he was a friend and welcoming face. I loved seeing him waiting at the end of the platform. He had that kindly character people warmed to, a proper East End boy. I always looked forward to being in his car, listening to him chatter away as we flew through all the backstreets to Chadwell Heath, West Ham's training ground. He seemed to know every shortcut in East London. While he drove, he talked constantly about West Ham, and sold the club to me with his warmth and his cheeky smile, never pushy.

To start with, I was only on trial. 'Come down and see if you like it,' West Ham said. Well, I quickly realised how genuine West Ham were, especially when I met people like Jimmy Hampson and Tony Carr, the academy director. I just sensed their honesty and that they'd do right by me. Brian Nichols was the Under-14s manager then, and he was so friendly that he immediately made me feel comfortable. From the start, I felt part of the family and played with a smile on my face.

West Ham excited me like no other club that I'd been around. I was very aware of their history as Dad told me all about Bobby Moore and West Ham's connection with 1966 and England's World Cup win. I quickly learned about the West Ham tradition of quick, passing football laid down by Ron Greenwood and John Lyall, whose names were constantly mentioned by the coaches at Chadwell Heath. The whole place felt genuine to me, whether it was the ladies in reception, the secretaries, canteen or coaching staff. Shirley and Dawn in the canteen were good as gold. Shirley always made sure I got an extra bread roll and it was just little things like that that showed me they cared. Ian Jackson, the groundsman who picked me up from the hotel to get me to training, also never stopped smiling. He passed away a few years later, which was very sad, especially as he was no age at all, just 38.

The kit men – Stan Burke, Pete Williams and Eddie Gillam – added to West Ham's family atmosphere. Jimmy Frith, one of the academy coaches, had been there for years, always around the place watching training and speaking to everyone. 'Don't move, son!' he'd say as he passed you the ball. There was also a guy called 'Tel', a disabled lad who was part of the West Ham family, chasing everyone around the canteen so he could tell you his new joke. Tel had the run of the place.

West Ham took me to their heart and that meant everything as I've got to admit I was anxious. For the first time I was far from home, on my own, mixing with new people. I knew I had to prove myself as a player and that I'd be judged every day on and off the pitch. I didn't feel intimidated, because my desire to make it as a professional overrode any fear and because of the welcome West Ham gave me.

Wherever you looked at Chadwell Heath, there were so many real characters throughout my time at West Ham: Ian Bishop, Trevor Morley, Les Sealey, Don Hutchison, John Moncur, Iain Dowie, John Hartson, Ian Wright, Slaven Bilic, Neil Ruddock, Paul Kitson, Trevor Sinclair, Stuart Pearce and Steve Lomas. I remember coming off after training one day, and Hutchison and the fitness coach, Tony Strudwick, were talking about working out in the gym.

'I'm better than you on the rower,' Hutch said.

'Are you?' Strudders replied. 'All right, yeah, let's have it then, 1500m row.' The lads jumped all over it.

We normally aimed to get in at 9.30 for a 10am start but the next day, everybody turned up at 9. Word had got around. We all crammed in the little gym, and they set up two rowing machines face to face and the winner was whoever rowed furthest in 10 minutes. 'Go!' Hutch went off fast into a lead, giving it the big heave, then blew up and hit a brick wall. Strudders plodded steadily on to win. Hutch just rolled off on to the floor. The place erupted, the lads were screaming.

Chadwell Heath was like that – the people built the atmosphere of the place. I used to watch out for Julian Dicks, whose hard-man reputation was no pretence. I was frightened to death of him. It was ruthless back then, a different environment to now, much more confrontational. Tackles flew in, and arguments broke out all over the place. You had to stand up for yourself. You had to be tough to survive. There was a drinking culture. 'Straight to the pub,' I'd hear some of the older players say after training, but they worked hard. Certainly, those who didn't have the right character didn't stay long. I loved all this constant drama but what I loved most was West Ham's commitment to good football, and Harry Redknapp's loyalty to the youth team.

During the holidays, it felt like a big privilege being a schoolboy of 13 or 14 years of age training with the youth team. They were years older than me and could have ignored me, dismissing me as, *A young kid from up North, what's he doing training with us?* But they kept me involved. Some of the lads were 18, and I did feel intimidated being in the changing room with them, so I kept quiet and listened hard to pick up any lessons I could. Frank Lampard and Rio Ferdinand were part of that team. Throughout my career, I've always tried to align myself with the best like Frank and Rio. Lee Hodges was the shining star at that time, a Plaistow lad, he was very skilful, and I looked at him in training and studied what he was doing. Frank was on another level. I was in awe of his technique and especially his volleys, and he was an unbelievable trainer too. Some lads don't train properly, they just do enough and don't make it as players or their careers just tick over. Frank always did extra, he pushed and pushed himself, and that's why he got to the top. I used to do extra training with his dad, Frank Senior, Harry's assistant. Frank Senior would be there, as always, pushing us to do more shooting, running, press-ups and sit-ups.

Basically, I tried to copy Frank, who was destined early for the first team. I remember the day he bought running spikes to do his sprints in, I just followed him and joined in as much as I could. West Ham fans sometimes got on Frank's back and moaned, 'He's only in the team because of his dad.' That was unfair. If the team struggled, it always seemed to be Frank who was made the scapegoat. Those fans who had a pop at him must have realised how wrong they were when they saw the rest of his career. He proved how good he was, and I'm convinced that all those jibes of 'He's only at West Ham because of his dad' toughened him up and made him determined to get to the top.

Although Frank was my first inspiration, as I got older, Rio became stronger. It's easy to warm to Rio because of his personality – he's very loud and assured, and he always seemed to be enjoying himself. The game came so easily to him. He was so confident on the ball, and noisy with it. He had a passion for nutmegging people and shouting about it. I loved his fearlessness and when he first got in the West Ham team, he'd come out with the ball from the back, doing all sorts of different skills and tricks, and taking on the centre forward. Yes, he got caught out a few times but those of us still in the youth team were in awe. Rio was inspirational. We'd say, 'How's he doing that? How does he have the confidence to do that!?' Not many managers would allow it, would they? But Harry Redknapp was different. I know there were times when he would give Rio a little warning sometimes to keep the right balance. Not many centre halves have Rio's quality on the ball and that was to be nurtured, not beaten out of him. Luckily, West Ham was the perfect place for that.

One other thing about Rio Ferdinand that people never appreciated, but I saw first-hand, was that he was probably the worst loser I've come across. Whether it was head tennis, video games or football – he was very competitive, always shouting and screaming. You'd want him alongside you every day of the week. I'm not sure many kids today work as hard as Frank and Rio did when I watched them at Chadwell Heath. We had an old indoor gym there with a five-a-side pitch, and two goals painted in white on the wall. We played this game called 'Ds', named after the D of the goal area. You had two touches – one D to the other – and the ball couldn't stop still in the D in front of the goal. If it bounced outside the D, you lost a point. It was just technique, technique, technique; left foot, right foot, half-volleys, dipping volleys, all sorts. Anybody without good technique was quickly found out and shamed. After training, we'd sometimes play Ds for ages, just backwards and forwards, honing our passing. Even now, when Rio and I chat, we often mention Ds and smile.

From the moment I first set foot inside West Ham, I understood they had a real star in the making in Joe Cole. Everyone talked about him. In my first Under-14 game against Norwich City, Joe was in the team. He was two months younger but a full school year behind me, and he was just doing tricks and moves I'd never seen on a football pitch before, especially a muddy one like Chadwell Heath. I scored a couple, but everyone was blown away by Joe's ability and audacity. Other teams tried to kick seven bells out of Joe, because he took the piss out of them. He would flick the ball over people's heads and do step-overs. He was the first player I came across who was genuinely all about skills. He'd roll the sole of his boot over the ball. He'd get his body in the right position to manoeuvre the ball, using his strength to shield it in that Paul Gascoigne way but Cole used more tricks than Gazza. He was able to roll and bounce off defenders, using contact from defenders to his benefit – he was so gifted! Joe was totally different to me. I never used contact from the defender. I always tried to make a yard or two of space. *Wow, who is this kid?* I thought when I first saw him. He was ridiculously good. He absolutely terrorised defenders in training. A few years later when he got into the first team Stuart Pearce would kick him and Joe would bounce back up. He'd moan about it, but he'd never shy away from it. Pearce was coming to the end of his career and had a fearsome reputation, his nickname was Psycho after all, and he was doing it to say, 'Don't disrespect me. You can't be doing this to me.' I also felt he was testing Joe, saying, 'Go on then. If you're that good, you're going to come back for more.' And Joe did. He just loved playing football and Harry kept telling him, 'Go on, Joe. Terrific, just go and play, son.' Joe went to Lilleshall so I didn't always see him at West Ham when we were coming through the system in those early years. Joe was that good he basically skipped the youth team and went straight into the first team. He took all the limelight off me and the others, and that suited me perfectly. I could continue my journey to the first team in my own way.

I could see a path into West Ham's first team and one particular event when I was 14 convinced me my future lay there. One night, Jimmy Hampson dropped me at King's Cross for my 8pm train back to Newcastle. I was sitting on the train waiting to leave when all trains north were cancelled. I was stuck in London on my own and began worrying a little bit. I called Mam and Dad from a payphone, and they rang Jimmy, who was nearly home.

'What? Michael's on the platform at King's Cross? Tell him to stay under the clock. Tell him not to move. I'll get there.'

Mam and Dad were having a bit of a panic up because I was on my own, no mobile phone, and they could contact me only when I rang them from a payphone. By the time Jimmy got back there, it was 9.30pm.

'Right, come on, Michael. You've got school in the morning. Don't worry. I'll drive you home.' Then he said, 'This is from Sue.' Jimmy's wife had some sandwiches and snacks. Jimmy then rang my parents to put them at their ease. 'Don't worry about Michael. I've got him. Put the kettle on in a bit!'

We headed out of London, up the A1 and Jimmy got me back to Newcastle at 3am. 290 miles! He came in, spoke to Mam and Dad, had a cup of tea, and went back to his car.

'I'm back at work first thing,' he explained. 'I've got a meeting at Upton Park at 8am.' Mam, Dad and me just looked at each other as Jimmy walked to his car for the long drive home. Another 290 miles. Jimmy hadn't made a big thing about it, he hadn't considered just sticking me in a hotel for the night at King's Cross, and telling me to catch an early train home in the morning. Jimmy cared enough for me that he drove almost 600 miles and he can't have got much sleep before work. Jimmy didn't want me to miss school, and he didn't want my parents, or me, to worry. He treated me like his own kid and that was the moment I told Mam and Dad, 'Do you know what? West Ham's the place for me. They'll look after me.'

After signing for two years from ages 14–16, the biggest decision was coming next. This is when it gets serious, moving out to play full-time somewhere. At the time, Mam and Dad were getting big offers from other clubs for me and some of the lads at the Boyza were getting offered contracts of two years' YTS (youth training scheme) and three years' professional.

'Why am I not getting any of this?' I asked. They never told me of the offers, they wanted it to be a football decision. Mam and Dad never thought of themselves even when some clubs offered to pay their house off, about £50,000. I really respect my parents for resisting that as they didn't have much money and they'd have been well within their rights to take the offer. I wouldn't have held it against them because it was life-changing. Dad worked away a lot, so he could have easily taken a scouting job off one of the clubs. As I've grown older and am now a parent myself I understand more than ever how big a decision that was for them, well actually in their eyes it wasn't their decision at all.

'Where do you like best?' they asked me, stressing the 'you'.

'West Ham,' I replied.

My parents were happy for me to go there as they saw how much Jimmy cared. 'He's going to get looked after,' Mam said.

On finishing school at 15 almost 16, I signed two years' YTS at £42.50 a week. Shortly before arriving, I spoke to Tony Carr on the phone. 'I've got into the England Boys Club team for this tournament in Blackpool. Can I go?' It was my first national honours. This was separate from the professional game. The team was made up from all the Boys Clubs in the country and as I played for Wallsend at Under-16s I was eligible. This was very unusual. Tony explained it clashed with pre-season here and West Ham were off to the Dallas Cup.

'It's a big deal for me, Tony.'

He understood that I was desperate to play as I felt it was the perfect way to end my playing days with the Boys' Club. Tony agreed and, again, it was that West Ham way of caring for players.

I also had to attend an England Selection Course at Lilleshall shortly before I was due to join West Ham permanently. I got the train to Lilleshall, and Mam and Dad and my girlfriend Lisa, now my wife, drove down to watch. Lisa has been with me from the beginning, always by my side for me to lean on; an absolute rock of support every step of the way. To think how young and innocent we were back then.

When the game finished, I'd arranged to be picked up in the car park of a local pub by a driver from West Ham. Mam and Dad brought all my cases down and the driver took them from Dad's boot and transferred them into the West Ham car. It must have been horrific for Mam. This was me leaving home for good. I was still 15 for a few more weeks. Suddenly, the last-minute fear kicked in. I panicked. 'Why didn't you let us go to Coventry?' I asked them. One of the lads from the Boyza, Steve Watson, was going there and Coventry had offered me a contract too. It would have been an easier option for me with Steve there, a familiar face.

'Mam, I don't want to go to West Ham.' It was a throwaway comment. I knew I'd be fine, really, so after some tears I climbed into the West Ham car and looked back at Mam and Dad, Graeme and Lisa getting in their car. The driver dropped me off at my new home in Salisbury Avenue, Barking, where I had digs with Pam and Danny Fletcher, a married couple whose kids had left home. Later that night, I rang my parents. It had been a horrendous journey back for them, with Mam and Lisa crying their eyes out.

'Mam, it's great here, I love it.'

'Michael, you don't know what you've done to me, son. That was the worst journey of my life.'

'This is where I want to be. Just having to leave you was absolutely horrible.'

I told them I was fine. In fact, I couldn't wait to get started. Most of the Under-17s and 18s were in Dallas, so I got on with settling in at Pam and Danny's. Four doors down was another family who looked after West Ham kids and this Aussie, Richard Garcia, moved in there the same day. It's funny looking back and realising that a strong, lasting friendship with a very different character to mine began on the No.

62 bus to Chadwell Heath. Rich and I were in each other's pockets 24/7 for the next seven years. I thought I'd moved a long way from Newcastle, but he'd come from Perth!

Rich and I both missed home, and became close, like brothers, and still are to this day. His wife Janelle and his two gorgeous children, Zac and Lauren, are like an extended family to me. I miss them a lot now they have moved back to Australia. We still meet up every two years or so when we can. The bond we have is very special. We've been through so much together, even being at the 2010 World Cup. At least he got to play. I've always been drawn to strong characters and Rich is fiery, he's got a snap on him whereas I'm calm. He'd get hammered off the lads about his clothes. Rich had long hair and was into bands like Green Day, Red Hot Chili Peppers and Pearl Jam. 'What's that?!' I'd ask dismissively when he played his music. He drilled it into me so much that I now enjoy some of it. I went to a Chili Peppers' gig recently – it was the best I've been to.

At the first day of training, when the boys returned, Rich marched straight into the changing room and sat down. Protocol for youth-team players was we collected our own kit from the kit man. This brash Aussie just sat there with his big mop of hair and said, 'All right then, who the fuck's going to go and get my kit then?' All the lads, especially the second years like Anthony Henry, Gary 'Trigger' Alexander, Alex 'Meatball' O'Reilly and Danny Fernley looked at him and absolutely abused him. 'Who the fuck do you think you are?' Then everyone started laughing and it broke the ice.

That youth team changing room was a special place. Some of my happiest memories are of sitting in there with the boys and the banter flying about. The spirit and camaraderie was amazing. One day, Craig Etherington, nicknamed 'Ugaz', got put naked into a metal, see-through crate, wrapped up with all the tape from the medical room we could get our hands on and wheeled into the canteen. I can still picture Danny Fernley's face chuckling away.

It wasn't all laughter. I remember as a first-year YTS, the youth team played Luton in some floodlit cup, and I wasn't great. Dad came down to watch and we were driving somewhere and Dad said, 'What's that sign say?'

'How am I meant to read that, it's miles away.'

Dad didn't reply, but I found out later that he said to Mam, 'Something's not right with Michael, he couldn't even read the sign and it was right next to the car, there is something wrong with his eyes.' Mam knew she couldn't say anything to me, because I'd say, 'I'm fine, I'm not going to get my eyes tested.' So, she rang the head physio, John Green, directly and said, 'Something's wrong with Michael's eyes.' He pulled me and said, 'Michael, I've had your mam on the phone.'

'You what?!' I phoned her as soon as I could. 'Mam, what are you ringing the physio for?' *I'm independent. I can look after myself*, I thought. But the club did get my eyes tested, and it turned out I was blind as a bat. In the space of three months, my eyesight had deteriorated, so I had to get contacts. I remember putting them in for the first time, oh my goodness, I can't do anything now without them. I get up in the morning and can make breakfast without my contacts, but driving not a chance. Before contacts, I'd look at the other side of the pitch, and it would be blurred, and I'd think when I passed to someone *that he's probably over there*.

West Ham got me sorted. 'We'll look after you,' Tony Carr said. 'We have a responsibility to you and your family.' When I think back on the many people who've helped me in my career, Tony Carr is definitely one of the first names to spring to mind. I think of the England squad in South Africa in 2010, and seven of the 23 owed a debt of gratitude to Tony: me, Frank, Rio, Joe, Jermain Defoe, Glen Johnson and John Terry, who was at West Ham briefly as a kid.

Tony took a long-term view of our development. He and Jimmy actually weren't 100 per cent sure whether to take me because I had a spell around 14 or 15 where my body grew at a rate I couldn't keep up with. I had this terrible fear that my body might let me down and destroy my career before it even started. I was terrible in training, really weak, and my coordination was horrendous. I struggled to get round the pitch because of problems with my knees.

'I'm miles away,' I told Mam and Dad. 'I don't know what's up with me here. I just can't play football.' West Ham's coaches were looking at me and probably asking questions in private, like 'Is Carrick going to be any good or not?' Tony didn't know if I was going to come out of this phase. I wouldn't have known his misgivings from his behaviour towards me. Tony was always supportive and encouraging. I knew he saw me as a player he had to train up to get into the first team, and one day might sell on, but he also saw me as a human being.

Tony certainly got us fit. Every Monday morning the first- and second-year YTS that made up the youth team had to do this run before training, five laps of the pitch called 'The Mile' to shake us back into life after a Sunday off. We all set off together, going as fast as we could. Some lads loved it. Danny Bartley, a tall centre forward, was instantly gone, quickly getting far ahead of everyone else. Danny was so fit, and ended up becoming a PT instructor in the RAF. I was all right at 'The Mile', usually in the top five or six, especially when my body sorted itself out. Tony totally believed in 'The Mile'. It was real old school training, partly for fitness but partly to toughen us up mentally. Tony certainly wasn't all nicey-nicey all the time. We did a lot of work on the 'third man run', one of his favourite themes. Tony organised possession work, where it was pass, pass, pass, and then a runner went in behind. It taught us movement and timing – the vital basics.

We were the last breed before the academies started when the system changed dramatically. With the old system of doing jobs, you had to suffer a little to reap the rewards. It taught values and gave you an extra sense of satisfaction in your achievements. Tony oversaw us doing the usual jobs, cleaning the boots and changing rooms, and gathering up kit. Tony made sure we did that properly and that was massively important for young players as it kept us at our level. At West Ham, I was really aware of the pecking order, and knew I had to work hard to get to the next level. That's such an important lesson, and it saddens me that it gets lost nowadays.

So much of my life and career has revolved around the importance of respect. It wasn't only my parents and the Boys Club who instilled respect in me, but Tony too. In the youth team at West Ham, if I was in the gym and a first-teamer came in, I'd stay out their way, maybe even leave the gym completely. They had priority. I wasn't at their level. I had to earn it. The culture was incentivised so I cleaned boots in the youth team, and when I got to the reserves, somebody cleaned my boots. I appreciated the huge amount of work I'd have to put in to get to the top. Football's forgotten a lot of this and is poorer for it. The rules have changed in academies, and they say young players can't do jobs, but there still needs to be a way of taking those steps up that ladder, rather than just gliding up without realising it. It's easier for young players now, they don't have to cope with such a harsh environment. I worked hard to climb to get to the top. I cleaned Tim Breacker's boots first, then Steve Potts's and then Ian Pearce's, because his boot boy was no good, so he headhunted me. I was tidy, quite fiddly with boots and they'd have to be cleaned just right. Doing Pottsy's boots was all right as he was a size six so it didn't take long.

Pearcey had a battered old pair of Puma Kings, massive things, size 12, which weighed a ton and took me extra time but I shined them right up. Pearcey promised me a tip at Christmas and then swerved me. Scandalous, isn't it? Pearcey – if you read this, I've not forgotten!

There was a big sink outside where we cleaned balls and boots in freezing cold water and my fingers would be in bits. The brushes were filthy. You had to be careful not to get the boots wet on the inside either as you'd never get them dry. There was a technique to it. I was a bit OCD, in fact more than a bit. I loved the feel of boots. Puma Kings were the best, so soft and classy, and I begged Dad to buy me a pair when I was 14, although it probably broke the bank account. I had an obsession with boots as a kid, I could tell you what every player wore. I liked the old Predators, not the big clumpy original ones, but the next version. I loved the Umbro Specialis worn by Alan Shearer and Michael Owen. West Ham gave us Pony boots, and then Fila, so my knowledge of the boot trade down the years was pretty varied.

As well as boots, we did all the usual apprentice chores. The absolute killer was moving the big heavy goals for the first team before and after training. It was backbreaking work lifting them, they were freezing cold and weighed a ton, not like the nice light ones now. If balls went missing at Chadwell Heath, Tony scrambled all the YTS lads to search for them. Sometimes I'd be relaxing in the canteen having done all my jobs, sitting there with my nice new Reebok Classic trainers on, and there'd be a shout from Tony, 'Get out and look for the lost balls.' If it was a winter's day, my new trainers would get ruined. I'd be carrying a goal in the middle of winter with my hands dropping off and getting my nice new tracksuit dirty. Tony ran a harsh school, but he taught us valuable lessons about doing jobs properly. If someone didn't do his job, the lads would hammer him. Some were wanting to get back to South

London, and if they missed the train or bus, it was an extra hour. It taught us responsibility and teamwork. It was ruthless and disciplined.

As a 16-year-old YTS, I cleaned the changing rooms after games at Upton Park. The home one was a ball-ache because the lads weren't in a rush. I'd think, *Hurry up*. If it was a night match, I'd miss the last train to Barking and then have to be back at training in the morning, so it was a disaster. I had no choice, though. I knew my place. I preferred doing the away changing rooms because they'd be dashing off, so we'd finish quickly. I also loved seeing all the superstars. I'd stand in the corridor with three or four of the other YTS lads. When Arsenal came, I'd stare at Tony Adams and Patrick Vieira. Adams always stood out because he had this swagger, this presence, really. After one game he was walking out, squeezing down that tight corridor, and he looked at us, nodded and said, 'All right, chaps?! Thank you!' He didn't need to, it was amazing of him to acknowledge us. I was buzzing after Tony Adams spoke to us and I'd never been called 'chaps' before, it seemed very classy at the time.

When Chelsea came, I'd look at Gianfranco Zola, Ruud Gullit and Gianluca Vialli and admire their aura. Chelsea games could be fraught as coming out of Upton Park Tube it got a bit naughty on Green Street. Quite a few times, I'd walk to the ground with it kicking off around me. Sometimes I'd come from a youth team game at Chadwell Heath wearing my tracksuit, so I had to keep a lookout. West Ham v. Chelsea could get tasty. It helped toughen me up and made me a little more streetwise.

The team I put on a pedestal most were Manchester United and it was here that I began falling in love with the club. Whenever West Ham played Manchester United, there was always a different buzz around Upton Park. I'd look at Roy Keane, Gary Neville, David Beckham and Ryan Giggs and analyse how they walked out of the changing room, seeing if they said anything or if they were just totally focused. I tried to pick up tips on how to be a top pro like them. When Manchester United came to town they'd be in their blazers and looked like they meant business. Seeing Alex Ferguson for the first time made a deep impression on me. He marched down the corridor towards the tunnel like a general eager for battle and utterly confident of winning it. I dreamed of playing for him. I actually did have a dream about playing for Manchester United when I was 19, and still making my way at West Ham. Becks was in the dream, Gary Neville too, I was in the team and we won the league. Dreams can come true! Generally, though, there was no time for day-dreaming at West Ham because they worked us, ran us and moulded us into pros. The difference of training once or twice a week at school and at the Boys Club, compared to a few weeks later training every day, even twice a day, was very tough to get used to. At times in the first two to three months I found it hard but once your body adapts it becomes routine. There were some horrible days, relentless days of training full-time, days that shaped me as a player. Often, we did double sessions and I'd almost be falling asleep on the bus home, and then having to go and watch a first team game or a reserve game, no matter how tired I was.

West Ham tested us mentally as well as physically. Sometimes, I'd be in the changing room after a reserve match, thinking, *That's my chance, and I haven't played well. Where's my next chance coming from? Am I good enough?* The pressure was endless. Looking back, I appreciate all that pain was the perfect grounding for a professional career.

I also look back and laugh as those youth team days are right up there with the best times of my life. My memories of all the lads and our various escapades will always stay with me. I remember Danny Fernley, who ended up in construction, just loved nutmegging everyone. He would pop the ball through someone's legs, and go, 'Oops! Sorry!' One game at Chadwell Heath, Fernley nutmegged someone right in front of the dugout, and did his usual, 'Oops! Sorry!' He got round the other side, gave a little look back to the bench and had a laugh with the lads. Tony Carr went mental and subbed him off. Peter Brabrook helped Tony with the youth team. He was a character and the lads loved him. He just wanted to play in the 'boxes' with us and nutmeg who he could. He used rhyming slang for everything. Even naming the team, he would say, 'Michael is in the sausage roll', meaning I was playing in the hole as a No 10. All the lads called me 'Spuggy', the Geordie out of *Byker Grove*. Brabs didn't have a clue what they meant and kept calling me 'Boogie'. He was a legend, Brabs.

Our youth team dressing room was the hive of all the banter, with the lads just buzzing after we came off the pitch. I'd hear the other players talk about all the things they got up to, life on the street, girls, getting in scrapes and it was a world I didn't know existed. Some of the second years had cars. Cars!! I didn't even have a bike. We'd get the bus. They'd jump in their Peugeot 306s. Again, seeing all that was an added incentive for me to push on.

Generally, they'd all hammer each other about something or another. Somehow, I escaped their abuse. Others got it relentlessly and were slaughtered for their gear, hair, looks, big nose, chin, stuff about their dad or mam. Someone would make a passing comment and Fernley would jump on it, 'You're not having that, are ya??' The other lad would reply, then the background hum would intensify and Fernley would be off again, 'You can't take that off him, he just said that about your mum.' It went back and forth, noisier each time and before you knew it, there would be a full-blown argument, Fernley laughing his nuts off and all the lads erupting.

We held a fight once a year in the gym, first years against second. One time, I fought Stephen Purches, an Ilford lad coaching at Bournemouth now. I wasn't a fighter, and nor was Purches, but the players' code demanded we go through with it. We pretended to wrestle, going at it with a lot of noise but without hitting each other, pathetic really. The fight was more a ritual, nobody got hurt, just a few dead legs and dead arms here and there. The second years were just trying to stamp their authority.

West Ham's youth team was a school of hard knocks. I wasn't dead soft, but I was never really outgoing. Nobody could sit there, quiet as a mouse, not saying a word, so I had to overcome my shyness because those who went into their shell didn't survive. Early on I thought, 'It's hard, this. I want to go home.' I never told anyone at West Ham, but I told Lisa. I didn't have a mobile, so we wrote to each other all the time and I told her how tough it was. I'd always get a little boost when one of her letters would drop through the door. Lisa always sensed what I needed, whether I needed to be left alone, or given a lift. She just *gets* me. One time I felt really low and wrote to Mam and Dad, 'I want to come home. I'm sick of it.' That was just the emotion on one day, one week, one month and I wouldn't have given up. I've inherited Mam's steely determination and desire to fight through.

I know we have a good life as footballers but there's a lot of sacrifice along the way. Being away from home was painful at times emotionally, but it's what made me. Going home after six months, and being around my old schoolmates again, I realised how much I'd grown up. West Ham made me a man. I'd been thrown into the real world while my Newcastle friends still lived at home, going to sixth form, and were playing out an almost extended version of our old school lives.

Harry Redknapp always went out of his way to speak to Mam and Dad. He was brilliant, bubbly and friendly, and he knew all the young lads by name. When I was 13 or 14, Harry would say, 'Bring them in' after a first team game, beckoning somebody to guide us kids into the dressing room. 'Come and see the boys.' There was no formal introduction, I just found myself being welcomed into the first team dressing room. That summed up West Ham, that strong link between the young boys and the first team. You could sense the genuine enjoyment, pride and satisfaction Harry and all the staff had at seeing a youngster rise to the first team. I knew I'd get the opportunity at West Ham, if I was good enough.

3 January 1998 was a day I'll never forget as I agreed with Harry and West Ham that I'd sign my professional contract. I was signing on for three years from 28 July, my seventeenth birthday. I've kept the contract, the print's fading but you can still make out the numbers. My basic pay for '98/'99 was £400 a week, going up to £500 in '99/2000 and £600 in 2000/'01. West Ham agreed to give me £700 for every start in the first team and £350 if I came off the bench. I'd get £2,500 on my full debut and £10,000 after 10 starts. My contract also had win bonuses depending on West Ham's position in the Premiership table. If we were ranked sixteenth to twentieth, I'd get £325 for a win, £500 for eleventh to fifteenth, £650 for sixth to tenth, £800 for second to fifth and £950 if we were ever in top spot. In the First Division, the bonuses were £300 max and nothing if we were below thirteenth. I also signed up to incentives in the FA Youth Cup: £10 for the first round, then £15, £20, £30, £40 on to £50 for each leg of the semi, and £100 per leg of the final. But money was never the motivation for me and still isn't. The chance of progressing meant more to me and now I knew there was a chance.

If the youth game was 11am at Chadwell Heath, Harry watched the first hour with Frank Senior and then dashed to Upton Park. All the teams felt connected. We only had three pitches all alongside each other – first team, reserves and youth. One day in '97, I was training with the youth team, when Harry shouted over, 'Tony, I need a midfield player. Can you send one over.'

'Michael, over you go.'

So, this was finally it – the chance I craved, training with the first team. I must have done OK because I heard later that Eyal Berkovic asked Tony who I was, and told him I was going to take his place in the team one day. That made me feel on top of the world because Berkovic was an unbelievable footballer. For him even to be asking about me boosted my belief that I could belong in the team. I watched Berkovic closely before he eventually headed to Celtic. I just wanted to learn as much as I could. I've played with better players, but Berkovic just had that sense of how to deliver that clever through-ball. He loved it, that little angle, and it was probably the best through-ball I'd seen up to then.

Because of my late birthday, my pro money didn't kick in until I was 17 so I stayed on £42.50 apprenticeship for what felt the longest six months ever. I'd little to spend my money on anyway, just clothes and Craig David or Usher CDs. I shared a room at Pam and Danny's with Anthony Hudson, son of Alan, the famous Chelsea, Stoke and Arsenal midfield player. I'll never forget the shock of waking up when Pam walked into our room after midnight on 16 December 1997 to deliver bad news. Alan got hit by a car and was in a coma for a long time. It was so tough for Anthony. So, I look at him now, a successful coach, so nearly getting New Zealand to the World Cup, and really admire how he got through it all.

After a year at Pam and Danny's, me and Rich Garcia had this brainwave of getting our own place. Stupidly, I thought we were men and got carried away. Really, we were still quite naïve. We wanted some independence so we found this flat in Chadwell Heath, but Jimmy Hampson got wind of it and went nuts. He knew what was best for us, far more than we did. Even Frank Senior talked to us about it and that showed me again the strong link between teams. Jimmy still felt responsible for us and by chance was in the process of buying a six-bed town-house on Kingston Road, Romford for the club, and got in an older couple, Bob and Val Rayson to keep an eye on us lads. On the top floor were two bedrooms, a kitchen and a shower so it was like our own little apartment, which Rich and I quickly claimed – our first step towards full independence! It was perfect, really, as Val filled the fridge up for us and two other Aussies, Mick Ferrante and Steve Laurie, were downstairs with Izzy Iriekpen.

Izzy could have been the youngest-ever player in the Premiership when West Ham played at Old Trafford in January 1999. It was last minute, the game was gone, we were 4–1 down, and Harry was going to put Izzy on, looking to the future really with a 16-year-old. But Izzy wasn't ready. He didn't have his pads or shirt on, didn't have his boots tied, and by the time he got ready, and was standing there, the ref blew the whistle for full-time. It was a harsh lesson. He never got to play for West Ham. You still see it now, managers turning round, telling a player to get ready and he isn't, even senior players. Their boots are untied, no shin-pads, no top. It's unbelievable the amount of times you see lads scratching around saying, 'Who's got my shin-pads? My shirt?' Sometimes, the shirt is even back in the changing room. Watching what happened to Izzy, I promised myself that would never happen to me, that I'd always be ready. I might have my boots undone to give my feet a breather, but otherwise I always had everything ready. Unfortunately for Izzy the chance never came around again.

After a year, West Ham bought the house next door and connected the two with a games room. Shaun Byrne and Adam Newton moved in, and soon there were 10 lads there – all the boys I'd known since I was 13, all living the dream. We were inseparable. I now had a support network at West Ham, mates like Rich, Mick and Byrney with whom I formed a bond that we still have today. Rich and Mick are living in Australia, Shaun's a roofer in Slough but we're still close. We all appreciate what we had at West Ham was pretty special.

One Christmas, everyone was sent home to have the day with their families, apart from me because I was needed for first team training. So, Mam, Dad and Graeme came down, and Mam cooked Christmas dinner for the four of us and we all had Christmas in my bedroom on the fourth floor. I lived there for two years and loved it, sharing with Rich. He had a decent contract, too, but we weren't flash. I did buy a car, a little silver Fiesta 1.4, it had a wooden dashboard and door trims, and cost me £7,000 second-hand – all very sensible. I was desperate to drive so I prayed my driving test went well. I was pretty confident, but still I knew that one or two mistakes at the wrong time and it would be game over. I was just about to do the parallel parking manoeuvre when the examiner started talking about West Ham's last game. I thought, 'Leave it out, mate. Put the ball away, I'm in the middle of my driving test and my hands are sweating.' He explained he was a steward at Upton Park. Happy days! I passed with flying colours – claret and blue. I think I passed regardless. The examiner just used the time for a one-on-one on West Ham!

I soon outgrew the Fiesta and decided to give it to Dad.

'No, no, no, I'm not taking it, son. I've got one.'

'Dad, just take the car. You can put the two in and get yourself a better car. I think it's due a service, so just put it in for a service, sell it, do whatever you want to do with it.'

'Oh, OK, brilliant, thanks, son.' When Dad took the Fiesta in for a service it cost him £400. The tyres were shot to bits and it needed new brake discs and pads. Dad was devastated. He didn't tell me for two years, mind.

'Did you realise you were driving the car like that?' Dad eventually said to me. 'It wasn't even roadworthy, the tyres were gone.' Dad wasn't telling me off, he was more worried.

'Sorry, Dad.' I felt I'd let him down. Just the fact that I drove around with four worn tyres was a bit of a wake-up call. I became more sensible after that. I'm a fast driver, but not erratic. I'm not one that flies everywhere, not any more anyway. I did when I was younger.

After the Fiesta, I bought a BMW 3 Series Coupé, blue, for £20,000 – it was nice actually. I'm not one for haggling. 'Is that your deal?' I'll say, and if I like it, I'll take it. After that, I got one of the early X5s. I had about three different X5s. I was still at West Ham when I bought a Mercedes SL 55 AMG two-seater, a lovely, beautiful hard top but it went back. I then bought a Dodge Viper, left-hand drive – it was ridiculous. The managing director of DaimlerChrysler, in Milton Keynes, brought it round. The lads were all there, Rich, Mick, Byrney and Steve Laurie, and they loved the Viper. 'You've got to get it,' they kept saying. 'Brilliant, something different, I'll get it,' I said. Cost me £45,000. I didn't know what I was doing. Beast of a car, grey with two orange stripes down the middle. One day, we'd been at Rich's house in Romford and decided to go to mine in Theydon Bois. I only had the Viper, a two-seater, but there were three of us, me, Rich and Byrney. We stupidly decided it would be a good solution to take the spare wheel out the boot and shut Byrney in, curled up in that space. It was a 20-minute drive to get home. The noise of that car was unreal. Me and Rich were crying with laughter while Byrney was shouting 'stop'. He could barely walk when he got out.

I look at kids at clubs now in cars like that and think, 'What are you driving?' The older lads at West Ham must have thought, 'Who does he think he is?' I was 20. I drove the Viper into Chadwell Heath one day and pulled in next to Tony Carr. He just looked at me with such a surprised face as if to say, 'What's going on here?' Tony didn't say anything, but I remember that look of almost disappointment in me. I realised I shouldn't have bought the Viper. I ended up hardly touching it and eventually got rid of it for £30,000. When I look back now, I think, *What an absolute idiot!*

My main outlay was getting my own place. I enjoyed it at Bob and Val's but life in the flat upstairs made me want my own place even more. So, when I turned 19, I bought a house for £280,000 up the road from the digs, on Brunel Close, the same street as Joe Cole. Rich moved in, paid me rent and it suited us both. I saw it partly as an investment. My parents have always been careful with money and I followed them. Lisa was at college and then uni in Newcastle, and came south when she could. Rich's girlfriend, Janelle, who is now his wife, would fly over from Perth. In the early days, we forgot to tell Lisa about Janelle. One day Rich and I were out training, Lisa was in the house on her own and there was a knock on the door. It was Janelle. Lisa never knew she existed. So, she opened the door and saw this woman standing there. Janelle said, 'Hello! Who are you?'

'I'm Lisa. Who are you?'

'Janelle.'

Lisa went, 'What's going on?' For five seconds, they stared at each other as if they were rivals. Then Janelle said, 'I've come from Australia to see Rich.'

'I'm here with Michael!' Lisa replied. 'All right! OK! Come in!' Lisa and Janelle have been best mates ever since.

I first met Lisa at the church hall in Wallsend where my parents and hers were having a party on New Year's Eve. I was quiet, shy and didn't really say too much to her. She was so differnt to me, confident and outgoing. I had my eye on her straight away, with her blonde curly hair, but I never thought I stood a chance. Lisa was friends with my mates Steven Bradley and Stephen Rutherford, who were more outgoing than me. We used to all meet up on our bikes to go to Wallsend Park and play tennis or cycle down to Whitley Bay and get the bus back to avoid cycling uphill.

Lisa's brother Glen is now a singer, but he played a lot of football as well, and played with Graeme for the Boys Club. That's how our parents met. There was a school play, *My Fair Lady*, on at my school and my mate Chris Hood was lead role. A few of us went to watch, Bradley, Rutherford, me, Lisa and a couple of her friends. I had meant to ask her out, but hadn't quite found the right moment. So, I rang her the next morning before school and she answered, 'Why have you rang me, it's ten to eight?' So I told her, 'The lads said I had to ask you out last night and I didn't, so I thought I'd better ring you before I went to school.' She told me, 'Well, I've got dancing tonight, netball tomorrow, I'll ring you back on Thursday.' She rang back and said she had her GCSEs starting in a few weeks and didn't have time for a boyfriend. We were good mates and I think she didn't want to hurt my feelings.

But then we started speaking on the phone all the time, just general chat. A few weeks later, after she'd finished her exams, she changed her mind. It must have been May, and then in July I had to leave to go down to West Ham. The timing was all off. I used to tell her, 'I can't wait until I make it and I'll fly you down.' I was on £42.50 a week, so I saved up, and flew her down on EasyJet. I'd ring once a week from my digs and, alongside the letters we wrote each other, we'd send some poetry too. I've got them all and Lisa's got all mine. When I'd get back home, we'd have a party at her place or mine.

Lisa stayed at school, did her A-levels and then got a degree in Business Administration. She worked in Romford doing a bit of accounting when we were down south. She used to dance quite a lot as well, in shows and pantomimes, and taught children. She fell into Pilates after I started it for my groin rehab and ended up studying a course. When I was at West Ham and Spurs, she used to go round to people's houses and teach Pilates to all sorts – young and old, men and women. She knew it was a skill she could take with her if I ever got a transfer somewhere else. Lisa has had to sacrifice a lot for us to have a life together. She had to move away from her family and give up on the career she would have had.

At West Ham, Rich, me and the lads were all close. Whenever we had an FA Youth Cup tie in the evening, we'd go to the same bakers in Romford at 11am, buy one sausage-and-egg sandwich and one bacon-and-egg sandwich, come back, wolf them down, have a little sleep in the afternoon, and go to Upton Park for the game. Those heavy, greasy sandwiches can't have helped much, honestly. We were never concerned with our diet or nutrition at that stage. It wasn't something we were educated on back then. It's changed dramatically over the years.

At night-time, we probably socialised too often in Romford. Some of the lads went out on a Wednesday night, even a Thursday, but I was always conscious of the game on a Saturday. Even at that young age, I understood the importance of preparation. I still needed a blowout, a respite from the pressures of the week. In the early days we'd go to The Barking Dog, bang next to the station, have a few pints there, and then on to The Golfer, a pub with a karaoke in Beckton, near the old ski slope. We'd start with normal songs and as it was West Ham territory and full of West Ham fans it always ended up in one big sing-song. We'd move on to Ilford, a club called 5th Avenue, and that was me unwinding on a Saturday night.

But I came south to play football, and my route to the top was first through the FA Youth Cup, a competition that obsessed everyone at

West Ham. I remember back in 1996, when West Ham played Liver-pool in the Youth Cup final – Frank Lampard and Rio Ferdinand were up against Michael Owen, Jamie Carragher and David Thompson – and it was all people talked about around the club. West Ham lost 2–0 at Upton Park but for the second leg at Anfield, Harry made sure I went along just for the experience. West Ham got beat 2–1 and everybody was disappointed. The Youth Cup mattered deeply. I'll never forget missing a penalty at York in the fifth round in March 1999 and Frank Senior absolutely caned me afterwards. We still got through, and even-tually reached the final against Coventry City. After we won the first leg 3-0 at Highfield Road, word got round that we were a good group. All the first-teamers at Chadwell Heath were asking about the second leg at Upton Park and wishing us luck. Harry and everyone at the club were rooting for us. Warming up for the second leg, I looked around and couldn't believe how many people were there. Upton Park was heaving. They only opened three stands and left one closed thinking that would be more than enough. Kick-off had to be delayed due to the amount of people who couldn't get in. The club opened up the East Stand, but they didn't do the turnstiles, just a gate, so people had to walk round the pitch before going up into the stand. When we kicked-off, there were still fans walking around the pitch, four or five deep. It was organised chaos. I'll never forget the atmosphere, a proper atmosphere, everybody singing like it was a big FA Cup tie. It was madness.

We were very close as a team and the spirit was unbelievable. I love thinking back to that team, because we had some really good players, not only Cole. We had Stevie Bywater in goal and I'd never seen somebody so confident in all my life, but likeable confident, not arrogant confident. 'You're not scoring past me,' he shouted at the first team when he was called up to train with them. The lads gave him stick for it, but he was a hell of a keeper at that age, streets ahead of anyone I'd seen at that time. West Ham signed him from Rochdale and he was brilliant, but he suffered bad problems with his wrist. I remember how frustrated Bywater got when he fractured his scaphoid (a bone just below the thumb) a couple of times and that knocked him. Hilarious fella, though. Defending corners, he told us, 'Don't worry, lads. I'm coming for this cross like a train.' When the cross came in, he shouted, 'Choo, choo,' and piled through to grab the ball.

We played good football and Tony Carr always encouraged us to play out from the back. We had three at the back, Terrell Forbes, Stevland Angus and Iriekpen – all strong athletes, who loved defending and who all wanted to pass the ball. When Stev was 15, I recall people around West Ham saying he was 'the next Rio'. Certainly, he was quick, powerful and could play off his left or right foot, but for all the ability he had, he never made an appearance in the first team although he had a good few years at Cambridge United.

The team had width and pace, too. Newtz was absolutely rapid up and down the right as a wing back. Byrney was left wing back, but was injured for the final, so Sam Taylor stepped in and played well. I know he's still at the club working with the Foundation. Just running through the line-up feels like the game was yesterday. It's emotional looking back because they weren't just teammates, they were real mates. We played with a smile on our faces, having the time of our lives, all on the same wavelength. Mick was a ball-playing midfielder, left and right foot and, of course, we had the great Joe Cole. Rich was upfront. Bertie Brayley was a chirpy, talented left-footed player who probably didn't have the application to make the grade and went on to play a lot of Non-League for the likes of Heybridge Swifts and Dorking Wanderers.

We were almost just messing around on the pitch, having fun. I hit a volley against the bar, turned round and me and Mick just burst out laughing. It didn't seem real. I hit the volley better than the goal I then scored, left-footed, after a pass from Rich. Everything just went right that night. As mates, as players, we just came together. Even to this day that 6–0 win is one of my best single memories in football. Somebody showed me the report in *The Times* the next day which said, 'Carrick and Cole were part of one of the most talented youth sides seen in England since the Busby Babes and Fergie's Fledglings.' It's a hell of a statement but, genuinely, we were. It was the FA Youth Cup, not exactly the Champions League, but it felt like the best of all trophies for us. The week after, we won the Under-19s league as well. That West Ham generation was just one of those great groups that you get, that just gel together.

The day after the second leg, we did our warm-down at Chadwell Heath, just jogging round the pitch where Ian Wright was doing some finishing. Wrighty's not quiet, is he? When we ran behind the goal, he went mental, singing and shouting, telling us how well we'd done. That was unbelievable seeing his reaction, how pleased he was for us. West Ham were that kind of club at the time. There was a genuine warmth and happiness for each other. We loved his reaction and it gave us even more energy and confidence. As we ran past, I watched him carry on his shooting and thought, *What a finisher he is.* He was a hero of mine growing up. I was drawn to him for his personality on the pitch, the way he seemed to be having fun and smiling, and most of all his celebrations. Graeme and I used to copy those when we played in the garden. I loved Wrighty so to see him that happy for us was very special. It summed up our sense of achievement. Two months later, instead of watching Wrighty, I found myself actually training with him.

5
THE WEST HAM WAY

Little did I imagine that within a month of the new season I'd find myself in a forest in Croatia being shown semi-automatic firearms by a local warlord. Harry blooded me gradually in the first team squad, and one of our trips in the UEFA Cup took us to Osijek. The war in the Balkans can't have long finished and Osijek was quite derelict. It was a real eye-opener for me and the others from our successful youth team who made the journey. We pulled up at this hotel in the middle of nowhere, and it was totally dark as if somebody had turned all the lights off. Even in the gloom, I could see the scars of the war in the bullet holes in the hotel walls. We were each given a poky, bare twin room, but Stevland Angus and Terrell Forbes shared with each other as they didn't want to be on their own in such an eerie place. An old lady shuffled along the corridors all night, she'd disappear and come back a few minutes later. It freaked us all out.

On the morning of the game, Igor Štimac wanted to show us around his Croatia so a few of the lads like Trevor Sinclair, Craig Forrest, Paul Kitson, Shaka Hislop, Steve Lomas, John Moncur and myself got into these cars driven by people Igor knew. It felt like being in a convoy driving through a war zone as we went on a tour of Osijek. We got out in what must have been the high street, there were bullet holes everywhere, potholes, half the houses were missing – we were right on the border with Serbia, in the heart of the war zone.

On the way back to the hotel, the first driver pulled off on to this dirt track and we all followed. He stopped the car and gestured for us to join him by the boot. When he opened it, I was speechless. The boot was full of guns. I let out a nervous laugh. I was scared stiff but excited at the same time. Apparently, one of the guys driving us around was a top warlord. This general and his mates put some bottles on a wall 50 yards away and some of the lads had shooting practice with a difference. The guns were little automatic-types, proper gear. Afterwards, the warlord shut the boot, drove us back to the hotel and dropped us off as calmly as if we'd just been on a nice morning stroll. It was game-day after all. Imagine doing that now! Shooting guns on the morning of a European tie!

I've one other memory from that visit to Osijek, and it's a memory that comes with deep sadness. Marc-Vivien Foé scored against Osijek and though I didn't know him that well, I could see he was a great character, always happy and smiling. He was such a supreme physical specimen that I just couldn't get my head round the horrific news in 2003 about his heart attack. For someone like him especially – the way he played the game, so athletic, strong and quick – to have been cut down so suddenly, it was beyond belief. Tragic.

West Ham qualified for the UEFA Cup by winning the Inter-toto Cup and the club gave us all a bonus. My eyes lit up when I checked my bank account to find an extra £20,000 had just dropped in there! Aged 18! I'd never seen money like that. Even the first team lads were buzzing. It was great, but money didn't spur me on, minutes on the pitch did – a balance I don't think all young players have right nowadays. I was obsessed with playing, knowing the financial rewards would follow later, and one of the reasons I came to West Ham was I knew Harry believed in youth. He put Frank in the team, then Rio, Cole was breaking through and I was a few months behind. That's four lads, 21 or under, forming the spine of that West Ham side. Not many managers had the courage to do that and Harry put his job on the line.

Harry gave me my debut in the Premiership in August 1999 when I came on for Rio against Bradford City. 'Go on, son,' Harry said. 'Go and play.' Harry's philosophy was: 'Express yourself, learn from mistakes. Be brave. Keep wanting the ball.' However much we were under pressure, Harry told us to 'demand the ball'. I owe so much to Harry for his coaching and his willingness to take a gamble on me. If I lost a ball trying to do the right thing, passing or doing a turn, Harry never got on my case. The West Ham Way was believing in flair, a bit of magic, to take risks. Soon after coming on against Bradford we got a throw-in right in front of the dugout. The ball came to me, I turned and played Paolo Di Canio over the top. 'Oh, what a ball. That's terrific,' I heard Harry shouting. I don't know whether Harry was excited about the pass or whether he was lifting me up more, and you know what – it didn't matter. My manager, a man I respected greatly, believed in me and that meant everything.

It was tough out there and I was a skinny, naïve kid up against hard midfielders in Neil Redfearn and Stuart McCall. Some of the Bradford players gave me verbals and tried to give me a kick or two to intimidate me, like you could in those days, but Harry's boys protected me. 'Don't worry about him, he couldn't lace your boots,' Steve Lomas said after one tackle on me. 'You're miles better than him.' Lomas could easily have thought, 'Here's this young kid, I'll let him fight his own battles.' But he didn't. I've never forgotten senior pros like him fighting for me at West Ham.

John Moncur was another who always gave me huge encouragement. I loved Moncs – one of the most two-footed players you'd see. I still don't know which foot was his strongest. Moncs knew I was going to take his place in midfield but he treated me like a son to guide rather than a rival. 'When I was at Spurs, somebody said to me, "Look, with the ability you've got, you need to get on the ball",' Moncs told me. 'You've got to do that, Micky. In a game or in training, just see how many times you can get on the ball. Now, go and get on the ball.' He was right, I could let the game drift around me, so I reacted. 'Get on the ball' became the motto hammering through my mind. Moncs helped me on the pitch even more by always passing to me. He could have killed my career right there, or certainly slowed it by never passing to me. A senior pro who doesn't really want a young player in the team can make his life tough but Moncs cared. I'll never forget his driving one day. In the first couple of years in pre-season, we used to go up to Hainault Forest with the first team and run. The lads would come back from the summer in all shapes and sizes. We used to go in a convoy and we'd jump in with them for a lift. On the way back, there's a roundabout where there used to be a bowling alley called Rollerbowl. As Moncs approached, the boys went left to drive round it as you would. Moncs drove straight over it, through the bushes and flowerbeds in the middle, straight over to the other side, bouncing all over the place and laughing his head off. It was always eventful at West Ham.

One day in late 1999, Harry called me in his office. 'I think it'll be good for you to go on loan. Get out there and play some games. Six weeks.' Harry did this with a few players, Frank went to Swansea and Rio to Bournemouth. 'Go pack a bag and get yourself over to Swindon,' Harry said. 'Jimmy will look after you.' Harry managed Jimmy Quinn at Bournemouth and trusted him to play me and develop me, just toughen me up. People didn't always see this side with footballers, heading off to prove ourselves on loan – just me, my boots and a desire to succeed. I was on my own now in the real world of football. No hiding. I had to accept Harry's challenge and leave my home away from home. I got in my little Fiesta, drove home, threw my boots, shin-pads and all my wardrobe in a couple of bags and headed west. I didn't ask any questions. I did exactly what Harry said.

I met Jimmy in a hotel-type bed and breakfast in Cricklade, a pretty Cotswolds town, all a bit different from Barking. Jimmy and his assistant Alan McDonald, God bless him he's passed away now, were there with their wives, having a drink in the bar.

'How you doing, Michael?' Jimmy said. 'Your room's upstairs. Do you want a drink?'

'I'll just have a Coke, thanks.'

'Not a beer?!'

'Coke's fine, thanks.' I wasn't trying to be appear ultra-professional on meeting my new manager. I just didn't like the taste of beer. I'd drink Smirnoff Ice if I was on a night out, probably far too much of it when I did. But only when I was out.

I obviously made an impression with Jimmy because one of the YT boys I knew from back home was at Swindon, a talented lad but one who messed about too much and liked a drink. He told me that Jimmy pulled him in the office. 'The first thing I said to Michael was "Do you want a drink?" And you know what he said? "No, I'll have a Coke." Look at his attitude, he comes in and works hard. That's what you have to do to make it to the top.' I wanted to give myself every chance of making it as a pro and Swindon helped massively. That loan spell taught me matches were physical battles as well as tests of technique. I was a nice, neat, tidy player who needed toughening up.

Going to the County Ground was a complete eye-opener, a glimpse of the other side of football, and I joined a side fighting for survival on and off the pitch. Swindon were struggling in Football League Division One and were skint too. They didn't have a training ground, so we'd meet at the County Ground, change and drive in our cars to a pitch down the road. All the lads even took their kit home to wash, something I'd never seen before. I was a kid on loan, so the kit man took pity and washed mine, but it was a world away from West Ham. Mam and Dad even bought me a club tracksuit. Some of the lads were fighting not just for their careers or to stay up, they were fighting for their livelihoods. With families to look after and bills to pay, any win bonus was vital. This was the real world I'd been sheltered from at West Ham. This was real football, living or dying with those three points on a weekend – it felt that extreme and I needed this wake-up call. What I experienced at Swindon shook me. I was pretty focused anyway, but I knew after Swindon I'd never take anything for granted in football and I wanted success even more. I stepped into a dogfight at Swindon and had to learn fast or I'd get hurt. So, I stood up for myself on the pitch. Swindon hardened me. After my debut against Norwich, I read what Jimmy Quinn really thought about me in the *Swindon Advertiser*: 'I knew he'd be good, but I didn't realise he'd be this good.' Jimmy was kind, and I appreciated his words, but I knew I had to be tough to survive in football at this level.

Swindon was a working-class community, like Wallsend where people also grafted hard. Everyone chipped in at the club because there wasn't a lot of staff really, only Jimmy, Alan and Dick Mackey the physio. Jimmy came on upfront sometimes, even at 40. He replaced big Iffy Onuora in that Norwich game. Lads like Iffy, the Aussie keeper Frank Talia, Mark Robinson at right back and Scott Leitch, a little left-footer who played next to me in midfield, could have thought, 'Who's this flashy Premiership kid who thinks he's going to be the next star?' But they welcomed me, and I was never the flashy type anyway. They realised I was there to battle alongside them. I mucked in. I didn't want them to feel like I was having a little dilly-dally about for six weeks, and then I'd swan back to the Premiership.

At Swindon, I encountered football at its most raw, the game was very physical with hard tackles going in, and at times it seemed that even Lady Luck didn't want to know Swindon. It was mad how many times Jimmy and Iffy kept hitting post and bar. For the last of my six matches with Swindon, we went to Manchester City on an arctic December day. I saw Swindon's loyal supporters shivering in a temporary stand in the corner of Maine Road with Mam, Dad and Lisa amongst them. Lisa severely under-clubbed on clothes. I admired Lisa's devotion if not her choice of clothes to keep out the cold, as she was wearing a tiny coat and was absolutely freezing.

It was blowing a gale but Maine Road was great to play at with that beautiful pitch and more than 30,000 fans packed inside. We got battered and I was taught a real lesson by Ian Bishop and Kevin Horlock, who were too strong and sharp for me. But I learned, and returned to West Ham a more competitive, clued-up player with a couple of goals to my name, against Charlton and Walsall.

I was buzzing when Harry quickly threw me back into the fray. 'You're playing tomorrow,' Harry told me when we travelled up to Newcastle. St James' Park! The place where I first fell in love with the game! I tried to be professional but the kid in me came out. Making my full debut was special enough, but the thought of doing it in front of the Gallowgate was beyond my dreams. I couldn't wait to ring Mam and Dad. As a family we normally play things down, never get carried away – that's not our way. Deep down, we all realised how amazing this was. For my parents, to see their son on the pitch at St James' Park was a dream come true. I spent the whole build-up thinking about what it meant to me and my family and friends. I couldn't sleep as I was too busy counting down the hours, minutes and seconds to kick-off at St James'. My focus was blurred by excitement and I got carried away about scoring the winner. I let my mind wander. Newcastle were a good team, I knew that. They had Gary Speed in midfield and an unbelievable front two in Alan Shearer and Duncan Ferguson but I wasn't so much thinking about the players but the stage and the occasion. I was going back home. *Who's watching? People from school. Where are they sitting? My family will be there. Can't let them down.* Warming up, I caught sight of familiar faces in the crowd, neighbours and school friends. All of this added to the commotion in my mind.

By kick-off, I was worn out emotionally and by half-time I was exhausted physically.

I can't go out for the second half, I'm gone, I thought. Staring at the floor, I wondered how I was going to last. I drank as much Lucozade and ate as many energy bars as I could to give me some help. I played tucked in off the right of a narrow 4–4–2 with Steve Potts behind me at right back. Alessandro Pistone was Newcastle's left back and he just kept galloping forward, while their left winger Kevin Gallacher was tucking in so I was chasing shadows. Frank scored, then Igor Štimac made it 2–2 with a header to rescue us and I was so relieved we'd drawn, and I wasn't a complete disaster. A point away for West Ham was amazing as we never travelled very well. Harry gave me a token 'well done' gesture. I learned an important lesson that day, a lasting one: don't get distracted by the occasion, just focus on the game. St James' also taught me that I could make it to full-time, however I was playing, and I prided myself in becoming a quiet fighter. People look at my career, and say nice things about composure, but I'm a fighter too. I don't give up.

My education at the Academy took in another placement. 'I think you'd benefit from going on loan again, Michael,' Harry said.

'Birmingham want you.' Birmingham City? At the time, Trevor Francis was manager and Andy Johnson was there, who I knew and rated from England Under-18s, so I got back in the trusty, slightly rusty, Fiesta and hit the road again. The traffic was a nightmare and I sat there stewing on the M6, knowing I'd be late for my first meeting with Trevor at a hotel near Birmingham NEC. I hate being late, it goes against everything Mam and Dad taught me about being respectful and organised. 'Oh, God, here we go,' I thought as I walked in to find Trevor and Andy waiting for me an hour and a half after the scheduled time. Thank God, Trevor was fine and very welcoming.

'I'll take you for dinner,' he said. Andy also came along to help me settle. Trevor took us to this really posh restaurant, well, that's how it felt to me, called Bank in Birmingham city centre. I wasn't used to eating in places like that and couldn't make head or tail of the menu. *What do I do? What do I order?* Reading down the dishes, I saw fish, so I asked for that.

'It's Dover Sole sir,' the waiter said.

'All right, brilliant, I'll have that,' I replied as though I'd eaten this Dover Sole all my life.

'Do you want it filleted?' Trevor asked.

'No, it's fine,' I didn't know what Trevor was on about. Fish and potatoes? Similar to cod 'n' chips, right? I can't go wrong, surely? I'd get through this. The waiter brought the Dover Sole, and I cut into it to find bones all the way through. Trevor stared at me as I tried to crunch the bones discreetly.

'Are you sure you don't want it filleted?' he asked.

'Actually, yes, do you mind?'

Filleting was a new word to me, but it clearly meant chucking the bones out. Trevor got the waiter to fillet it, but the fish was a mess and

I cringed in embarrassment as a plate of ruins was placed back in front of me. I felt so out of my depth.

My poor start to life at Birmingham never improved. I never felt as comfortable there as I had at Swindon. I couldn't deny that Trevor was good, and there were some real characters in the Birmingham dressing room. Stan Lazaridis had been at West Ham and still lived in Loughton so he and David Holdsworth, drove me up and back. I'll always remember their kindness, but I played only 83 minutes in total there and didn't even get off the bench at home to Portsmouth.

My frustration lifted after the match when I was called up to the England Under-18s to play France. I later found out I was going to be captain. I'd never captained a team before. Trevor told me after the Portsmouth game that I had to play in the reserves at Tranmere on Tuesday night, so I couldn't go with England. I never answered back, I was too young and respectful, but I was raging inside. I was still fuming by the time I rang Dad to complain, something I'd never done before or since. I started swearing down the phone to Dad, 'It's a fucking joke.' I'd never sworn to Mam or Dad like this before. Even to this day Mam will clip me or pull me up if she ever lip-reads me swearing on the pitch. But I was furious, 'I don't fucking believe it, Dad, he's not letting me go.' Dad tried to calm me down, but I was still livid when I phoned Jimmy Hampson.

'Why am I playing in the reserves at Birmingham?' I asked. Jimmy spoke to Harry, and called me back. Harry didn't know about the England captaincy and thought I was just being a prima donna and moaning about playing reserve games at Birmingham. 'Tell him to play in the reserves and get on with it,' was Harry's message back to me.

So, I played against Tranmere. I went up for a header, landed awkwardly and felt all sorts of cracks and crunches as I twisted my ankle badly, bang – I was out for a month. I'll never forget that feeling of helplessness and anger as I lay on that stretcher, injured in a meaningless reserves game when I should have been representing my country.

After four or five weeks out, I was back in the West Ham team and coming up was Arsenal away in the Premiership on 2 May 2000. This was my biggest test by far, against a top team with some of the very best players around – they really were an intimidating opponent. That Arsenal side could do everything – pass, run and fight. They could be ugly and aggressive but also had flair in abundance. What a team! Players like David Seaman, Tony Adams, Ray Parlour, Patrick Vieira, Marc Overmars, Dennis Bergkamp, Emmanuel Petit – they were one of the best sides in Europe. These were the games I loved playing – against great players presenting a real challenge, on a grand stage, with a full house, and Highbury was special. Don't get me wrong, I never supported Arsenal but I loved watching Wrighty when he was there and Highbury had a classy feel. The bus dropped us on Avenell Road, we walked up the steps to reception, through the marble halls, past the bust of Herbert Chapman and to the changing room, which I remember had a heated floor. Highbury was a proper football ground, full of history and smartly dressed staff, and I felt as though I was entering some aristocratic hall.

Changed, I walked down the stairs and into the tight tunnel, squeezing in with the other players like Adams. It seemed only seconds ago he'd called me and the other apprentices 'chaps' at Upton Park. The referee, Paul Durkin, led us out, and we rose up towards the noise, the light and the challenge. My thoughts were always the same: this was what all the hard work was for. Graft, play well, and win. I wasn't nervous, just incredibly excited. I loved Highbury, even if the pitch was cramped. You almost couldn't breathe out there, especially when Vieira wouldn't give you an inch. I had to fight to gain respect from my own teammates and to show Vieira and all the Arsenal lads that I was no kid who could be bullied. What a monster of a player Vieira was, all arms and legs, six foot four inches of ability and aggression. That first confrontation was a test of my fighting qualities that I hoped had improved at Swindon. I needed to be physical to stand up to Vieira or I'd be brushed aside like a weak child. Football's changed now, it's gone soft. Back then, the pitch was a battleground, a brutal environment. When I tussled with Vieira, I asked myself, *What am I doing here?! Fighting Patrick Vieira?!* I had to grab his shirt to stop him turning away from me, and Vieira gave me a death stare that flashed 'Who the fuck are you?' Me? Just an 18-year-old kid, trying to give you some. Just trying to wrestle with a World Cup winner. Vieira was strutting his stuff, and I tried everything I could to disrupt him, pulling his shirt again, hounding him and every second learning more about the mindset needed to survive in midfield. I had massive respect for Vieira so that's why I got in his face. It's disappointing that this way of playing the game has virtually gone. I'm not naturally aggressive but I loved that physical rivalry – tackles flying in, squaring up, pushing each other in the chest, which was classed handbags then, and is probably a red now. 'Look at you, trying to fight Vieira!' Coley laughed at me. He was right, though. I got caught up in the moment but that was good. I was back in the schoolyard, refusing to be pushed around. If I'd shied away from confronting Vieira, he'd have walked all over me. This was me saying to Vieira, 'I'm still here. I'm not going away. You might have a better game than me, you might win, but you're not going to bully me.' This was me slowly coming of age.

Each game brought a new challenge. On the opening day of the 2000/01 season, I ran into Dennis Wise which I discovered was never a pleasant experience. The Chelsea midfielder was a real nuisance, trying to wind me up and get me booked. He stood on my toe and constantly nipped me behind my arm. Wise put a few tackles in on me too, just making me know he was about, so I gave him some back. You have to understand it was fight or flight and no way would I let Wise intimidate me. During my career, it annoyed me to hear people claiming, 'Oh, Michael Carrick doesn't tackle enough.' Back then, I loved a good tackle.

That season marked my first encounter with the hardest of them all: Roy Keane. We played Manchester United at Upton Park but the game that really stood out for me was the fourth round of the FA Cup at Old Trafford in January 2001. That match pitched me completely against Keane's power and also showed me the sheer size and strength of Manchester United. On the bus from the Worsley Marriott to Old Trafford, I couldn't believe the tens of thousands of United fans streaming to the ground. I realised Manchester United were more than a football club. They were a religion. I saw all these fans hurrying into Old Trafford as if it were a cathedral and it was time to pay homage, and I began to understand what United meant to people.

In the crowd by the tunnel, I saw Mam and Dad standing there with Stevie Bywater's dad David and Coley's parents, George and Sue. Always there, always loyal. Most games my parents liked to be there to give me a wave as I got off the coach. I waved back, and headed into Old Trafford, excited and curious. I hoped United would put a good team out as I wanted to play against the best. Looking at the team sheet, I could see the quality: Fabien Barthez, Gary Neville, Jaap Stam, Mikaël Silvestre, Denis Irwin, David Beckham, Roy Keane, Nicky Butt, Ryan Giggs, Teddy Sheringham and Andy Cole. Hell of a starting XI that, quality subs too: Dwight Yorke and Ole Gunnar Solskjaer both came on.

Harry warned us to be wary of United because they'd been slaughtered for not defending the FA Cup the previous year when they decided to play in the World Club Championship in Rio. They'd be up for this and nobody gave us a cat in hell's chance. Running out from the tunnel in the corner, the stand seemed to go on forever and I couldn't believe the size of the pitch. *Imagine playing here every week!* I thought. I was swiftly introduced to the Manchester United of Sir Alex Ferguson, coming for us, going for the jugular. I kept thinking, *These guys are just relentless, what a team!* They played with such confidence, almost an arrogance that I admired straightaway. Keane clattered Coley, but Joe is fearless and gave him some back. I never really had any bad run-ins with Keane. I always found him an honest competitor, hard but fair. When I put in a good tackle, Keane got up and gave me one back. He was like Paul Scholes, Butt and Vieira. If I put a fair, hard tackle in on them, they appreciated it in a way. They returned it with a bit extra, but it was an old-school, honest battle, nothing underhand. There was no cowardice, like trying to do someone cynically, it was just the ball was there to win, and each man went all-in. Those days you had to be smart and tackle in a way to protect yourself.

Getting close to Nicky Butt, I was soon thinking, my God, why isn't he given more credit for how good he is? Butt shared pitches with great passers like Scholes and Beckham, and people didn't fully appreciate how good a passer he was himself. I saw the passing man, as well as the running man – he was always on the move, back and forth, a box-to-box midfielder and a complete nightmare to chase. I came away from Old Trafford delighted with the win which Paolo Di Canio got us. I also came away thinking, *This is where I want to play my football.* It was a distant dream, of course, but I promised myself I'd become as good as I could and one day I might have a chance of playing for Manchester United.

Looking back, I appreciate how fortunate I was to have so many good influences early in my career. I was surrounded by charismatic figures in that West Ham changing room, like the goalkeeper, Shaka Hislop, who was always bubbly and helpful. Trevor Sinclair also always had my back. Lisa even stayed with his wife Nat a few times when we played away so they weren't on their own. Paolo Di Canio was so up and down. When he was up he was unplayable but when he was down he was unmanageable. That famous image of Di Canio signalling to Harry to take him off at Upton Park in February 2000 will stay with me forever. We were losing 4–2 to Bradford and Di Canio was fuming that the ref, Neale Barry, hadn't given us penalties for fouls on him by Gunnar Halle and David Wetherall. Di Canio waved his finger in the air, marched 50 yards towards the bench and then sat down on the pitch, demanding to be taken off. It was like a protest.

'I cannot play on,' he shouted to Harry. 'The ref's crazy. Take me off now.' I was sitting on the bench with almost front-row seats to the drama, and couldn't believe my eyes.

'No, Paolo, please, we need you!' Harry told him. 'We're losing. Get back on.' He did eventually and he scored.

Joe got the equaliser and then Frank scored late on to make it 5–4. It was Stevie Bywater's debut for West Ham, and Stevie, being the lad he is, turned around to watch the replay of Frank's goal on the big screen behind him and celebrated with the fans. Bradford kicked-off, and somebody saw Stevie on the corner of his 18-yard box and had a shot, the ball flew through the air and Stevie panicked but then realised it was going wide and jogged away with his hands up as if to say, 'Calm down, everything's all right'. Harry went mental. We were pissing ourselves. What cheek, for an 18-year-old as well!

Paolo Di Canio had a split personality: the true pro training properly one day and the next day something would get to him, he'd end up arguing and walk off. 'PAOLO!' Harry would shout after him. He'd come back the next day and be completely back to normal. Harry put up with these manic fluctuations because of what Di Canio offered when he was on it, especially at Upton Park. I'd listen to Harry cajoling him and telling him how much he meant to the club, to him and to the fans. I loved watching Harry deal with mavericks as he was a complete master of the art. He varied his response depending on the psychological make-up of the player. Paolo Di Canio needed careful handling, like defusing a bomb. Jimmy Bullard was an altogether different type and I'll never forget him asking Harry for a day off to go fishing. You can imagine the short answer he got off Harry! Jimmy signed from a Non-League side, Gravesend & Northfleet, and didn't fully understand the demands of the professional game.

Harry quite often announced the team right before kick-off. We'd meet at Upton Park for a 1.30pm meeting in the changing rooms for a 3pm kick-off. Harry pinned the line-up on the board in the changing room, and then retreated to his office next door as if he'd lit a fuse. When Harry left someone volatile out, they'd pile into his office and we'd hear all the shouting through the wall. They'd have a right tear-up in there – all par for the course! That was the type of character and culture we had at West Ham. No holding back!

Stuart Pearce was one of the players I respected most. What impressed me so much was Stuart's unflagging dedication and every day he'd drive in from miles out west in Wiltshire. *Why's he still doing it?* I wondered. *What's his motivation at 38?* I couldn't believe how he almost sacrificed his body to play, as though injuries and illnesses never registered with him. In one of his last games, against Chelsea in March

2001, Pearce twisted his ankle and was subbed off after 11 minutes. I looked at his ankle in the changing room and it was black and blue, so I thought that's him out for four to six weeks minimum – and I was being optimistic. Like everybody, I was aware how tough he was, but I was totally gobsmacked when he hobbled back in four days later. We were playing Spurs in the FA Cup and he must have thought, *This could be my last Cup game.* So, he strapped his ankle up and said, 'I'm playing.' Nobody argued. You didn't with Pearce as he had that edge to him. He got on with preparing for kick-off as we all looked at each other in amazement. It was outrageous how he played that game; he even scored. He was just so driven, even every day in training. He hated losing and I could see why he got nicknamed 'Psycho'. I'd watch his temper spill over and some of his tackles bordered on GBH, even in training. He was one of those strong characters I was instinctively drawn to and wanted to learn from. I'd watch his warm-up, which was so meticulous. He'd put a clock on his peg in the changing room so he knew the precise time for each part of his routine. One day, John Moncs nicked the clock and Pearce went mental. He was a perfectionist, just slightly scary with it.

Whereas, Moncs was a madman, the joker of the pack. One freezing cold day at Chadwell Heath, Stan Burke, the kit man, was in his little room, counting socks or something. Stan was very protective of the kit and trying to get an extra top off him was like trying to pull his right arm off. Moncs kept asking for another top but Stan was adamant. 'No.'

'Bollocks to that,' said Moncs, ran outside and did a lap of the pitch in only his socks and boots. I could tell Moncs grew up with Gazza at Spurs. West Ham fans adored him.

We were brilliant at Upton Park because the supporters were so close to the pitch, and looking up at the steep stands it felt like the fans were almost on top of me. The old Chicken Run terrace would really intimidate the opposition. It scared me a bit and I played for West Ham. I never went in the Chicken Run but it felt like it came to me a few times with the abuse we got.

'Carrick! You're shit.'

'Fuck off back up North.'

'What you doing playing here?'

'Sort yourself out, Carrick.'

That kept me on my toes.

Upton Park actually suited the showmen we had like Di Canio. Away was a different story, mind, as needing to be more resilient and boring didn't suit West Ham. Our chances of keeping clean sheets were significantly damaged when Rio Ferdinand left for Leeds United in November 2000. I guess Rio was so good, and so far ahead, that he had to move on. Knowing it would happen one day didn't lessen the blow of losing our best player. I respected West Ham's attitude. I knew how much the club wanted to keep him, and they kept giving him better deals, but they understood the way of the world. Leeds were a different level to West Ham at that time, so to hold Rio back would have been cruel. The beauty of West Ham at that stage was that they were like good parents, nurturing players like Rio, loving them, and understanding when they wanted to leave home. West Ham felt a duty of care to players and that came from the very top, from Harry and the chairman Terry Brown. Leeds were fighting for the Premier League and the Champions League, so West Ham could hardly stand in Rio's way and £18m seemed great at that time.

When Harry followed Rio out the door six months later in May 2001, I was stunned. Harry's time at West Ham had maybe run its course, and I quickly learned in football to get on with life. It's brutal, yes, but realistic. As a pro, when a manager goes, it's a case of 'goodbye and thanks for the memories'. I'll always feel respect and appreciation for Harry because he gave me my chance and helped me believe in myself more, but I was now committed to the new man. I knew Glenn Roeder well because he took the West Ham development group – lads like me, Coley sometimes, Rich, Mick, Byrney – and we all loved him. When Glenn got the manager's job, the dynamic changed and a barrier went up. We all understood Glenn couldn't be the friendly guy he was before and needed some distance from us. Everything was good in the first season under Glenn, and we finished seventh.

That July, the club offered me the No. 6 shirt – Bobby Moore's old number! Naturally, I said, 'Yes!' What an honour! I understood what No. 6 means to people at West Ham. 'No. 6!! Bobby Moore wore that!!' fans would say to me. Personally, I was never fussed about numbers and never felt weighed down by the history, but I totally respected the No. 6 shirt.

Going into the 2002/'03 season under Glenn, there was a mood of optimism. I've always believed 24 August 2002 was the turning point under Glenn. We were fantastic against Arsenal, 2–0 up and playing terrifically, but Thierry Henry scored from nowhere and Sylvain Wiltord equalised with two minutes remaining; the whole of Upton Park was deflated as we'd got so close to beating the champions. We never got that momentum back, and the fans turned. They're so passionate that when things go well, they're a fantastic crowd. But, because they care so much and are desperate for West Ham to do well, when games don't go well they let you know very quickly. West Ham fans started having a go at Glenn and somebody even threw a brick through the window of his home. That was out of order. That's not football, that's not about the game, that's not about love of the club any more. No football manager deserves to have his house attacked. That's crossing the line and it sickened me. That's about someone's life, that's someone's family they're threatening. Imagine if the shattered glass had cut one of his three kids? Fans can go to Upton Park, voice their concerns, of course, but there's ways of protesting, respectful ways and no one deserved to go through what Glenn did.

West Ham still had powerful personalities in the changing room like David James and Christian Dailly – really vocal guys – and there was Lomas, Moncur, Sinclair, Di Canio, Hutchison, Nigel Winterburn and Tomás Repka, senior players who'd been round the country, let alone round the block. I feared if we lost a few games that it might become difficult for Glenn to manage a group of players with so many strong opinions. Personally, I let Glenn down in a way because I couldn't contribute enough. Even before that season, I'd started getting problems with my groin, hernia-type trouble. I battled on, playing game after game but eventually came off at St Mary's in January 2002 as the discomfort was too much. Every time I side-footed the ball an excruciating pain ripped across my pubic bone. The surgeon, Mr Steven Snooks, operated and put some mesh in both the left and right side and gave me a prognosis of 'six weeks out'. I rushed back because I wanted to help Glenn and the team, even though a nagging discomfort remained. My first game was against Manchester United at Upton Park, and we lost 5–3, and I still don't know how the hell I got through that game. I wasn't right. I played against Portugal for England Under-21s a while later, we lost 4–2, and I'll never forget passing a ball and suffering a shooting pain that crippled me in the same area. So, I went under the knife again.

I didn't know it until the surgeon cut me open again but the mesh had peeled away and rolled up. A second op that summer still didn't sort it and West Ham fans lost patience with me. I thought I had a good relationship with the supporters and I knew they loved seeing young players coming through. They felt all that emotion that comes with nurturing one of their own, but I learned that honeymoon periods end and us home-grown kids eventually got judged like anyone else. By now, we were near the bottom of the league under Glenn, I wasn't playing great and the Chicken Run was unforgiving. As a kid, I could have shrunk into my shell, but I told myself: the best response is just to keep doing the right things and come out the end of it. Frank got a lot of stick from the fans, and he just showed how tough he was, so I vowed to do the same. It was so frustrating, though. I always really liked West Ham fans because there's a quick humour to them that comes with that Cockney swagger.

With me in the middle of a lot of the fans' anger, I felt the storm around Upton Park wasn't going to blow over any time soon. 'Michael, you're on the bench tomorrow,' Glenn said. It was Tottenham away, I'll never forget the date, 15 September 2002 – a big game, and the first time I'd been dropped, probably deservedly. I limped on, but my groin still wasn't right and after mid-March I couldn't help at all in the fight against relegation. By then, West Ham were caught in a downward spiral and the fans really turned during the game against Boro at Upton Park in April 2003. Glenn blacked out afterwards and was raced to hospital, straight into the operating theatre and the surgeon found a non-malignant brain tumour. Thank God, Glenn was in good hands and he was safe. That was all that mattered. He was a good man placed in an intolerable position. What happened to Glenn put football, and our situation, in perspective. West Ham were in turmoil and the team were leaderless. Somebody had to step in and manage the side so Trevor Brooking, a club legend we all looked up to, took over for the last three games of the season. This may surprise people who associate Trev with calm and politeness, but he has a steely, stubborn side, which we needed at that stage. What really shone through with Trev was his love for West Ham, although we needed more than love to stay up. We needed a miracle.

On the last day of the season, West Ham faced Birmingham and we had to beat Bolton Wanderers' result against Boro to stay up. Still injured, I travelled up on the morning to St Andrew's with Ian Pearce. We sat in the stands and shortly before the end, Di Canio equalised to make it 2–2, but Bolton won at the Reebok, so we headed downstairs. As we walked down the stand, Birmingham fans on both sides booted me and Ian. We were taking kicks left, right and centre – even though I'd played for them! They'd probably forgotten all about that. We had no chance of defending ourselves, so we hobbled out of there as quick as we could.

In the corridor outside the dressing room, we saw the other players and everyone looked devastated, silent with shock really. None of us in the changing room could escape the painful truth that we'd all let the club and the supporters down. Some players left in the summer and when I returned to Chadwell Heath for pre-season, there were only about 10 or 11 players out there. We lost some massive players, Di Canio to Charlton, Fredi Kanouté to Spurs, Les Ferdinand to Leicester and Trevor Sinclair to Man City. Glen Johnson came from nowhere, up from the youth team, played the last four months of the season, and left for Chelsea with Coley, joining Frank Lampard who'd gone there the year before. Rio Ferdinand had long gone north. It felt like the end of an era at West Ham. Jermain Defoe put in a transfer request pretty quickly after the final whistle of the season. I understood why he wanted to leave but his timing was off, and I suspect he realised this after he'd done it. I watched my mates heading out the door and it was hard to take losing all that talent, but I couldn't blame them. They had to think of their careers. I'd not played a part in the relegation battle, and my season was a disaster, so I felt it was my duty to remain and help out. I stayed almost out of guilt as much as loyalty.

Newcastle did come in for me, but they didn't have the money. 'We'll offer two million for you but it'll have to be in the next transfer window, so you'll have to hold on,' they told me. It seemed a strange way of doing business, as if they weren't completely sure they wanted me, so I decided to stick it out at West Ham.

At Chadwell Heath for pre-season, I found a club in mourning. It was horrible to see people losing their jobs, victims of relegation. I'd wonder where certain familiar faces were. 'Oh, they've been laid off,' came the sad reply. I hated to think of the impact on their lives and their families, the financial and emotional cost to them, and I became even more determined to get fit and get West Ham back up. I was still having the same problems with my groin and, fearing I'd never be pain-free, in August I went to Leicester to see Mr David Lloyd, a surgeon who operated on me with a different technique. It was keyhole and would only keep me out for two weeks as he placed the mesh on top of the groin instead of underneath. Mr Lloyd had this clever procedure to nick a ligament to release pressure. It worked and since then I've been fine.

Glenn was already back at the club and I admired him for that. He could have called it a day, not put himself through all that pressure again after what happened. However, Glenn loved the game and missed it, so he came back. I enjoyed his training sessions, Glenn was a hell of a coach but sadly the board sacked him after three games as the circus continued at West Ham.

Trevor Brooking stepped back in as caretaker and before we played Derby away on 4 October 2003, he pulled in Rob Lee as a senior player to pick his brains about me. I was still feeling my way back after the operation. 'Do you think Michael is ready to be back involved tomorrow?' Trev asked. Rob's reply was, 'Yes, we need him. You have to play him. Put him straight back in.' Rob was thinking we'd play together in midfield. Trevor's response was, 'Oh, thanks Rob. I think you're right. You're now on the bench tomorrow,' and he walked off. Rob told me the story straight away. It was hilarious. Rob wasn't laughing too much, mind. We won at Derby and shortly after Alan Pardew arrived as manager in September 2003. I liked Alan's training as it was bright, intense and well organised. I know Alan divides opinion because he's very confident, but that swagger was just what West Ham's bruised dressing room needed at the time. His personality lifted the team and he was always good with me, trying to get me on the ball as much as possible but I found that season a real grind. I was 22, didn't want to be in that division, out of the limelight, and felt my career was at a crossroads. It hurt to see England squads announced and not be named. It was tough seeing Glenn Johnson and Coley at Chelsea, doing so well. *Am I getting left behind?* I kept asking myself. *Where's my career going?*

It was physical down there in Division One and tackles flew in as people wanted to prove a point against West Ham, just to show how the mighty were fallen. I've still got a scar as a souvenir. We played Stoke City in December and one of their players, John Eustace, went over the top and punctured my ankle and at half-time the Doc put stitches in to hold the skin together. I should have come off, but I wasn't going to be kicked out of a game, so I went back, played on but it was a struggle. At the final whistle, West Ham fans gave us a bit more stick. I was thinking, *I can hardly feel my ankle, there's blood everywhere. I gave all I could.* It was a lonely place, constantly asking myself what else could I do. *Am I good enough?* West Ham fans didn't know the pain I was in. They just shouted, 'You're not trying, there's no passion.' Well, I knew I put my body on the line out there and still got abuse thrown at me. What really got to me at times in my career was hearing 'there's no passion'. Just because I wasn't playing well doesn't mean I don't care. This was one of those occasions when that shout of 'there's no passion' really pissed me off.

When West Ham fans were with us, mind, they lifted us higher and I can almost still hear the unbelievable noise at Upton Park when we took on Ipswich Town in the First Division play-off semi-final. We were down 1–0 from Portman Road, but Upton Park was rammed for the return and even warming up, I smelled the hope, almost the desperation, for us to reach the final. Upton Park was extra-special under the lights. Driving down Green Street towards the ground when it was all powerfully lit up really stirred me. Big nights were off the scale, even more so against Ipswich when Matty Etherington and Christian Dailly scored. Matty's was a great goal from the corner of the box.

We were off to Cardiff for the final against Crystal Palace, a moment that shaped my career, really. I knew if we beat Iain Dowie's side, I'd still have a year left on my contract and I'd stay at West Ham. Back in the Premiership, job done, so why leave? West Ham were desperate for cash, but promotion meant around £30m in those days so there would be no fire sale of players. I reckon there were more than 35,000 West Ham fans there to greet us when we came out at the Millennium. They knew the significance for their club and I was acutely aware of the implications for me: win and I stayed, lose and I left. My conscience is clear. I gave everything I could to get West Ham up. I set up Bobby Zamora for a chance he didn't take and as we chased an equaliser I definitely should have had a penalty with seven minutes left. I got into the box, nicked the ball past Mikele Leigertwood and he caught my ankle – 100 per cent penalty, no shadow of doubt. I was in bits on the floor with my ankle a mess, in too much pain to appeal, but Graham Poll waved play on. The ankle blew up straightaway, the same one I'd done on loan at Birmingham. I managed to get up, but my ankle was so sore that I couldn't move for a couple of minutes. We'd played all our subs, so I hobbled about up front for the last 10 minutes. One bad decision by a ref can influence the whole future of a player and a team. If Poll gave that penalty, we could've got back in the game, might have won, West Ham would have gone up and I'd have stayed.

To clear my head, Lisa and I disappeared to Jumeirah Mina A'Salam in Dubai. The first person I saw around the pool was Iain Dowie. I couldn't escape the play-off, even 3,500 miles away. I had a brief chat with him, congratulated him, hid my pain over the result and all the uncertainty over my future. It was a horrible situation for me and West Ham. If we'd got back to the Premiership, there was a chance people would have got their jobs back but not now. As callous as it sounds, I had to think about myself. This had to be about me now – my future and my ambitions. I'd had a good season and got in the PFA First Division team. So, I talked to my adviser David Geiss.

I had been introduced to David as a 17-year-old. It was after I had signed my first pro contract, but felt I needed some guidance. My parents had been keen for me to get some help as it was a whole new world for us. I had had agents before coming up to me in car parks and approaching my parents after games, promising me the earth, but I wasn't comfortable with any of them. I always like to go with my instinct on bigger decisions, be patient and let things fall into place. I've always thought it's up to me to perform and if I do that it doesn't matter what agents promise. It's my own responsibility. Dave was sound and

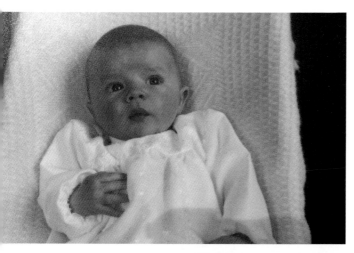

Left: Early days: Even as a baby, I was always concentrating!

Right: Grandma and Granddad Carrick. My Granddad had a trial for England, and was also a war hero.

Below: Graeme and I wore out the grass in our garden playing football.

Growing up: Wallsend Boys Club became my second home.

Above: Lisa has always been by my side, supporting me.

Below: My Grandma Towers was always there for us.

Above: Dad, Mam and Graeme join me as I sign schoolboy forms for West Ham. I couldn't have asked for a better place to develop as a player.

Below left: The indoor gym where I played hours of 'Ds' working on my technique.

Below right: Hanging out at Bob and Val's, the digs for the youth players.

The FA Youth Cup gave me a taste for trophies.

Left: Always learning: I didn't expect to be taught how to shoot on a trip to Croatia!

Right: I was emotionally drained by my first start against Newcastle.

© Michael Steele /Allsport

Left: Facing Arsenal's Patrick Vieira was a huge test.

© Laurence Griffiths/ALLSPORT

I was so lucky that Martin Jol believed in me at Spurs.

National service:
I was honoured to play
for England, it's every
schoolboy's dream, but
I never felt established.

grounded, a chartered accountant by profession, which immediately gave me confidence in him looking after me financially. We would have loads of people coming into the training ground at West Ham in those days trying to offer all sorts of things to invest in. It can be very dangerous, and I was out of my depth. The biggest factor for me was that I could tell he had my best interests at heart. He was interested in playing the long game, which was important. I look back and realise I was so lucky to find David so early and stay with him through my whole career. He's more of a family friend than an 'agent'.

David is a West Ham fan but we both knew this was it. I had to get back in the top division and West Ham needed money. West Brom and Portsmouth came in for me and Iain Dowie tried hard to get me to Palace. I never spoke to any of them because none of it felt right. Everton were interested and I spoke to David Moyes on the phone but that just faded away. After a few weeks, Portsmouth came back in again. Portsmouth were a decent team at the time, a solid Premiership club. Harry was there, and so was the chief executive Peter Storrie who I knew from West Ham. I was well into the pre-season so with time running out I agreed to meet Harry.

'I'll get my head round it, get in the Premiership, have a good year and then see whatever,' I told David. So, we went to meet Harry and Peter at a hotel near Heathrow on 6 August 2004, a couple of days before the season started with the Community Shield. On the way, David got a call from David Dein which really threw us. Dein was the main man at Arsenal and very close to Arsène Wenger. There was nothing concrete, and we didn't know the strength of their interest, but, still, Arsenal! It was just a call, sounding us out really, so we carried on, and spoke to Harry and Peter. 'Come down to Portsmouth tomorrow,' Harry said. 'Have a medical.' That seemed sorted, I was going to

Pompey. Then on the way home, we got another call. Arsenal again, asking us to meet Arsène. As it happened we were driving past his home in north London, so we arranged to call in on the way. Within an hour I was sitting in the front room of Arsène Wenger's house, pinching myself. Could this really be happening? Arsenal! Could I really be on the verge of signing for The Invincibles who'd just gone through the season unbeaten? Arsène Wenger was at the peak of his powers at the time, a giant of management, and it felt surreal to be there talking to him in his front room. 'Tell me about yourself, Michael,' Wenger said. 'What are your strengths? What are your weaknesses?' It all seemed quite formal as if I was undergoing a job interview with the Civil Service. It was quite a contrast to the relaxed chat I'd just had with Harry.

'All right, OK,' I began, and just outlined my strengths. I felt self-conscious talking about them as I'm not into bigging myself up and I didn't want to come across as arrogant to Arsène Wenger. I understood why he asked me, though, as he wanted to get to know my character. We talked for almost an hour about football. Wenger had the Community Shield at the weekend but was spending an hour with me, so surely he had to be interested in signing me?

'Let's get Cardiff out the way, and we'll see you Monday,' Wenger said as we left. Things were moving so fast I needed a few minutes to put it all into perspective. That night, I sat at the bottom of my bed and talked it through with Lisa, just running all the possibilities through my mind. It came from nowhere. My head was spinning. Arsenal were finishing either first or second in the Premiership. Lisa knows I'm not a big talker and tend to keep things to myself and find a way to deal with it. This was different. This was a decision that affected the path our lives would take.

I was overjoyed Arsenal wanted me but very conscious of treating Harry with respect. First thing, I called him. 'Look, Harry, I'm not coming down, it doesn't feel right now, my head's a bit all over the place. I'm just sorting a few things out. It's Arsenal. I'm sorry, it's off.' I almost felt guilty over how calmly Harry took it. He knew the attraction of Arsenal.

Arriving at Chadwell Heath on the Saturday, I was thrilled to hear that Dein and Terry Brown had already spoken about a fee. Wow! I was moving from the First Division to a team in the Champions League. I'd heard Vieira was leaving Arsenal and that opened up a space in midfield, so it seemed nailed on that Monday morning I'd be an Arsenal player. I went out training, and it was good because Graeme was there at the time, and Rich threw me a red bib, just messing about. 'Red? Very funny!' Rich knew about Arsenal's interest.

On the Sunday, I settled down at home in Theydon Bois, Epping, to watch Arsenal, my team to be, in the Community Shield against Manchester United. I saw that a kid, Cesc Fàbregas, only 17, started in Vieira's place. Fàbregas played a blinder but I didn't think too much about the significance. I sat at home on Sunday night waiting for the call to arrange details of the next day. Arsenal! I couldn't wait. But I waited, and waited, and that call never came. The next day, I had to go into training at West Ham instead and on the way David phoned to say he'd had a call from Dein. David relayed the gist of his message, like, 'I'm sorry, the manager says we don't need Michael. Fàbregas is coming through like he is. Sorry, the deal's off.' Fàbregas' performance changed Wenger's mind about needing me. I was totally devastated as I had my heart set on Arsenal and playing with all that talent. My head was gone. Arsenal had swayed me, and I didn't have a clue what I'd do now.

When I got in, Alan wanted to see me. 'We'll offer you a two-year contract, Michael.'

'Thanks, but my head's not on that. It's best for me and for everyone that I leave.'

'You're not getting a top four club, Michael. They're not going to come in for you. You need to go to one of these Premiership clubs still interested. Or sign the deal. I need a decision.' If I was leaving, Alan wanted me gone as quick as possible. He didn't want it dragging on and then having to sort out a replacement last minute, so I understood his need for a decision. But there was no way I'd be rushed into a decision by Alan Pardew or West Ham United. I wanted to make sure I chose the right club, not any old club, just for the sake of getting out. Alan was right in a way. I'd just played a season in the First Division, so why would a team heading into the Champions League chase me? Arsenal had been interested, and that gave me hope. The moment I left Alan's office, I rang David and said, 'What happens if I stay and we don't go up? I'll have lost a year. I need to go now.' But where? I didn't want to go to a relegation club. My head was so messed up.

Harry hadn't given up and I got a call from him later, 'I'm on my way up to see you.'

'Harry, please, don't.'

'I'm in the car.'

'Honestly, Harry, there's no point you coming up to see us, and I don't want to mess you around.' Which was true, I didn't want to be disrespectful, I was just stuck in the middle, but I eventually managed to put Harry off. It just didn't feel right to go to Portsmouth now.

Out of nowhere, Spurs' sporting director, Frank Arnesen, called, 'We're bringing in good young British players, and we want you, Michael.' I knew Paul Robinson and Sean Davis had arrived. Spurs were on the up, and it was surely a good time to join. Arsenal's rivals wanted me! I looked at Spurs' playing style and thought, *This is going to suit me.* I'd been thrown a lifeline. I rang Lisa and then Mam and Dad, who were on holiday with Lisa's parents. 'Oh, by the way, we're going to Tottenham!' I told them.

'All right, OK!' they said, very relaxed.

There were still details to sort out and dealing with Spurs was weird, to be honest. All the phone calls with them seemed to happen about 11pm. I'd be lying in bed at home and David would be ringing to keep me informed. 'I've just spoken to Frank Arnesen again,' he'd say. It was madness. Quiet all day, then after 11pm the phone started ringing, either Frank or David.

Alan Pardew kept me in the reserves while all the talks went on. At least that gave me the possibility of playing in the same side as Graeme, who'd joined West Ham. I remember Graeme phoning home, and saying, 'Dad, I'm in the reserves tomorrow night against Norwich and Michael's back from injury. Me and Michael are playing in midfield!'

'Great, son.' Dad never gets carried away, but it was still a big deal – both of us in the same team. On the coach travelling up to Norwich I got a call saying I couldn't play as the deal was close to being done. West Ham pulled me out and I sat in the stands. Graeme couldn't believe it. Like me, Graeme hoped we'd finally play together but the word from the club was that I was signing for Tottenham the next day. West Ham didn't want to risk £2,750,000 going up in smoke if I went down injured. Mam and Dad travelled to see their two sons play but found me next to them in the stand. It was such a shame I never got to play a competitive game with Graeme.

The next day, 24 August, I was finally a Spurs player. I felt it was a summer of sliding door moments. I was close to joining Arsenal but ended up at their rivals. If I didn't get that call off Arsenal, I could have signed for Harry at Portsmouth that next day and then where would I have been when he walked out that November and Portsmouth hit financial problems? The only strange thing about joining Spurs was that I had no contact with the coach I was to play for. Jacques Santini had nothing to do with the negotiations, but I was so keen on just getting to Spurs I didn't think twice about that.

6

EARNING
MY SPURS

'He doesn't know who I am, David.' I shook my head in disbelief as I spoke to David Geiss after we visited Jacques Santini at Spurs' training ground for the first time. I couldn't believe the scene that greeted me at Chigwell or, more accurately, didn't greet me. My new head coach, the man supposed to guide the next stage of my career, didn't recognise me, didn't have a clue about me and didn't seem interested at all in a new signing who'd cost Spurs £2.75m. David shared my dismay at Santini's indifference. 'You're right, Michael. I don't think he does know who you are.' Why? What the hell was going on?

Fans see players switching clubs and think it's a smooth process, but they don't understand the hold-ups, nerves and tensions that go with a transfer. To start with, my medical was delayed because of the groin problems I suffered at West Ham. I became edgy as it took so long, even though I felt 100 per cent. I knew my injuries were behind me, and Spurs could surely see I was moving freely, but clubs get jittery. Docs are under pressure not to miss something. If you sign and a month later a problem flares up and you miss games, it's on the doc's head so all these medics pored over my scans and held a big discussion. Spurs' doc told me the club kept asking him, 'Is Michael all right? Or is he not all right?' The doc told them, 'Look, he played 43 games last year for West Ham. He's all right.' Spurs sent me for more scans, just to double check and, of course, I cleared that hurdle. However, I found the obstacle course was just beginning.

Heading into Chigwell, I was buzzing about catching up with some of the lads I knew from West Ham like Jermain Defoe, Fredi Kanouté and Jamie Redknapp, who I knew from playing for his dad, as well as Sean Davis, 'Davo', from England's Under-21s. Frank Arnesen was really welcoming and I chatted with him for a bit. 'Go and speak to the coach,' Frank suggested. That's where I ran into this problem of Santini. A French defender, Noé Pamarot, signed the same day as me, and was already in with Santini. I could see it was quite lively, friendly, smiling and messing about, light-hearted, as you'd expect. When I entered the room, it was really awkward. Frank introduced me, which wasn't a good sign. Surely Santini knew who I was? I shook his hand and tried to talk to him but he didn't speak great English and made little effort to engage. I felt like an imposter and I left Santini's office with an empty feeling.

That's when I talked to David. I remembered all the sound advice Mam and Dad gave me growing up about being respectful, working hard and never complaining. OK, I'll tough this out. At training the next day, Pamarot was in the first team squad but when I walked over to join them I was pointed to where the reserves trained. I felt so small, embarrassed even, with all the first team looking at me. What was I meant to do? At least Clive Allen was taking the reserves, and he understood the situation and made an effort to help me.

'Keep training hard,' Clive said, and then picked me to play against West Ham reserves, of all people, at Stevenage Borough. I'd just left the club as one of their better players and here I was now playing against their reserves. I'd gone to Spurs thinking big things were happening, I wasn't expecting to start immediately but thought I'd be in contention, surely? I thought it best to speak to Santini to try to understand his thought process. I came out his office none the wiser. He said anything just to get me out of there. 'Keep training well. I've got a few players at the minute who are playing well.' Yeah, yeah. Something else was going on.

I then twisted my ankle training with the reserves which ended all debate about me and the first team for a few weeks. I began to think my move to Spurs was the wrong one. Would I have been better off in Division One with West Ham? I was pretty low for a while. I wasn't going to surrender, so I drew on all my determination to get fit with the physio and get back training as hard as I could with the reserves. I started training with the first team a bit more and finally Santini gave me 18 minutes against Portsmouth, 30 minutes against Bolton Wanderers and seven against Fulham. It was still a struggle. I couldn't make sense of it at all as I wasn't a poor player or a troublemaker. I discovered later there was a power struggle between Frank Arnesen and Jacques Santini, and I was caught slap bang in the middle of it. I was obviously Frank's signing rather than Santini's. Spurs' coach didn't rate me, but we never had cross words and I never actually fell out with Santini. It was painful but professional.

I made sure I didn't give Santini any excuse to cold-shoulder me. I didn't make a fuss, I kept my head down. I'll always be grateful to Frank and Santini's assistant, Martin Jol. If I trained with the first team, Martin always had a kind word with me, trying to lift my spirits. If I was dumped back in the reserves, he sought me out, and told me to keep going as my time would come.

On Bonfire Night, David Geiss rang with surprise news. 'I think you're starting tomorrow,' David said. He'd heard a whisper that Santini was putting me in against Charlton Athletic. For David to find out before me was weird in itself. It's not happened before or since, thankfully. At last, I'd have a chance to show my manager what I could do from the start, and I quickly called Mam and Dad so they could come down. For the first time in weeks, I smiled. Typically, it didn't go to plan! That night Santini walked out after only 13 games! I didn't know whether to laugh or cry because Santini finally seemed to appreciate me and now he was out the door. And there was another twist, of course there was! Frank pulled me out of the team as he feared it would look like they'd put me straight back in with Santini gone. Confused? Not half as much as me. I knew it must be politics. In the end, I came on for Jamie Redknapp, we still lost and it wasn't until Martin was promoted to head coach that everything changed overnight for me.

Martin Jol rescued me, he really did, and I'll be in his debt forever. He gave me my first start for Spurs at White Hart Lane in a tear-up with Arsenal that turned into total chaos. Nobody needed to tell me about the importance of Spurs v. Arsenal – a fixture that's part of the heritage of football. A full house at the Lane for a North London Derby was the sort of occasion that stood out for me watching TV growing up. Derbies mean everything to fans. Emotions are pushed to extremes. It's a chance to scream abuse and nick the bragging rights. Liverpool v. Everton – huge. West Ham v. Chelsea – big. Tottenham v. Arsenal – always massive. I was well aware of the historical edge with Arsenal doing well in the league and Spurs always considered a cup team, going back to Gazza's FA Cup semi-final in 1991 that I watched as a kid. I'd missed the buzz of a big game. I couldn't wait to feel the butterflies in my stomach again. You didn't get games like this in The Championship. I'd moved to Spurs for challenges like this. In the tunnel, I remember being still, no eye contact with the opposition, no emotion. I never spoke to the other team, even if it was one of my best mates. If I'm leading the side out, I might shake the hand of the other captain in the tunnel, or if someone comes up to me, but I never go out of my way to say 'hello'. All I could think was: 'first tackle, first pass'. Impose myself. I'd suffered for two years with injury and relegation, so this was me back on the big stage going up against Fàbregas, who'd stopped me going to Arsenal. This was the first of many battles I had with this terrific footballer. The Arsenal player I admired most was Dennis Bergkamp. At one point, Bergkamp tried to get away from me when I lunged in with a real sliding tackle, thinking, *I've got him here.* Bergkamp just lifted the ball over me and danced away, boom, 'See you later.' I felt myself giving a nod of appreciation, like, *Yep, well played Dennis, you've done me there.* We lost 5–4. I hate losing, but after all I'd been through I was happy to be back and setting up a couple of goals for Noureddine Naybet and Ledley King. It gave me a sense of belonging again. I was back on track.

The North London Derby brought out the best in me. I remember playing at Highbury in April 2006, one of my best games for Spurs, and going on a dribble, which was not really like me. Martin kept encouraging me to seize games more so I got round three Arsenal players, and thought I'd beaten Jens Lehmann, but I hit the side-netting.

Martin Jol was a huge influence on me and got me to the next level. His wife Nicole would come up and say, 'He's a big fan of yours.' Martin cared. He always put so much faith in me. By my second season he gave me the responsibility of being the focal point of Spurs' midfield. All players get compared to players of the past at some point. I knew all about the Glenn Hoddle legacy at Spurs. I'd seen enough clips to appreciate how good he was, what he did for Tottenham and the amazing career he had.

I settled at Spurs, the team were moving forward under Martin and it was big news that second season when we signed Edgar Davids, a genuine superstar. I knew all about Davids' track record, his Champions League with Ajax and Louis van Gaal, the three titles in Italy with Juventus, and how brilliant he was with Holland at France '98 and Euro 2000. Davids' peak was two or three years earlier but I learned playing alongside him, and most of all from his desire to win. All those trophies had not diminished his hunger. Spurs had developed a good little midfield with me, Jermaine Jenas and Davids mixing it around with Aaron Lennon flying down the wing at the time. Azza was some talent when he was younger, so quick, and in my second season at Spurs, he was almost unstoppable. We had plenty to aim at with Fredi Kanouté, Jermain Defoe and Robbie Keane playing well and a real character in Mido, who did a decent job up front. Ledley was our leader at the back with Michael Dawson. He was top drawer, Ledley, even then when he wasn't training much because of his knees. I never saw him down over the injuries, but then Ledley doesn't say much anyway. I just had loads of respect for the way he got on the bike at Chigwell, kept himself ticking over during the week, turned up on match day and delivered. Football came so easily to him, passing with either foot, quick and strong, calm and confident. God knows how good he could have been if he'd had full fitness for longer. He was up there with the best I've played with, not far off Rio Ferdinand level. Ledley could have played for Manchester United quite easily.

They were a good bunch off the field, too, and camaraderie goes a long way in making a team. Keano and JJ – great lads, Ledders, Daws and Andy Reid too, the heartbeat of a club. I was closest to Keano, always the life and soul of the party. We'd all go out for dinner with the girls, go into town and end up in a sing-song with Keano because he loves his singing. He doesn't need any encouragement, absolutely anything, all sorts of Irish folk songs. He's not got a bad voice, actually.

I became very happy at Spurs. It's a fantastic football club. The Lane was a great ground to play at, so tight with the stands so steep that the atmosphere stayed in. I really believed we could achieve something special under Martin and we set our hearts on qualifying for the Champions League. For the final game of the 2005/'06 season we were playing West Ham away. Everyone knew the maths as we checked into the Marriott West India Quay in Canary Wharf the day before: if we matched Arsenal's result against Wigan we'd finish top four. That would be huge for Spurs and the thought of beating Arsenal to the final Champions League place added to the excitement. As we gathered for dinner at the Marriott, it all seemed so routine, the usual meal and team meeting followed by bed. So, began what the press jokingly called 'Lasagne-gate' but which was far worse. I woke up in the middle of the night struggling badly and throwing up. I'd never endured agony like this. It felt like a fire was lit in my guts with petrol poured on it again and again. The pain kept flaring up and I curled up in bed, praying for it to pass. Get through the night, I told myself, then see the doctor in the morning. As bad as this was, I didn't want to make a fuss. That's not me. At 7am, I couldn't wait any longer, so I eased myself downstairs to try and have something to eat, hoping that would put out the fire. I managed a banana, and that was a struggle, just forcing it down and hoping it would stay down. It didn't. A few of the lads began drifting in to the breakfast room, looking pale and weak. They'd had sleepless nights too, and been chucking up.

I couldn't stay there any longer, so I shuffled back to my room and collapsed on the bed. Why this? Why now? Of all times. I lay there for an hour, telling myself, I'll be all right, I'll get through it. I knew Martin and the boys would soon head out for the usual pre-match walk. By now, my idea of a walk was no further than the difficult steps to the bathroom: stagger, vomit, sleep, repeat, except with no sleep. No chance of that. My body screamed at me to stay in bed rather than report downstairs, but I had to. I forced myself back down and entered a meeting room that looked more like a hospital waiting room. Seven or eight of the lads were badly affected. Nobody knew what it was. A virus? Accidental food poisoning? Or worse… deliberate? The police arrived to investigate potential foul play. Officials from the Premier League turned up and went into immediate talks with Martin Jol and the chairman Daniel Levy. When Martin re-emerged, he told us, 'We're asking for the game to be postponed for a day, or at least by four hours to give some of you a chance to recover.'

Daniel Levy rang Richard Scudamore at the Premier League, but he wouldn't budge. 'We have to play,' Martin told us an hour later. I understood the Premier League's unsympathetic stance. Where do you stop? Two people ill? Four? Six? What's the cut? When do you say, 'Right, that's it, game off.' This wasn't just any normal game, as all the work we'd put in all season rested on this and I was desperate to help.

'Can you play?' Martin asked. I was drained and weak, My guts screamed 'no', but my conscience demanded I answer 'yes'. I didn't want to let anybody down, I felt a responsibility to get out there. I'd made more crosses and passes than anyone at Spurs that season.

'I'm struggling… but I'll play,' I told Martin, who was really grateful. He was close to getting 11 now. I climbed gingerly on the bus, and positioned myself strategically within dashing distance of the toilet. At Upton Park, I tried to listen to Martin's team talk but ran off to throw up again. I tried to focus on the game but all I could do was try to stem the flow of diarrhoea and vomit. I remember trying to shout encouragement to the lads in the changing room before kick-off, I guess I was trying to motivate myself more than anything. It must have seemed so feeble because I can still picture JJ, who was out injured, sitting in the corner, giggling at me. I must have looked so weak. Looking back,

I appreciated what Jermain Defoe told the press afterwards, 'I really respect guys like Michael. He went out and played even though he was struggling.' God, I was struggling. I couldn't move out there and I couldn't get close to anyone. I was so weak and lethargic, the tank on empty. I focused more on stopping myself throwing up on the pitch than concentrating on the game. I heard West Ham fans singing, 'One–nil to the Arsenal' and assumed they'd scored at Highbury. West Ham supporters went quiet when Wigan made it 2–1 but we knew Arsenal were 2–2 at the break. We were 1–1 after I'd set up Jermain's equaliser. As it stood, Spurs were in the Champions League but standing was soon no longer an option for me. My body was shot, I was playing from memory and when Martin went to sub Davids after an hour I quickly put my hand up and said, 'You're going to have to take me off.' I felt like I was waving the white flag, a horrible feeling of surrender, but I had no choice. It was the only time in my career I asked to be subbed, because I'm too proud, but I was that bad. Without even waiting for Martin's approval, I walked straight off.

I felt helpless watching the remaining life drain from our players and from our season. West Ham scored, Arsenal won, we fell short and West Ham fans gave it to us big time. It was massive for West Ham to stop Tottenham getting in the Champions League, so Upton Park was rocking. All of those West Ham fans bouncing in the stands couldn't have made me feel any worse anyway. Downstairs, our dressing room was like a morgue with everyone sitting there motionless, almost frozen. I just wanted to curl up and sleep off the feeling of emptiness. Football is hideously cruel at times. I'm convinced Spurs would have qualified for the Champions League with everyone fit at Upton Park.

The health inspectors went into the Marriott, tested the lasagne leftovers and declared it wasn't food poisoning that had struck us down.

They reckoned we were suffering from norovirus, so it was nothing to do with the hotel. I heard all the crazy conspiracy theories but never dreamed it was suspicious, anyway. If someone wanted to nobble a team, it would be easy to do, just go and throw something in the food. That never happened here. Everybody banged on about Lasagne-gate but it wasn't. Lasagne-gate just makes the story sound better. But the sour taste in our mouths had nothing to do with the Marriott's pasta.

The other frustration for me was that the new deal Spurs offered me wasn't a good one. I was really happy there and at Christmas time, we spoke to Daniel Levy about extending and improving my deal, which had two-and-a-half years to run. He didn't agree and we were too far apart financially. His position annoyed me as I'd come in at quite a low price from West Ham, actually for the same money I was on in the First Division. Everyone knew Tottenham's wage structure was strict, but I felt I deserved an increase. Ledley was looking for a new contract at the same time, so Daniel was busy juggling the money as usual. He always thought we had it lined up to leave but I can honestly say, hand on heart, that wasn't the case. I 100 per cent wanted to re-sign for Spurs at that stage. I know it sounds horrible saying 'if the money was right I'd have stayed' because money's not what I'm about. But, seriously, if Daniel had made the deal fairer, I'd have stayed.

For me, a principle was at stake here, about a player being properly valued by his employer, and Daniel Levy didn't seem to realise that. I'd come back in for my second season really motivated. It felt like now or never, that this was the time to perform otherwise I could easily fall by the wayside and be a 'nearly' player. It was the crossroads in my career. Without exaggerating, this period shaped the rest of my life. I was totally committed to Tottenham and had no reason to leave. We finished fifth where would I go? Would a bigger club come in for me? I didn't think so.

Arsenal showed some interest again and David Geiss knew their chief scout Steve Rowley well, so there was dialogue and unofficial-type stuff, like 'What's Michael doing… would he be interested?' But could I really go to Arsenal from Spurs? That would've been a tough move. I never seriously considered it. Liverpool enquired, half-heartedly. What really excited me was David revealing that Manchester United quietly joined the hunt. My head filled with all those images of me playing United and standing in the corridor at Upton Park in awe as they filed past, in their blazers. Could that dream of playing for United actually come true?

I went off to the World Cup in Germany in a hopeful mood, and left negotiations to David. I got frustrated over how protracted it became because of the issues United had dealing with Daniel Levy. On 10 June, Daniel rejected a £10m bid from United and I was stunned by the size of the offer and Spurs turning it down. Play fair! Spurs paid £2.5m for me, going up to £2.75m, so two years down the line, I thought they'd be happy to take a healthy profit, especially as West Ham were due only a small percentage. I feared Spurs were pricing me out of my dream move. 'Twelve million is surely the max,' I said to David.

I learned later that the United boys out with England in Baden-Baden reported back to Sir Alex, saying that I trained well and was a good pro. I never sensed Gary Neville particularly watching me train or how I conducted myself around the lads and around the hotel, but he must have been. I never had a conversation with Gary but I heard he recommended me to Sir Alex.

Still Daniel Levy played hardball. OK, I understood – Daniel's a good, tough businessman driven by getting the best deal for his club. But Daniel had just got warmed up. The two sides were locked in a game of poker and Daniel was a master at it. Leading negotiations for United was their chief executive David Gill, who liaised with the club's owners, the Glazer family in Florida. I discovered later that Sir Alex was on the golf course when David Gill phoned to update him that Daniel wanted more than £12m for me. God knows what that did to Sir Alex's putting. A couple of times I thought, *This might not happen.* But David Gill kept saying to David Geiss, 'Don't worry, we'll get it done. Just tell Michael we're not leaving him, we're not going to run away.' I dreaded United going cold so I was greatly reassured to receive a phone call from Sir Alex himself on 30 June. I was sitting in the garden of the England families' hotel, Brenners Park in Baden-Baden, having a cup of tea with Mam and Dad, Lisa and Graeme when David Geiss phoned. 'Fergie's going to call in a minute.'

Exactly a minute later, the phone rang again. 'Dad, it's him, it's him!' I whispered as I picked up the phone from the table. For Mam and Dad, Lisa and Graeme, this was as surreal an experience as it was for me. My heart started racing a bit and I paused before answering. He's Sir Alex Ferguson, isn't he? The most important manager in English football so I was really nervous. I bent over the table, trying to hide the call, in case anyone was listening. I knew reporters were all over Brenners Park. Once I started speaking to Sir Alex, I was fine, and it was a brief conversation, a minute max. 'How you doing? Are you playing?' Sir Alex asked.

'No,' I replied. It was after the Ecuador game in Stuttgart, when I'd done well, but I knew I wasn't starting the quarter-final against Portugal.

'How are you not playing, son?!' Sir Alex said. I appreciated the support. We talked briefly about Manchester United, but Sir Alex never had to sell the club to me, no chance, I was obsessed with it already. All I wanted was for him to know how keen I was to join.

'Hang in there, Michael,' he said. 'Tottenham are messing about but we'll get it done.' That was the biggest phone call of my life, by a mile. I looked round at Mam and Dad, Lisa and Graeme and said, 'What's just happened?!! I've just spoken to Sir Alex Ferguson!'

'What did Sir Alex say?' Mam asked.

'He says we'll get the deal done.' That's all we needed to hear. Tea never tasted so good. When I got back to the England hotel, Schloss Bühlerhöhe, I didn't tell Gary Neville. I kept it a secret. I've never been one for telling people things, anyway. I didn't even tell my best mates about Sir Alex's call. They'd have gone, 'Who's he??'

When occupied my thoughts more and more as negotiations dragged on into July. I was in Cannes with Lisa on holiday after the World Cup, and I just felt as though we all needed closure on it. I was due back in training at Spurs the following week and was desperate to get the deal sorted. So, I decided to call Daniel Levy for the first and only time. I pulled myself off the sun lounger and sitting on a bench on the boardwalk, I pleaded with him. 'Look, I really want to leave, Daniel. Can you please accept the price they're offering? This is quite fair. You paid two and a half million for me, they're offering twelve million plus.'

I found that such a hard phone call to make, because it's not in my nature to say, 'Look, I want to leave.' But it had reached the stage where I had to act because I was in limbo. Football careers are short and opportunities like this one wouldn't come along again, especially as this was the perfect time as I was turning 25. It was now or never.

'Well, they need to pay the money,' Daniel replied. There you go. It was all about the money for Daniel, just driving the price up and up.

'I didn't think I'd have to come to you, Mr Chairman. I didn't think I'd be asking you to let me leave the club, because I was happy – but this is Manchester United.'

'Well, Manchester United need to pay the money.' Arguing with Daniel was pointless. I would have got more joy talking to a brick wall.

'Please, Daniel, this is what I want. I just really want to go.' He mentioned the money again and we ended the call. It was civilised and I respected Daniel for fighting Spurs' corner, but God I was frustrated.

On returning to Chigwell, I went in to see Martin Jol. Martin was a good, honest man and he was great with me, as usual. 'Look, I really don't want to lose you, but I fully understand,' he said. 'There's no way I'd stand in your way. You deserve to go.' Spurs weren't in the Champions League, United were. United had won leagues over the last 10 years and it was an obvious step up. Martin saw that. He also needed time to get a replacement in so Daniel Levy delaying things didn't help him. The players understood, too. Manchester United! Anyone would jump at the chance.

I felt some sadness at the thought of leaving because I had a great time at Spurs. At last, on 24 July, David Geiss called. 'The deal's agreed.' YES! The Glazers had ok'd an increased bid of £18m. £18m! Way over the odds, I thought, but the fee had nothing to do with me. My immediate reaction was relief. I'd heard whispers that United were interested in Marcos Senna of Villarreal and Owen Hargreaves at Bayern Munich as well as me. I'd heard there was a debate inside the club over whether they wanted a ball-playing midfielder or a more defensive midfielder. Whether I was United's first choice or not, I didn't care, I was just thankful to be joining them.

When the transfer was announced, I saw supporters from Spurs and United questioning it and it reminded me I still had a lot to prove. Bernie Kingsley, a Spurs fanzine editor, was interviewed by the BBC about whether Spurs supporters were sad to see me go. 'I don't think fans will be desperately upset,' Kingsley said. 'For that sort of money, and with Tom Huddlestone and Didier Zokora at the club, it has got to be good business.' The BBC also interviewed Mark Longden of the Independent Manchester United Supporters Association, who said, 'I've not spoken to anybody who, when £18.6m became available, would have spent that on Michael Carrick.' Rightly, there was a debate about me. If I'd had £18m I probably wouldn't have gone out and bought me. With Daniel Levy lifting the price bit by bit, United almost got hooked into it. At that point, as a Tottenham fan, you'd say, 'Eighteen million is a good deal.' As a United fan you'd think, 'He's a good player, but it's a lot of money for someone who hasn't really done much.' As I headed north with Lisa, I was very aware of everyone asking questions about me and my worth.

7

PROVING MYSELF

I'll admit to more than a few butterflies in my stomach as I headed out for the first time to the Manchester United 'boxes' at Carrington. These squares of grass measuring eight yards by eight were the first test. Did I have the technique? Did I have the temperament? Yes, all clubs do boxes, but I'd heard about the demanding nature of United's. It's essentially a game of piggy in the middle, but more intense. Between five and eight players pass the ball to each other, pinging it first time, while two lads in the middle try to intercept. If you nick the ball, even divert it, you swap with the shamed passer on the outside. Boxes at United were quick, ferocious and unforgiving and were, I soon realised, steeped in an underlying culture of players constantly challenging each other. Boxes develop technique and teamwork and sort the serious players from the pretenders, so which was I?

The first question I faced was which box to go in: young or old? At 25, I qualified for either. I made a beeline for the older box as I wanted to get as close as I could to be able to learn from the best. I wanted to be like them, and I saw the older box as the heart of Manchester United. I challenged myself to live with the best. I'd seen flicky and flimsy boxes before, lads rolling their studs over the ball, a messing-about box full of fluffy skills, and I'd switch off and think, *What's the point? This is crap. We're not getting anything out of it*. Sometimes it was just a case of walking around in the middle and eventually you'd get the ball back, not the full-on intensity I knew I'd find in United boxes.

The old box was such a high standard and was totally run by the lads, no coaches invited or required. Sir Alex Ferguson watched from 20 yards away, always observing. My new workmates were Ryan Giggs, Paul Scholes, Ole Gunnar Solskjaer, Gary Neville, Nemanja Vidić, Patrice Evra and my old friend Rio Ferdinand. Louis Saha would be there and when I first started Mikaël Silvestre and Gabby Heinze were there too. Entry policy to this exclusive club was mainly dictated by age but over the years the members changed. Ji-sung Park joined and Wayne Rooney eventually ventured over to the older box. He'd got so frustrated with some of the lads messing about trying to nutmeg him that he flew into tackles. You'd hear cheers and turn round to see him chasing around in the middle like a madman. That was Wazza. Two minutes later he'd be laughing about it. That aggression and determination helped make him great.

Our box wasn't so much about taking the piss out of people. Scholes did take the mickey but he wasn't deliberately belittling you, it was because he was so good. When he did do something outrageous he'd just chuckle away to himself and not say a word. As I drew closer to the older box on my first day, I heard shouts of 'this is Coutts box', 'that's Barclays box' and 'this is Champions League', 'that's Championship'. Rio jogged towards the old box, yelling 'this is Coutts, this'. The moment I reached it, Scholes lashed the ball at me, in the way only he does, with a little smile on his face, properly testing me but having fun at the same time. Those boxes were ruthless environments. Rio told me that after he joined for £30m Roy Keane drilled a pass at him, he didn't control it and Solskjaer cut him down with a little, 'Fucking hell! How much?!' Rio's a confident lad but he said that hit him. That edgy mocking warned every player he had to hit a level. Boxes may seem a simple exercise, just a warm-up, but it summed up the culture in the squad. It swiftly became clear to me that life for the players at Manchester United was about having pride in yourself and a desire to push each other, to enjoy football, embrace high standards and have the staying power to do it every day. It was about hunger to improve, to climb that ladder, to get in the old box – the Coutts box, to get in the team, win games and win trophies. And then to do it again and again.

Any player who went in the middle of the box twice in a row got a little shout of, 'Oh, he's in again! Season ticket! He's in again!' It was light-hearted but it nevertheless cut to the quick and I absolutely hated to be 'in' again. Scholesy was merciless and he'd rap one in at me now and again. He'd fire one at my chest and I'd have to deal with it, there was no margin for error, which I liked as it made sure I was switched on. Giggsy loved giving you the eyes to send you the wrong way, whereas Rio talked his way through it and I swear Ji-sung had three legs and could read your mind. Ji was ridiculous at winning the ball back. Try and give Ji the eyes or even double-bluff him, didn't matter, he'd still be waiting for that pass with a big smile on his face. While Solskjaer was the silent assassin who'd launch bombs at you and expect you to deal with them.

The competitive nature of the players Sir Alex gathered meant that a few people in the middle dived in on tackles. Don't get me wrong, we weren't going around smashing each other to bits but every day was like, *boom* – 10 to 15 minutes, full-on, setting the tone for the whole session.

Stepping into the box, I knew I had to earn the trust of the United lads. I had to prove I had the ability and the hunger to be with them. The impression I got from my new teammates was, 'We've got to win the league this year. What are you going to do help us?' That mindset stayed strong throughout my time as a player at United and soon I'd be looking at every new signing, thinking, *How good is he then? What's he going to bring?*

I wanted to bring everything I could to United, and then improve to bring even more. Such was my desire to sign for Manchester United that personal terms were not even discussed until late on. I suspected that United waited to discover how much I would cost from Spurs. The higher the fee the easier it would be for David Gill to say, 'We haven't got as much money to give you.' I agreed a deal very quickly that was more money than I was on at Tottenham. We didn't get weekly win bonuses in the league because we were expected to win, we were Manchester United after all. In the Champions League, we got a bonus for each win in the group stage but then the whole thing changed and we only got bonuses in the later stages.

Around the time of my signing, I became aware of a BBC interview with my old coach at West Ham, Frank Lampard Senior, in which Frank said I was a 'nice, easy-going lad' who'd have to 'push himself more at United because he's stepping up a level and there will be demands on him all the time'. I agreed there was no hiding place now, I needed that push and doing well for United became a cause that took over my life. Later, I read that Sir Alex described me when I came as 'a shy boy who needs to be shaken at times'. I get where he's coming from. I wouldn't necessarily say shy, maybe quiet. At that time, he could have gone and bought anyone. I might not have been his No. 1 choice, in fact it's more than likely I wasn't. Sir Alex wouldn't necessarily just go, 'Who's the best midfielder in the world at the minute? Right, I'll take him'. I've always felt more appreciated by managers and players than supporters. Half the time English fans prefer a player to give the ball away and then storm back in, make the tackle, *bang*, win the ball back and the crowd go wild. It doesn't makes sense. Still, signing a new player is always about the balance of the team. Understanding that balance comes from having a clear philosophy of how you want to play, what you value and how you see the game.

I know some lads struggled to cope with the pressure of playing for a club with the history and ambition, let alone size, of Manchester United. The weight of the shirt dragged people under if they had any mental frailty. At Spurs, I could play well every three weeks and everyone raved, 'Oh, Michael, you're a good player'. Spurs could have a bad game and there still wouldn't be much criticism, whereas defeat was unacceptable at United. On that first day, I remember very clearly wanting to let the players know, 'You can trust me, I'm ready, I'm with you'.

Sir Alex explained the expectation levels at United to me. I'd got to Carrington early. I stayed with Lisa at the Lowry Hotel and got up in the morning, put the postcode in the satnav and set off super early for my first day at my new job. No way was I going to be late. I also thought it would be easier to go into an empty changing room and seeing the lads arrive gradually. I was eating breakfast in the canteen when Sir Alex came in and I jumped up. 'Come and have a word in my office, son,' he said. We sat on a couple of sofas at the side of his desk in the corner office, which gave him a prime view over the pitches and the players' car park.

'Welcome, son, I'm glad it's all sorted,' he said. 'You'll love it here, it's a great place to work. The lads are brilliant. Keep working hard and I'm sure you'll do great.' That was the first and certainly not the last time I'd hear the Boss say, 'Keep working hard.'

'We're used to winning at Manchester United, you know? The scrutiny is different to what you're used to. Everyone looks at you differently when you're at Manchester United and when you're winning like us and the standards we've got. Everyone wants to beat you, everyone wants a piece of you, everyone wants to criticise you, everyone's after you.'

I still can't believe, even now, how stupid my reply was to Sir Alex's emotive portrait of Manchester United. 'Similar to Chelsea,' I said. Chelsea had won the title for the last two years and I was just thinking as champions everybody also wanted to beat them.

Sir Alex gave me a withering look, 'No, son. This is Manchester United. We're different to the rest.'

I thought to myself, 'Why the hell have I just said that? What does he think of me now? What a start to my United career.'

In welcoming me, Sir Alex mentioned that he thought 'Geordies travel well' and named Sir Bobby Charlton and Bryan Robson. He was funny like that, the Boss, he'd get an idea in his head and it stuck there forever. Someone from Newcastle did well somewhere, and Sir Alex went, 'Right, Geordies travel well'. It didn't surprise me to learn such a meticulous manager ordered background checks on my character, and talked to other managers as well as his England players, and maybe he thought my Geordie blood would help me settle in well.

I listened spellbound to this legendary manager and noticed little things like he always said 'Manchester United', never just 'United' – always the full name as a mark of respect. He had a passion and a pride in Manchester United, not just the team, but the club and not just the present but the past too. Sir Alex always wanted Manchester United to do things with a touch of class, and he went out of his way to know all the members of staff, their families and backgrounds. The great man at the top cared for everyone at Manchester United, so everybody gave everything to the job. Before I left his office that first morning, Sir Alex asked me which shirt number I wanted.

'I'm honestly not fussed.'

'There's No. 16 if you want it?'

'Yeah, fine. No problem.' Roy Keane's old number meant this was no ordinary shirt and other newcomers might have been tempted to ask what other numbers Sir Alex had spare.

'You sure, son?'

'Yes.'

I knew the legacy and challenge I took on with Keane's No. 16. Later, I learned Sir Alex felt I showed 'courage' in taking on No. 16 as I could have been superstitious about the Keane connection. In fact, my desire for Keane's shirt was a deliberate statement that I had no fear. I knew the inevitable questions that came with ownership of No. 16. For my first few months at United, if I didn't play well, people said, 'Ah, he's not Roy Keane.' Every day for my first few months, I was asked, 'What's it like replacing Roy Keane?' I still got that question every week after three years. 'Well, it's not really an issue, I just get on with it as normal,' I'd reply. I tried to make out that the shirt was just a piece of material, rather than an important part of the fabric of Manchester United's history. Of course, I knew No. 16 was a big issue, partly because Keane left in fairly acrimonious circumstances after criticising players in an MUTV interview, which, apparently, was too controversial to broadcast. Nevertheless, what Roy Keane did for the club was amazing and his great legacy is still there for all to see. He was integral to Manchester United's success. I understood fans wanting a new Roy Keane but you can never replace a player like that like for like, so you do it another way. Best, Charlton, Cantona, Scholes, Giggs, Ferdinand, Neville, Ronaldo, Rooney – you can't find another of any of them. And Keane's in that bracket.

It's not a difficult exercise to put Keane in the top level of Premier League midfielders though I couldn't say he was the best because, for me, Scholesy was a genius. But Keane was up there. I rated him as an opponent and all the United lads told me that people didn't appreciate how good a passer Keane was. 'He was so good getting the ball to the forward's feet,' Rooney once said to me. Keane's technique got overlooked because he was so aggressive, and people fixated on that. His willpower was in your face, snarling at times, and he was just so demanding of his team. Rio told me how Keane once gave him a bollocking shortly after he arrived. 'Pass it forward, take risks. You're not at Leeds or West Ham now, you're at Man United.' Keane's legacy lived on in those high standards and I knew I had to step it up, I couldn't pass sideways, I had to go forward, be bold.

After I got my new shirt, I collected my match-day suit from the player liaison officer Barry Moorhouse. Opening this little cupboard out the back, Barry picked out some jackets and trousers and said, 'Do these fit?' Well, it was hardly bespoke, made to measure, and it's different now, but putting on the jacket with the large crest on the breast pocket gave me a sense of arriving, of achieving, really. I'm sorry if it sounds cringey but it made me feel taller and more confident, as if my back instinctively straightened after putting it on. It took me back to those days standing in the corridor at Upton Park, seeing United players walking in all smart and thinking, 'Yes, they look the best.' At Manchester United, we took great pride in how we presented ourselves in public. 'When you're travelling through an airport, people will see you,' Sir Alex said. 'You represent the club. You wear your blazers.' The Boss wanted to send a message, that we not only looked the part, but we also meant business. That look creates an aura.

As we chatted, Barry mentioned he'd followed United home and away since the Busby Babes, and I noticed very quickly on my first day that all the staff were lifelong United fans. Many of them came from

The Cliff – the old training ground in Salford dating back to the days of the Babes. That length of service always shone through for me, whether it was Cath on reception, the girls in the laundry or Carol and Rita in the kitchen. 'What the fuck was that?' Carol and Rita shouted at us if we lost or even drew. If I didn't go up to the kitchen for a couple of days, Carol was on my case. She still is. 'Where the fuck have you been? Why are you not coming up and eating? Are you trying to avoid us?' Nobody was safe, academy kid or knight of the realm, when Carol was ranting. She's probably the only one at United who could get away with giving Sir Alex an earful.

I then met Mick Phelan, the first team coach, who knew the culture of Manchester United profoundly having spent five seasons in midfield here. Mick often said to me, 'Be arrogant when you play.' He didn't mean be arrogant towards the opposition, just be arrogant on the ball, as if to say, 'Yes, I'm the best here. Give me the ball, I want the ball.' Pulling on that red shirt, I felt, 'We are the best. We do things the right way.' You have to understand this wasn't being arrogant and behaving like knobs, so people didn't like us for it, it was about being confident.

Behaving properly was an unwritten rule. I didn't really need to be told as conducting myself well was how I had been brought up by Mam and Dad and at Wallsend Boys Club. United's standards were set by Sir Alex and the old guard like Nev, and there were obvious things like we'd never, ever comment about other teams' players. If United were going to Anfield in two weeks' time, you wouldn't say anything to stoke the fire in the press or on TV and that ethos shone down from Sir Alex. I knew the Boss sometimes had a little wind-up in a press conference, and only rarely was it premeditated, about the next opposition, but as players we never said anything that might come back to haunt us. I know there was the controversy of United players surrounding refs like Andy D'Urso in 2000 and that was a case when they overstepped it because of their hunger to win – another trait Sir Alex had in abundance. Sometimes he'd get aggressive on the touchline, sometimes at the fourth official or the ref, but it was simply due to the Boss's drive to succeed. We had to win and if we could do something that might influence the ref and get us a decision, we'd try it. We'd be nice to the ref, be his mate, and see if that worked and he might be nice back. Other times, we'd put pressure on him, telling him he wasn't doing a good job. Occasionally, I'd prod the refs and let them know I wasn't happy about them not giving certain decisions – it didn't always work. We just tried to get any edge we could. Some outsiders believed that the aura around United, especially at Old Trafford, led to some refs feeling pressured into giving us decisions but that was total nonsense. Visiting teams did so much defending there were inevitably fouls, so refs awarded free kicks and penalties to us. Simple.

From that first-day meeting with Sir Alex, I knew I was in the presence of a genius, especially because of his ability to instil the right mood in the build-up to a game. He possessed this phenomenal capacity for preparing players psychologically. The day before the game, the Boss would show us a short video, 10 minutes max, on the opposition prior to training. It was all so simple. Sir Alex never told us how to play. We were his players, Manchester United players, and we were there because he trusted and believed in our strength and character.

Still, his team talks were special. For a 3pm kick-off, we'd have a meeting at 1.30pm in the changing room and when Sir Alex spoke, you could hear a pin drop. The Boss would have the opposition team on the board and he'd talk about their main strengths, mention one or two players and say, 'keep an eye on him', but a lot of the time he just brought up one of their players, and went, 'He can't run. He can't run!' A favourite of his was, 'He couldn't run a message.'

The theme of teamwork ran through his talks. A regular story he told us was about migrating geese and how they flew thousands of miles in a V formation, basically in a slipstream, and when the goose at the front tired, another took over. The geese looked out for each other and shared the workload. He told this story to the European team at the 2014 Ryder Cup and apparently all week at Gleneagles the players were saying to each other 'remember the geese'. It obviously helped as there's that great picture of Rory McIlroy and the rest of the boys pointing to the sky after they beat the Americans. They were laughing because a flock of geese was flying over!

The Boss was a master at telling seemingly random stories that were all linked by a common message – working hard – particularly if it was a big game. When we played Arsenal at Old Trafford in 2010, the Chilean miners were invited – the ones who'd been trapped underground and stayed strong as they were winched one by one to the surface. Sir Alex talked about Sir Matt coming from a mining background, the strength needed to work underground and gave this really inspiring speech about how the Chilean miners survived. It had nothing to do with the game football-wise, it was a lesson about character, sticking together and grafting hard. The Boss spoke passionately and at length in the changing room about the shipyards on the Clyde where his father worked. Sir Alex knows so much about history and he'd throw stories about the past into his team talks, about brave soldiers fighting for a cause. He would start off nice and calm and sometimes talk himself up into a whirlwind of aggression, like a heavyweight climbing impatiently into the ring. He held that room with his delivery and eloquence, and he'd finish by saying, 'It's the easiest thing in the world to work hard. Nothing stops you from working hard.' The three things he always mentioned were: 'Don't be afraid to work hard. Concentration. Penetration.'

We're professionals, dedicated to Manchester United, and were always going to give everything but Sir Alex made us give even more. His insatiable hunger set the tone for everyone and I was soon shown the danger of dipping below the highest levels of commitment at United.

My first start in the Premiership was Watford away – I played 75 minutes, we won 2–1, and I thought, *Three points, happy days*. But the Boss was not happy. He'd shouted something to Giggsy on the pitch, Giggsy responded and that triggered Sir Alex, who went mad afterwards. He came into the changing room and yelled, 'I'm not having that! That's not good enough.' The message from the Boss was clear: 'It's not about winning away from home, it's about how we win and how we play.'

Going into my first game at Old Trafford, against Spurs of all people, I sensed immediately the desire, almost the demand, to win. Standing in the banked tunnel for the first time as a United player was a huge moment for me. I felt 10 feet tall alongside lads I'd played with just weeks before. We beat Spurs 1–0 that day and hearing our fans before, during and after the game had a powerful effect on me. That feeling never left me during my playing days at Old Trafford. I recognised how lucky I was to have this stadium as my place of work. Behind the scenes, Old Trafford was quite low key, and the dressing room was basic, nothing flashy really. At Carrington, in the changing room, I found myself in the incredible position of sitting between Giggsy and Ronaldo with Scholesy one along. It was a different order at Old Trafford for matches but I almost couldn't believe that I now rubbed shoulders with some of the best players in the world – serious stars. I'd watched them on TV, faced them on the pitch – usually on the losing side – or trained alongside some of them for England. Now this!

Fans often ask me why United were so formidable during this period, and I often mention the energy and camaraderie that spread from Cristiano Ronaldo to Darren Fletcher, to Wayne Rooney and Rio Ferdinand, all the way round the room. The team were a family with Sir Alex as the father-figure, and I soon relaxed and thought nothing of chatting about the most mundane things, like asking Giggsy about restaurants. Lisa and I were staying in the Lowry Hotel and wanted to get out occasionally. 'Do you know a good Italian restaurant?' I asked Giggsy. He recommended Stocks, the old bank converted into a restaurant which he and Gary Neville bought in the end. Players really helped each other out at United, and Giggsy, Nev and the others went out of their way to welcome me.

I saw that togetherness in every look, word and pass between Rooney and Ronaldo, and what happened at the World Cup with Ronnie's wink when Wazza got sent off against Portugal simply wasn't an issue. It's football. It's win or lose. End of. That bond was strengthened through this army game 'Socom' we played as a group on PSP (the old handheld PlayStation). The lads all had different names and I was 'Havoc' because I caused havoc with grenades. Rio was 'Brrrap', Fletch 'Keyser Söze', Wazza was 'Jack Bauer', Nemanja Vidić (Vida to us) 'Arkan', Wes Brown was 'Wade baby', John O'Shea was 'Cobra' and Kieran Richardson 'Vendetta'. You'd play in a team, sometimes two v. two but it could easily end up eight v. eight. Richardson was the best, the one we sent out to kill the others. We'd never play on the way to a game but the day before we'd all be at it when travelling, usually a little four v. four, and it was unbelievably competitive. Some of the older lads like Giggsy, Scholesy and Edwin van der Sar decided it wasn't for them, and they just put their headphones on and ignored us because the shouts were ridiculous. We'd be screaming 'Press Square!', 'Revive me!', 'Get me up!' and 'I'm in the generator room!' Now and again, the Boss would turn around and have a scream-up. When we got to the hotel, we'd gather in adjoining rooms and as long as the walls weren't too thick the wireless could get through, so we'd play on for hours, not like silly hours into the morning, but until 9pm or 10pm. Some of our goal celebrations came from 'Socom', and I remember Vida scoring against Inter Milan, dropping down on one knee and pretending to launch a rocket. A few PSPs got smashed up in the heat of battle. None of us liked losing.

Games like 'Socom' helped me settle in fast, as did the Boss' instructions. A month after my arrival, we faced Arsenal at Old Trafford and I was sub as maybe the Boss didn't think I was quite ready. I rarely missed a game after that, especially big games. 'Make sure you get in their faces, be aggressive, watch for the 1–2s and go with your runner,' the Boss told the lads. I learned that it was before games like this, especially against flair sides like Arsenal, that Sir Alex gave one of his specific team talks.

'Today, boys, it's a running game,' he'd say. 'Run more than them, run over the top of them and fucking beat them. They don't like it. Run forward! Pass forward!' That would be it, the thrust of the team talk – not tactics but heart and mindset. 'It's sheer aggression today,' Sir Alex would say. We'd storm out there and press them, run, be aggressive, tackle, play forward, run forward, support. The running game didn't work against Arsenal that day, but it usually did. When the Boss went 'running game today', I'd always tell myself, *We're going to win. Physically it'll be a hard game, but we'll beat them by running over them.* We always had the quality to play with intensity.

We did what the Boss ordered us to do, not out of fear, but out of total belief in him. He caught us all off guard when he was raging at half-time at Bolton Wanderers that October. By this point, I'd bedded in well, I thought, and had already played 10 games. I knew Bolton away in those days was a tough place to go with serious competitors like Gary Speed, Ivan Campo and Kevin Davies playing. I picked out Rooney with a ball through the middle, he added a second and we were 2–0 up at half-time, although we should have been four or five up having played some unbelievable football. I strolled off the pitch with Rio and Giggsy going, 'Fucking hell! How good was that!?' As a team we'd brilliant passing, movement, timing, speed, intensity – it all clicked. Rio, Giggsy and I were chuckling, almost in surprise.

But the Boss was waiting for us, raging, 'Yous lot fucking took your foot off the pedal. That last five minutes was a fucking disgrace. I'm not having that.' I sat there, stunned, not risking eye contact with him, trying to recall what went wrong, and couldn't think of anything. Speed went close with a free kick and Abdoulaye Faye headed a corner over but that was it. Seriously, Edwin didn't have a save to make, yet Sir Alex still tore into us. 'Whoa, this is different,' I thought. At West Ham or Spurs, if I came in 2–0 up at half-time, Harry Redknapp or Martin Jol would be clapping and going, 'Brilliant that!' Not Sir Alex. He rattled us to keep us going, I felt. We went out in the second half and, OK, didn't play as well but Ronnie scored, Wazza got his hat-trick and it ended 4–0 – job done. Sir Alex strolled in and just said, 'Well done. Brilliant.' I felt like I'd been standing in a storm that blew in out of nowhere, crashed through the dressing-room, shaking us all, and disappeared just as quickly. The Boss gave us each a little pat on the head, and I can almost feel the affectionate touch now. I was leaning forward, taking off my boots, and Sir Alex just tapped me on the head and moved on. He never said much after a win, just a few words. If I hadn't played very well I'd get a pat on the head, if I played all right I'd get a 'Well done, son' and now and again, I'd get, 'Brilliant'. You can imagine how proud that one word made me feel. Scholesy always got a little slap on the side of the face as if to say, 'You've done it again, Scholesy, you're brilliant.'

Scholesy could do no wrong. I mean, like, he usually was brilliant but there was one game at Old Trafford when he had an absolute beast of a first half, and Sir Alex sighed and said quietly, 'For fuck's sake, Scholesy.' No one laughed as we knew it was a serious one. With anyone else, the Boss would have screamed, 'What the fuck's wrong with you?' and there would be a bit of an inquest. That was it from Sir Alex to Scholesy, just four words. The Boss was probably shocked.

It wasn't just us who got it. I remember we led 1–0 in our first game at the Emirates in January 2007, but ended up losing 2–1, and were all raging as we went to the changing room, arguing and shouting, and it was probably as aggressive and angry, as I ever saw the Boss. He was having a go at one of us when this old guy came in. He was doing the doping, with his vest on to show he was drugs, and he tried to get one of the lads to go straight to doping control. The Boss nearly ripped his head off: 'Get the fuck out of my changing room, who the fuck do you think you are?' I thought the Boss was going to fight him. The poor guy didn't know what to do. Whoever he was supposed to be testing was sitting there. But he just got ushered to the door, and the manager carried on shouting.

The Boss would sometimes have a pop at Giggsy, who'd have a little go back and then go out and play as if nothing happened. There was no special relationship with Giggsy as I felt Sir Alex was pretty similar with all the senior lads: Giggsy, Nev and Scholesy. He'd pick their brains, ask them about certain lads, 'How's he? What's happening in the changing room, how are the lads?' He'd ask their view on particular players he was looking at, like with me. 'What do you think about him?' The Boss had a real trust in those three to keep hold of the changing room. At Carrington, the Boss never really came into the changing room, but he ran the place and we knew he saw everything. As I noticed on my first day, Sir Alex's office looked on to the main training pitch and the first team car park at the back, and if he saw a young lad with what he thought was a flash car, like a Range Rover, he wouldn't have it at all. 'What are you doing driving that?' I loved that from the Boss. That sent a message that everything in life must be earned so don't get ahead of yourself. I'd see the young lad meekly return the car, unless they parked it round the front, or pretend they'd sold it and still drove it. Giggsy, Nev and Scholesy had a word, too, just to reinforce the manager's point.

Really, in those days, anybody who went round the back at Carrington and saw the players' car park would be surprised. Don't get me wrong, they were nice cars in there, but there weren't Ferraris, Bentleys and Aston Martins lined up. Some of the lads had them at home, but in the car park were Audis, family saloons, Mercedes saloons, quite low-key really but Carrington really wasn't like car parks at other Premier League training grounds which looked like super-car showrooms. We'd pull into an away ground, into the main car park and see all their players' cars – all top of the range, kitted out with blacked-out windows and big alloy wheels. At United, our cars were more understated, quite business-like really, and that was just the way the Boss liked it.

The more I worked under Sir Alex, the more I understood why he was the greatest manager of his generation. So much of his greatness was in how he treated his players. I was coming off the pitch at Carrington once, Sir Alex walked past and said, 'Well played Saturday, son. That was your best performance of the season.' There was a game the next day, so I thought, 'Brilliant. I'm playing. I'm up for this.' I was sub! The Boss gave me those nice words because he was dropping me the next day. It was calculating, yes, but it was his way of keeping my spirits up when he was about to rest or drop me, depending on how you look at it. He often picked his teams in advance, then he'd pull you and tell you he's resting you this week, but to be ready for the next one or a week on Saturday. He managed the squad and individual players' emotions incredibly well. He'd drop you but make you feel like his most important player.

Playing for Manchester United was like riding a train that never slowed, it just kept rolling on, stopping for no one. There was an unspoken message from the Boss which I soon picked up and that was, 'On to the next game'. That was the Manchester United way – don't dwell on wins. It's always the defeats that kill you the most and I knew the Boss never stopped thinking about them. If there was a really bad result, Carrington was down for a few days and everybody was very aware of the Boss's fury. 'That's not happening again,' screamed his every look and word. I know there were times when United lost two on the spin, and those games at Roma and Portsmouth in 2007 are a painful memory, but we hit back by thrashing Roma 7–1 next up. It was a point of burning pride that we fought back and we never lost three in a row during my time under Sir Alex. If United did have a bad result, you wouldn't want to play us next because we'd come at you like wounded animals, desperate to prove ourselves. We lost at FC Copenhagen the game after Bolton, and took out our anger on Portsmouth three days later. I could see and hear the desire in all my teammates to avenge that loss. 'All right then, let's have it then, next time out.' Our sheer determination after a defeat summed up in, 'Well, that's not happening again.' We never sulked, we just hit back stronger.

At United, it was us against the world. What got written in newspapers or said on TV or radio, positive or negative, never really got talked about inside United. In England squads, hell, that's all that got talked about because the outside dictated the mood inside the England camp. That's what was special about the culture at United – no one really gave a damn about the outside. All we cared about was, 'We have to win the next game.' Yes, the papers were in the canteen at Carrington and the lads flicked through them, but I never read the back pages, and wouldn't touch the United match report or look at any stories about us. I just didn't believe what was written because the truth, for me, was what the Boss thought or what the lads felt.

I was like a kid in a sweet shop. The environment was stimulating and I was learning all the time, but even in those early days, Sir Alex never sat me down and said, 'This is how I see you playing.' He just trusted me and, yes, he talked about getting forward and shooting more but it wasn't a tactical command, more encouragement. 'You can score more,' he said. In my first year I scored six goals, not bad for a midfielder settling in, but I always sensed this quiet demand from the Boss to score more. Score more, give more, do more – the Boss was relentless. His advice was sparing but inspiring, and there were pearls of wisdom like, 'When you're trying to stop a counterattack, and closing the ball down, defend with your arms out as it makes you look bigger.' Such was my belief in the Boss that I didn't even pause to think about hand-ball. The Boss often came up with little nuggets of advice like that, but he'd never tell me where to stand, how to mark a man or pass a ball. He never coached and we never really did much set-piece practice at Carrington. All that tactical stuff, the pattern of play, was the preserve of the Boss's assistant, Carlos Queiroz, who worked with us on shape, and was seriously good.

Behind every great manager, there's often a studious coach and Sir Alex and Carlos were almost like a powerful blend of heart and head. Carlos was more cautious, measured and quick to point out pitfalls, while the Boss was a natural risk-taker. Carlos was big on forward runs from midfield, and we'd work on that but mainly it was quite free-form on possession. We never did tactics the day before a game, just boxes, some crossing and then, for 15–20 minutes, we'd have a match that was often so intense Sir Alex stepped in to call a truce. 'Save your energy for tomorrow,' he'd shout.

I remember Louis Saha pulling his hamstring stretching for a long ball over the top and the Boss going berserk with Wes Brown, who'd flown in to tackle Saha as the Boss thought he'd injured him. 'Right, that's the end. Finish, lads.' The Boss knew what Wes was like and thought he'd smashed Louis. Wes's tackles were legendary, old school – he'd take everything, ball, player and even linesman all in one go if he could. Wes had terrible luck with injuries but what a player he was. Wes never touched Louis, though. Louis just injured himself chasing a ball because everyone gave everything in those matches. 'They're sometimes harder than the real game,' Nev laughed as we walked off one day.

Under Sir Alex, my preparation for games became far more meticulous. I'd done some work in the gym at West Ham, a bit more at Spurs, but it wasn't until I joined United that I really hit the gym properly. I wasn't banging out heavy weights, just keeping my body at a peak level to perform. We even did a mini pre-season in January at United, two weeks of solid training while matches went on. 'Right, we'll get through the game this weekend, we'll win that but these two weeks are preparation for the rest of the season,' Sir Alex said. I was stunned. *Two weeks of January doing this?!* It was dead hard training too. *Are they mad, or what?* I asked myself. We trained fiercely Monday, Tuesday, Wednesday, Thursday, normal Friday, played Saturday with heavy legs but were good enough to win, then repeated the workload the following week. It was knackering. The Boss trained us like racehorses, so we'd be fit and fresh to let loose towards the end of the race. As usual, Gary Neville was super vocal about the importance of stamina and conditioning work as he felt it fired us up. 'We'll overrun teams at the end of the season; we'll have more energy, we'll run over the top of them,' Nev told me. History tells you how Sir Alex's sides always finished strong in games and in seasons. April and May was our time. Everyone else tapered off at the end of the season while we kicked up a gear. 'We're different from the rest,' Nev said. 'This is when we finish strong; this is where we come good. When it really counts.' Nobody else did this at that time and that's why nobody could contend with us.

Thinking back on my playing career, I know I'd have got more headlines if I'd been more selfish but that was exactly why I was so suited to Manchester United. I sacrificed myself for the team. I'm not looking for praise. It was just that was my nature, and also the club's. The ego at United was always collective; we believed we were the best but it was not an ego where it was 'All About Me'. The greatest footballers, like Giggs and Scholes, were all about the team. That first season I was there, it was insane how good those two were. Giggsy did everything he could to be the best, stretching, gym, yoga, diet – whatever it took, he made that sacrifice. Scholesy had no ego. He wasn't obsessed with being the best player in the world. He played football because he was good at it, loved it and adored Manchester United. Every day at Carrington, Scholesy was probably the best in training.

Cristiano Ronaldo was different. He was driven to be the best player in the world, and it was almost a mission for him from a young age. Especially in the early days, Ronnie played for the team and individual honours followed. I played against him three times at Spurs and respected him, but when I reached United I saw how Ronnie came back after the World Cup in Germany at just a different level, a different character – more mature and physically a beast as if he'd been on the weights all summer. What shone through with Ronnie was how unbelievably hard he practised. His appetite for self-improvement was ferocious. Ronnie was one of the first in the gym before training, strengthening his ankles with resistance bands, then going outside, working on his skills and constantly practising free kicks and shooting. He put little weights around his ankles and off he'd go, dribbling between cones. He was so dedicated and I know people talk about his nice cars and the image, but I promise you, Ronnie wasn't a show-off. Sometimes when someone had an over-the-top car, I thought, *You flash so-and-so.* Never with Ronnie. He was really likeable and also he'd earned that nice car with hard graft. In my first season at United, Ronnie's performances were as good as I've seen. He got hammered left, right and centre because of what happened with Wayne Rooney at the World Cup but Ronnie won everyone over and ended up Footballer of the Year. He got kicked and got back up. He got booed and abused, yet he still wanted the ball, and when he got it Ronnie just ran at defenders again and again. He had persistence and resilience. He had that hunger to use his skill to create a chance or score himself. Nowadays, I see too many players do a trick but it's harmless and they'll lay the ball off. Not Ronnie. He just drove at defenders and made things happen. His technique was so good, and he worked so hard at it, that he could go both ways and I almost pitied the full back trying to stop Ronnie. Nev put himself up against Ronnie every day in training just to challenge himself. 'Come on, Ronnie, what have you got?! Come on!' I'd hear Nev shout. Half the time, Ronnie would beat Nev, and laugh at him but Nev would come again. Ronnie and Nev pushed each other to be better.

If you asked me to name the greatest competitors, I can't think of many I'd put ahead of Gary Neville. Watching him closely in training, I grasped how amazingly dedicated he was. Whenever we'd break in a session, Nev started doing some mad runs, zigzagging, sprinting and doing fast feet. 'What an absolute numpty he is!' I heard one of the younger players saying once. 'What's wrong with him?' Nev didn't give a monkey's what anyone thought about him. He maximised his ability. He did whatever it took to reach the top and then stay there. I've never met anyone as driven as him. He was an unbelievable captain, too, because he cared. The Boss wouldn't entertain speaking to agents for the young kids so Nev went in with every kid from the youth team and reserves, and did their deal with the Boss. Nev was involved in everything, making decisions and influencing outcomes. Devoting his time to advising kids on their career paths, and getting them the best deal, showed how much Nev cared. He was a big, big voice in the dressing room, where he was always moaning, and believe me, Nev could moan for fun. He'd moan at the players. 'You didn't pass it right.' 'You didn't run hard enough.' He'd moan at the staff. 'The massages aren't good enough.' He'd moan at the kit men. 'This kit is shit.' All this moaning wound everyone up but it was also invaluable because Nev kept standards up, and if anyone dropped below those standards, then Nev would moan at them again.

Giggsy was never as vocal. He'd pick his moments to make his points and everyone listened because of the respect we all had for him. Scholesy was dead quiet, really, but when he had something to say, everyone knew it was worth listening to and his one-liners could destroy someone. I always sat next to Giggsy on the bus and opposite Scholesy with Tony Strudwick, the fitness coach who'd moved from West Ham, also on the table. Strudders was always giving banter or spotting someone, looka-likes walking down the street. Mike Donnelly, the chef, would be up and down the coach after a game with chicken wings, pasta or sausage and mash. First off, it used to be fizzy drinks, sweets and a bar of choco-late after a game but now it's far more controlled and scientific. Protein this, carbo that. Sitting there after a win on the road, chatting and eating away, were some of the best of times. Nobody had headphones on. We talked and that bonded us together even more. With United, it wasn't a case of getting on the coach and the lads going, 'Right, what are we doing tonight?' None of that. We'd talk about the game, debate the good and bad points – a players' debrief really, and Giggsy and Nev would have these really deep conversations about football. Just listening to them was a priceless education. They spoke of games I'd watched with Graeme on the TV and now here I was, playing with them and my sense of privilege at being at United deepened further. Everything I'd hoped for when talking to Graeme about joining Manchester United was coming true.

8
THE WINNING HABIT

Manchester United were into 'marginal gains' long before they had a name. They worked on my vision. When people talk about my vision, I almost have to stop myself laughing because I'm actually as blind as a bat. On joining United, they took detailed preparation to another level. I had my eyes tested by the club's vision expert, Professor Gail Stephenson, a lovely lady, who sadly passed away in 2015. Gail put four shapes on a ledge to either side, then moved one slightly forward and asked, 'Which one's forward?' I got really good at it, so Gail shifted it a fraction and I'd still get it. 'Your peripheral vision and perception of depth are amazing,' Gail said.

Playing in the centre, my peripheral vision stayed pin-sharp as I looked left and right pretty equally. Picking out players came easily as they were never a blur even if the angle was tight. I saw them even more clearly after Gail gave me exercises for my eyes during the warm-up. 'Pick out objects short and far, and keep focusing on them to get your eyes adjusted to the light in the stadium,' Gail said. Just before kick-off, I'd look at a blade of grass, something close, and then focus on an object further away, a hoarding or a sign, whatever, to sharpen my vision. Gail found a real difference between my vision and Gary Neville's. She noticed a big difference in peripheral vision of those who played out wide. Nev's left-side vision was stronger than his right because as a right back he looked to his left most of the game.

I defy anybody to find anyone who is as hardcore a Red as Nev because he got the bug as a baby, but soon my life too became consumed by United and nobody in the changing room needed to give me a history lesson about games against Liverpool. Before our 3 March 2007 fixture, I definitely sensed the mood intensifying among the local lads and Sir Alex. The Boss's team talks at Anfield were his most mesmerising. You knew how much it meant to him, just listening to his words, which crackled with electricity. You could see how desperate he was to beat Liverpool at their place. You could feel the depth of his hunger as he talked so powerfully about the rivalry between the clubs, even the rivalry between the cities, the economic history and the Manchester Ship Canal. 'We have to win,' he said. The Boss spoke about our responsibility to United supporters, and how they'd go into work the next morning with their happiness the next day, week, even month resting on our effort over the next 90 minutes. 'Don't let them down,' he'd demand. 'Work hard.' Always work hard. The Boss built the game up and up, so each of us pulling on the United shirt knew it was win at all costs. 'This is the best place to win, here,' he'd remind us before the buzzer sounded from the ref summoning us to battle.

Walking out of the tunnel at Anfield was something else. The difference between being there in a United shirt, rather than a West Ham or Spurs one, hit me like a giant wave of noise, insults and hatred. Liverpool fans on all sides were standing up, abusing me, shouting, 'You Manc Twat', 'Carrick, you're shit', 'You Geordie bastard', which made me smile. Most of it came during the warm-up when it's quiet and I'd hear shouts, someone trying to get a laugh off his mates by abusing me, harmless really. I've had it where the ball's gone out, and a Liverpool fan throws it back hard at my chest, trying to be clever and make his mates happy. I'd smile back, just to show them they were wasting their breath, which wound them up even more, so, good, job done. It's great all that. It gives me a buzz and makes me laugh. It's football rivalry at its best.

I don't even pause before claiming that that March match at Anfield is an occasion I'd place among my three favourite moments during my time with United. We were top of the Premiership, pressure was cranking up and this was the time of year I heard Nev talk about when United really went to work. We were actually horrendous that day, absolutely hopeless, I got booked for fouling John Arne Riise, Scholesy got sent off and we were holding on grimly. Thankfully, Edwin made an unbelievable, one-handed save from Peter Crouch to keep it goalless and a point looked good, so we thought let's just take it and get the hell out of there. The board went up for four minutes' stoppage time when Giggsy was pulled back to the left of Liverpool's area. Ronaldo lined up the free kick, and we only put four in the box – O'Shea, Vidić, Saha and Ferdinand – while I stayed outside the area, waiting for a loose ball or to see off a breakaway. What a moment. Pepe Reina fumbled, Sheasy rammed in the rebound, and it was utter bedlam, as we'd won it in the last seconds, in front of the Kop, and life doesn't get much better. Sheasy turned and ran past me, the full length of the pitch to our fans. Sir Alex was on the touchline, celebrating, and we ran past him to our fans at the final whistle, down the Anfield Road end. I celebrated first with Giggsy, Nev and Rio, then I hugged Vida and Wazza. Nev ripped his shirt off and flung it to our fans. Sir Alex marched on to Liverpool's turf like a conquering general, surveying his captured land. He clapped our supporters, who were going wild because victory at Anfield meant everything, the three points meant everything, and it felt like we'd won the Premiership there and then. Chelsea were second and needed us to lose but our grit saw us through. We were one big step closer to the title and to have that feeling in our rivals' backyard was even sweeter.

Some wins mean more than others. Seeing what it meant to our old guard as well as the Boss and back-room staff, not to mention our fans, rammed home the significance even more to me. I gazed at our brilliant fans partying in the Anfield Road end and felt at one with them. I'd only been there nine months but United was my religion now. I watched Nev celebrating with the fans and knew that United was his life, his family, his mates, his everything. Nev embodied United for me. He was born with two fingers up to the rest of the world and I loved him for that defiance. Nev's passion for United rubbed off on me. One of the most treasured pictures on my phone is of me, Nev, Giggsy and Rio at the end of that Anfield game in front of our fans and I look at it from time to time. That feeling we had back then was special. Nev, Giggsy and Scholesy were the heart of this passion for United but everyone was in on it. Solskjaer was massively into it, Sheasy too, and Wes was there through and through. Fletch, Wazza and Rio absolutely bought into the belief big-time. Alan Smith came from Leeds United – the enemy – but it was like he had been born in Salford he was that into Manchester United. Patrice Evra and Ji-sung Park had no attachment to United growing up but still had this deep love of the place. Evra was well respected by the younger, foreign lads and would quite often have a go at Anderson and that type, and pull them into line if they needed it. He was a big character and full of life. Ji was his best mate. The strangest three friends in the world were Patrice Evra, Ji-sung Park and Carlos Tévez – they were totally inseparable, playing one touch, two touch in training together every day. God knows how they communicated – one from France, one South Korea, one Argentina – but they just loved being together, and being at United.

That win at Anfield pushed us closer to the title and when Ronaldo scored a penalty against Manchester City on 5 May 2007, Chelsea had to beat Arsenal at the Emirates the next day otherwise we'd be champions. I'd never been here before, so close to the prize, and I didn't know what to do. So, I went into Carrington for a warm-down, then back to the flat Lisa and I had in Alderley Edge. Lisa was away on her hen do so there was only Graeme and me in the flat, watching the Chelsea game. For such an important occasion, the set-up had to be dead right and we rearranged the room so we could lie across two sofas just staring at the telly. It was a rollercoaster. Chelsea went down to 10, Arsenal went 1–0 up, Chelsea equalised, and it was 1–1 with 20 minutes to go. Graeme and I talked all the way through and then fell silent for the last 10 minutes, just lying there, not moving a muscle. When the ref blew the final whistle, we erupted. We jumped up and down for a minute, hugging each other. My stomach did somersaults and my heart thumped out of my chest. I went absolutely mental and nearly put a hole in the floor. God knows what the lady down below must have thought. 'Championes, championes, ole, ole, ole!!' we sang manically. There's only so long you can do this between two of you, so we stopped after a couple of minutes and just looked at each other in silence, panting, getting our breath back.

'Wow, man, you've just won the league! I'm proud of you!' Graeme said. Sharing the moment with Graeme was brilliant, because he knew the sacrifices I'd made. 'What do we do now?!' I said. Winning the league was what I'd wanted since I was kid, and I just didn't know how to react. Fortunately, we were sorted by Nev, always the party organiser, who rang and instructed us, 'Right, get to the Living Room.' Within 45 minutes we were in town, in the Living Room bar on Deansgate and all the lads were there to a man. Academy staff, and some from the training ground, had all been out in town, and they piled in followed by Brian McClair, director of the academy. The first team coaches were invited over to the Boss's house, and into his dining room probably, which was definitely a bit more civilised, but everyone else crammed into the Living Room. Nev's old man, Big Nev, came with all his mates. Giggsy's mates were all there and they're all Mancs, big Reds, then all the other lads turned up and it was absolute chaos, the biggest sing-song ever. Big Nev, who made Nev look quiet, took charge, standing on a bench and all of a sudden he'd go, 'Shushhhhh', and start another United song. The lads stamped on the floor, banged the ceilings, and I was bouncing around, singing, sweating and totally bollocksed by the end. I knew we'd have the public moment of lifting the trophy but this was the real celebration, the private one – a team partying as if there was no tomorrow. We'd been through this battle together, trained hard every day, gave everything every game, so to have a beer and a sing-song with mates was the ultimate.

I stood in the middle of the Living Room and had a moment, taking it all in. I loved that whole United team and all that camaraderie. I'd never be disrespectful to United teams of the last few years, but the buzz about that group of players was unbelievable, we were almost like brothers. Believe me, that spirit is tough to get and we had so much of it, more than any other team. Those parties were moments in time, captured in my memory only as there were nowhere as many camera-phones then as there are today. I'd give anything just to see some of the scenes again and get taken back to that magical time. The best dos were when I first signed, when all the players knew all the words to all the songs. Christmas parties ended up in a pub with a band and punters joining in. We'd sing proper songs, but within half an hour we'd be going through the United songbook, hammering away at all the great tunes, 'Yip Jaap Stam', 'Nicky Butt, Nicky Butt, Nicky, Nicky Butt', 'Oh, Keano's fucking magic', 'We are the pride of all Europe' and old classics like 'Ooh, aah Cantona'. We'd go round the room singing a song for every player. As crazy as it seems, these are the times I miss the most.

Graeme and I often talk about that United team and I was buzzing my brother was in the inner sanctum that night to see how unique it was. I remember him telling me as we finally left the Living Room, and I probably haven't got all his words down exactly because it was quite a night, but Graeme said something like, 'It's a massive privilege being invited in there.' Graeme was right, it was.

That first season started my love affair with the Champions League – a relationship that was to bring me heartache as well as joy. Falling in love with the Champions League was easy because of the atmospheric venues, that stirring anthem, playing under the lights and the great names of players and clubs we'd take on. The noise at Celtic Park that November was outrageous. When the UEFA anthem finished, the roar from the Celtic fans was something else, absolutely spine-tingling. I'd admired Celtic as a kid because Dad's Catholic and he followed them and told me all about their passionate fans. I played at Celtic Park with West Ham in a pre-season friendly in 2000, when Paolo Di Canio ran out blowing kisses to the Celtic fans, and that was quite an atmosphere but nothing like their reaction when Manchester United rocked up. More than 60,000 people were in there, rammed to the rafters, all desperate to win, to make the knockout stage. When Shunsuke Nakamura's free kick went in, the noise was so deafening my ears rang for a while afterwards.

We made the knockout stage eventually and it became really lively again with Roma in the quarters. The first leg was in the Stadio Olimpico, and I remember the atmosphere ramped right up. Our fans were warned about ambushes by Ultras, especially on the walk over the Ponte Duca D'Aosta towards the ground. It was a rough night all round as we got ambushed on the pitch. Sir Alex warned us Roma exploited the multi-ball system brilliantly.

'Watch their quick corners,' the Boss said. 'They get the ball back quickly.' A few minutes in, I started to suspect the selection process for ball boys at Roma involved sprint trials. At every Roma corner, the ball boy raced over, planted the ball by the flag, and Francesco Totti ran in and smashed it across. They must have practised the routine with the ball boys in training because it was a slick, well-drilled oper-ation. Within five seconds of the ball going out, it was flying into our area. The first couple of corners Roma got, it was madness in our box. Incoming! Real life 'Socom' with balls as grenades! Rodrigo Taddei scored from a quick corner, and Roma's ball boys never moved that fast for us! When the ball went out and it was ours, it took ages to come back. I'd not take anything away from Roma, though, they were relent-less. Everything went through Totti, their main man who wouldn't beat you in a foot race but could beat you with his vision and technique. Roma had almost a set attack of playing it up to Totti, he'd flick it on, one touch around the corner, and everyone ran forward, especially the two wide men. That was a hard, hard night. Scholesy got sent off for a late challenge on Christian Wilhelmsson and then tripping Totti. I hear plenty of debate about Scholesy's tackling, but I never heard the Boss tell him to tone it down as that was just the small price to pay for Scholesy's genius. With Scholesy gone, I spent the rest of the evening protecting the back four. Our fans got a terrible beating off the Italian police at half-time, shocking really. We got out just about in one piece, only 2–1 down, and I returned with Totti's shirt. Those was the days when I collected shirts, something I drifted away from as time passed.

Rooney's away goal was massive and made us feel we could turn the tide around at Old Trafford. I get a tingle just thinking about what happened on 10 April 2007. We didn't have Scholesy, and we didn't have a chance in some pundits' eyes, but we had our fans and Sir Alex knew how to unleash them. 'Get the early tackle in, get crosses in early, get running forward quickly, take a throw-in quick, get shots off early, get the fans going,' Sir Alex told us. He knew this would create an energy for the fans to feed off. Lining up in the tunnel, we could tell our fans were already flying, cranking up the volume and turning the place into a fortress. Old Trafford can be quiet at times, that's only natural, but not on make-or-break European nights like this. Maybe our fans were still angry over the harsh treatment meted out to them in Rome and wanted retribution for the batons and the abuse. Maybe they'd also seen the trouble outside Old Trafford as Roma fans ran riot. Maybe they knew how much the players needed them. They certainly didn't let us down, backing us raucously, and we responded by tearing into Roma. Everything was high tempo, we just pressed and pressed, following the Boss's orders as well as the fans' pleas.

'Play on the front foot, get at them,' Sir Alex said. We played with emotion and energy, and were pretty much unstoppable. We felt invincible as individuals and as a team, playing with freedom and the belief that anything was possible. Every single player and every single supporter was up for that game. The togetherness was unreal. It was as if it couldn't get any better or louder but then we'd score again and it would get better and louder. It was heaven. This was the night when I felt I truly arrived at Old Trafford, when I was accepted into this powerful community of supporters and players. When Ronaldo passed inside, I took a touch and the ball was under my feet with Roma's keeper Doni coming off his line, so I had to dig it out. There was no way I could get the power into the shot to beat Doni, so I had to do it through the air. I had to flight the ball perfectly because I couldn't get the backlift to just drive it in with force. So I scooped it out, floated the ball over Doni and Old Trafford just went mad. That lit the touch paper.

It was one of the great nights at Old Trafford, and will remain forever in my memory, as we unleashed attack after attack, goal after goal from Alan Smith, then Wazza after a great move between Giggsy and Ronaldo, then Ronnie himself just before half-time. Relentless aggression and movement, just as the Boss ordered. 'Don't worry about giving the ball away, just be positive all the time,' he'd said. Sir Alex's tactics worked, with Smudger on his own upfront, Giggsy in behind, Wazza and Ronnie wide and me in the middle with Fletch. Wazza made it 5–0 and still the United fans chanted 'attack, attack, attack', it was like they really wanted Roma to suffer, so I obliged with one of those shots you take on when you're firing on all cylinders and the ball just flew in the top corner. Wazza came over and we just started laughing because it was that sort of extraordinary night.

My first was a massive goal, one of the biggest I've ever scored, but by the time my second, our sixth came around, the game was dead. We'd beaten them up. Roma had had enough by then. They didn't even bother celebrating Daniele De Rossi's volley. The Boss brought me off, and the fans' loud applause lodged deep within me. I can still hear it now, just a long, emotional seal of approval. As I reached the bench, I had a chuckle with Mick Phelan. 'Any chance of leaving me on for my hat-trick?' I joked.

'How much did we pay for you again?' Mick said. 'I think you've just paid it back!'

Patrice Evra rounded off a special night and at 7–1 up, everyone just waited for the final whistle and a quick 'Well played, lads.' That night, I did get a pat on the head off Sir Alex and a 'Brilliant.' Lisa and I went into town with Mam and Dad and popped into Wing's Chinese restaurant quickly as my parents were driving straight back up to Newcastle – one of the many late-night road trips they've done over the years. When we entered Wing's, everyone stood up and clapped me in. It showed how much it mattered to United fans that we won in style. Even now, I can be out and about and United fans rush up to tell me that Roma 7–1 was one of their favourite nights.

Sadly, our shot at Europe started to fizzle out that season against AC Milan in the semi-final at Old Trafford as Kaká glided over the pitch, so smooth and so quick, and scored twice. It was 2–2 with 10 minutes remaining, and Giggsy said to me, 'We'll get a chance, keep going. We always get one chance.' That's what we genuinely believed. We always did get a chance and no way was that luck. I heard Giggsy say it many times, and he was so often right. In the last minute, Giggsy sent Rooney through and he smashed the ball past Dida at his new post, so we travelled to Italy with high hopes. I absolutely loved the San Siro. Coming out to warm up, many of the 78,500 supporters were already in, and it sounded like every single Milan fan whistled at us. It was a brilliant feeling to get abused by so many, very satisfying really. Milan's fans were just getting going. Gennaro Gattuso catapulted from the tunnel and sprinted towards one end with everything he'd got, ran into the corner, and the San Siro just went absolutely nuts. It must have been a ritual because they were all waiting for it. Gattuso was like that all night; he ran everywhere and spent much of the evening kicking the life out of Ronaldo. Gattuso clattered him early on but the ref, a Belgian called Frank de Bleeckere, only gave a free kick when it was a booking at least, and then Gattuso knocked Ronnie into the hoardings. Everybody, except the ref, could see what Gattuso's game was – stop Ronnie by any means. Credit to Gattuso, he did his job to perfection. Milan were class though, especially Clarence Seedorf. I knew Seedorf was good, from watching him over the years, but didn't realise how incredible he was until that night in Milan. He was just a level above, playing with both feet, and walking all over us as they won 3–0.

Elimination was hard to stomach, and I didn't sleep that night as I went over and over the match in my head. Over the years, I've realised it's a form of grieving I suffer after defeats. *Why didn't I make that pass? Why didn't I stand in that position? Why didn't I make that decision?* I'm a bad sleeper after games anyway, horrendous really, and there was no chance of sleeping that night when all I could see when I closed my eyes was the wreckage of a whole season's work in Europe.

Nights like that – being so close to the final, but so far – you just want to hide. Bad nights in the San Siro taught us more than good nights at home to Roma as it made us appreciate the concentration and mentality required and made us even more determined. Only Giggs, Neville, Scholes and Van der Sar were really experienced in Europe. Solskjaer too, yes, but he was coming to the end of his time at United. I knew Evra had been in the final before, in 2004 with Monaco, but me, Ronaldo, Rooney, Fletcher and Vida were new to this level, and we had to learn. Sometimes you have to suffer first. Sir Alex took going out of Europe really to heart as the Champions League was his great love. League was No. 1, because it told everybody in England that United were No. 1, but Europe was a rare prize. At the time, United had won it only twice, in 1968 and 1999, and that rankled Sir Alex.

'Manchester United should have more European Cups. Look at Real Madrid – nine European Cups. Look at Bayern – four. Look at Ajax – four.' He mentioned it many times. We then lost the FA Cup final to Chelsea and that hurt, and I remember leaving Wembley vowing again to come back stronger. Even now, I shake my head in disbelief when I hear people say about Cup finals that the important thing is to 'enjoy the occasion' as I couldn't enjoy defeat however nice the surroundings. I took nothing from that Chelsea game, just emptiness. I gave my loser's medal to Graeme as soon as I saw him. I didn't want to be near that medal. Win or nothing. As kids, Graeme and I talked so often about the Cup. 'Whoa, imagine playing in the FA Cup final one day!' he'd say and I'd laugh and quietly dream about it. Once I was there, all that mattered was winning. It was quite a dead game, roasting hot, Didier Drogba scored, Chelsea won, we lost, so let's lick our wounds and move on quickly. I hate even recalling that day but it's important to remember the suffering. Defeat shapes you, it drives you. I know I was perceived as this calm pro and a level-headed lad and all that but, believe me, I was churning up inside at defeat, and felt deeply wounded. You can't accept setbacks. You have to want to put it right.

Defeat erased the elation of winning the league and brought me back down to earth. The Boss was constantly going, 'Next year, next year.' Pre-season for Sir Alex was *boom* – time for hunting trophies again and that attitude was driven by the players, too. I'd listen to the experienced lads saying that 'We have to be better.' It was relentless at United: more effort, be better, fight harder. A summer when I should have been celebrating the title, all I could think of was the FA Cup final loss. I was itching to get back into the new season, to make amends. United's desire to go again was unbelievable and I realised that's why they'd won so much. These lads were something else. Unbelievably gifted, yes, but what set them apart was their hunger.

That summer Lisa and I got married. The previous autumn I'd proposed. Just about. I'd organised to go to the ballet on Lisa's birthday. She'd never been and always talked about it. I got tickets for *Swan Lake* at the Coliseum in London, booked the St Martin's Lane Hotel, and was just checking on the tickets as we arrived at the hotel. We'd got the wrong month. *Swan Lake* wasn't on! I went to the concierge and the only tickets we could get for that night were for *Mary Poppins* at the Prince Edward Theatre. The only gear I had was a suit for the ballet, a brown suit, because I wanted to do it properly. I put that on. Lisa had a beautiful dress. We were totally overdressed for *Mary Poppins*! The show was great, we got one of those little rickshaws back to the hotel and I'd asked the hotel to put flowers and candles in the room. There wasn't a chance in hell I was asking Lisa to marry me with anyone around, like in a restaurant, so I left it until we got back in the room. I'd ordered champagne, which wasn't like me, so I thought she might guess. I wasn't nervous. I just kept checking my pocket to make sure I still had the ring. I got down on me knee in the middle of the room, there were a few tears, it was beautiful. We rang our parents straight away. My one regret was I hadn't asked Lisa's dad for permission. I still don't know why I didn't. We got married in a church in Leicestershire and I would go through the wedding all over again tomorrow if I could. It was the best weekend of my life. We smiled non-stop from Friday to Sunday, never leaving each other's side just how we had planned it. It was perfect. We honeymooned in Bora Bora, and then had four days in Vegas, where we ended up bumping into Wayne and Colleen!

Going into my first full pre-season at United opened my eyes to the club's staggering popularity around the world. When I toured South Korea with Spurs in 2005, it was quiet and nobody bothered us, really. When I visited the Far East with United in 2007, it was mental. We played Urawa Red Diamonds, FC Seoul, Shenzhen FC and Guangzhou Pharmaceutical and it was a circus and marathon combined. These tours were draining: travel, train, train, match, travel, train, train, match and in between the travel, matches and jet-lag we'd try to fit in training. The staff were bollocksed and they didn't have to train and play, so it took its toll on us. After two weeks, people were short-tempered and niggling at each other. Jet lag and packing/unpacking were two of the constants on tour, plus the local fans' utter obsession with Manchester United. When we flew in to Seoul, thousands of fans besieged Incheon airport. I read somewhere that there were like 27 million people in South Korea who loved United, and their population is around 50 million. Koreans used United credit cards and ate in United-themed restaurants in Seoul. Outside our hotel, hundreds sang 'Glory, glory, Man United'. It was gratifying and surreal at the same time. Even the rain didn't put them off at training the next day and there must have been another thousand there.

Nowadays on tour we have to fulfil many duties to commercial partners, but on that 2007 trip, we did more work with the Manchester United Foundation and UNICEF. I went with Patrice Evra and Darron Gibson to the Young Suk Sco Bo Rin orphanage in Seoul and had a kickabout with the kids there. We visited hospices with UNICEF on that trip to Asia, which I found very humbling and, to be honest, very hard to take in. My playing career has always been built around health, fitness and a feeling of invincibility, and here I was going into places where people were dying. I felt so small and weak because there was nothing you could do to help them, nothing at all. These poor kids suffered so much and some had only days, even hours, to live. It made me feel so powerless yet at the same time the kids were so happy to see us. We're so protected as professional footballers, and we're taught how to act and be strong, and then we go into an orphanage, a hospice, a blind school or a camp where there are people with HIV/AIDS and all that certainty is torn away and we stand there so vulnerable. It was difficult to go training afterwards, almost impossible, as I couldn't forget the torment I'd seen in the hospice.

It's a myth that the club are distant from the real world and disinterested in those worse off. United care. I know so many people at the club, and in the Foundation, who use United's power to help, and often rescue, those in need. We just don't boast about it. I mention it now because the image of Manchester United Football Club matters greatly to me and I want people to know that the club do so much for the community at home and abroad. Visits like the ones on that Asian tour, and going round hospitals at Christmas, also teach the young lads what to say to people in tough situations but I'll confess to never finding it any easier. I'd always come away from an orphanage, hospital or hospice devastated for the children and having kids myself now further heightens that emotion. I think of the bond between the father and his sick child, and know how devastated I'd be if that were Lou or Jacey.

It was difficult to return to football, but I had to be professional. The day after our trip to the orphanage, we played FC Seoul at the World Cup Stadium and the place was rammed with 60,000 Koreans, mainly there to see Ji, even though they knew he wasn't playing. That's how mental they were for Ji. He'd just had knee surgery, but Ji wasn't going to miss the tour to his homeland, and I'm sure the organisers wanted Ji there, probably demanded it. Before kick-off, I laughed as the camera panned along the squad and focused on Wayne Rooney, and there was a cheer, then Cristiano Ronaldo, an even bigger cheer, and then it got to Ji-sung Park who was standing there and the whole place just went absolutely crazy. No matter how much I love Ji, I never thought he'd get a louder cheer than Ronnie, but then I realised Ji's like a god in Korea. Ji just laughed it off. Ji's remembered fondly at Old Trafford. If you're picking players from great United teams, Ji's not necessarily one you'd choose, but he was a dream to play with. He worked so hard and was so clever, so economic with the way he played – his movements, touches and turns, everything was just textbook.

From Ji's homeland we flew to China and when we pulled up outside the hotel in Guangzhou, the reception was unreal. The Chinese put garlands round our necks, a steel band almost exploded they hammered away so hard, dancers leapt around and security guards held at least 500 fans and TV crews back as we walked into the hotel up this huge staircase. Seeing fans wait for hours and then burst into tears when we arrive makes you realise how much United affect people's lives in every corner of the world. I still find it very hard to get my head round it. The reaction was the same at training at the Guangdong Olympic Stadium the next day when a couple of the thousand watching fans ran on to the pitch to get close to us.

We got home from those trips shattered and quite often I was ill for a few days. Tours had to be done for financial reasons, even more so now, but it certainly didn't help us start the season fresh. We drew in the Community Shield against Chelsea and in the Premier League against Reading and on the morning of our next game, at Portsmouth, the Boss beckoned me to his table at breakfast in the hotel. 'You're nowhere near where you were last season,' Sir Alex said. 'Me and Carlos both notice it.'

I was like, 'Really?' It caught me off guard.

'Yes, you can't drop your standards,' the Boss added. I don't know whether he genuinely believed my form had dipped or whether he was playing mind games like, 'I'm going to give him a little bomb just to keep him going.' Either way it was a message to me to keep pushing and never be satisfied. I bet the Boss felt I was at risk from second-season syndrome and thought, 'I need to get into him and make sure he's not complacent.' And I responded. Sir Alex was a genius at man-management.

That January, the Boss took us all away to a mid-season training camp to freshen our minds and bodies. Because of United's huge appeal, we got invited everywhere, to extraordinary events, and that January we flew to Riyadh for a testimonial to celebrate Saudi Arabia's most famous footballer, Sami Al-Jaber. There was plenty of social stuff, like meeting dignitaries, and we got invited to one of Prince Abdullah's palaces. Evra and Rooney joined in the dancing, holding knives. The prince gave us a tour around the palace, through the garden, and out the back where the desert stretched off into the distance. Giggsy went on a camel into the desert and then one of the prince's staff casually asked, 'Does anyone want to go on quad bikes?' *Yes, yes, yes.* The lads were all over it. United staff went into meltdown and I heard them conferring, 'We can't put the lads on quads.' Too late. We leapt on quads and sped off into the desert and it was carnage in that sweltering heat. Everyone zigzagged across this huge sand dune, and some went up it. I saw Tony Strudwick go over the top of the dune and then heard a bloodcurdling 'Aaaaaaaaargh.' I raced up there to find Strudders lying in a heap, trying to get up. He'd hit a concrete block, some marker in the desert, and was a mess. 'No, I'm all right, I'm all right,' Strudders kept saying, trying to play it down. I was in tears, because I just couldn't stop laughing. The quad was battered but still worked and Strudders took it back to the palace, praying nobody noticed the dents. He got on the coach, still going, 'I'm all right, I'm all right.' But as he tried to pull his shellsuit bottoms down, they stuck to him because of the blood oozing from this massive graze in his leg. No offence to Strudders but I was thinking, 'That could have been one of the lads.'

Even meaningless games like the next day against Al-Jaber's side, Al-Hilal, at King Fahd Stadium gave me another glimpse into Sir Alex's greatness, and why this United team were always so competitive. More than 65,000 people turned up to salute Al-Jaber and we should have drawn when we had a penalty in the last minute. Danny Welbeck paused as he ran in and tried to dink it down the middle but he got it wrong and it went over and casualness like that sent the Boss nuts. Welbz was a kid, only 17, but the manager was proper raging with him. I just stared at Sir Alex as he tore into Welbz. There was nothing forced or fake about the Boss's anger. No one cared about the game. But it was a point of principle for Sir Alex. It was because Welbz was a young kid, coming on for Anderson in the second half, and the Boss expected him to play properly.

United fans also received the occasional wake-up call from the Boss. I remember the headlines that January when we beat Birmingham City at Old Trafford because Sir Alex described the atmosphere as 'like a funeral'. I understood what the manager was saying – the atmosphere was flat if United fans didn't feel inspired by the occasion or the opposition. If we played Liverpool or City or it was a big European tie, a natural buzz was generated. Matches against the so-called lesser teams were also more challenging for a player because I have to admit I didn't have the adrenaline that flowed in a big game. I knew it was my responsibility to overcome that and I couldn't just rely on supporters to get me going but the fans' mood was really important. I'd make these games just as important in my head to exaggerate the concentration, challenging myself to do certain things in the game to not get complacent.

It felt like destiny when we sealed the Premier League at the JJB Stadium on 11 May 2008 – the day Giggsy equalled Sir Bobby Charlton's record of 758 games for United with Sir Bobby watching on. Giggsy's goal summed United up, really. We kept pushing for the second goal to kill it off rather than holding on to our goal lead. I was involved three times in the move, Carlos Tévez and Owen Hargreaves were in there, too, and then Wazza played the ball through for Giggsy to score in front of all our fans in the North Stand. So many wanted to be there that it is still the stadium record of 25,133. Giggsy slid on his back, I was first to him, then a fan joined in. Sir Alex charged down the touchline with his wet, white top on, raising his arms in the air, smiling away – one of his best celebrations that, and hugging Carlos Queiroz and Mick Phelan. The last 11 minutes were a party, really, but typical United, we kept attacking. At the final whistle, I again looked across at the bench and there was Sir Bobby standing in the tunnel, all smart in his suit, his usual figure of calm as the celebrations exploded. All the players sprinted to the centre circle, Vida jumped on my back, and we got in this huddle, shouting and celebrating because we all knew that winning back-to-back titles was so tough and we'd delivered what we'd promised in pre-season. I'd constantly pushed myself, asking myself, *Have I got the mentality to do it again? Have I got the drive? Or am I settling for winning it once and thinking that's brilliant? No chance.* Confronting any doubts about myself, I answered those questions and it was the best feeling, so satisfying.

United's American owners, the Glazers, were there at the JJB. They came around the changing room at the end, shook hands and spoke to some of us, some of the staff. Before I came to United, I was aware it was a huge deal for the Glazers to be taking over the club and there was a big reaction to it. I think the Glazers have been great owners. Couldn't really ask for anything more. They throw some money out there for transfers and have never interfered. I see so many owners of other clubs picking teams, I hear other owners talking about their players and their manager but I never heard the Glazers coming out and speaking. They let everyone get on with the job, which needs to be applauded. The Boss went on record so many times saying that for him they were fantastic. You see some horror stories throughout football, people take over clubs and almost destroy them, so the Glazers need a lot of credit for how they've gone about it. I hear people say that English clubs should be owned by English people, but those days are gone now. If you want the Premier League to be as big as it's become, foreign owners are inevitable. United have progressed under the Glazers on and off the field.

Six days after doing the title, I signed a new four-year deal. United were everything I'd dreamed of and more – excitement, pride, trophies and the challenge I wanted. And four days later came the greatest challenge of my career – Moscow.

9

MUNICH AND MOSCOW

Gathering in the centre circle with the lads is the moment my stomach tightens. It hits me, a horrible jumble of nerves, anxiety, fear and excitement. I've watched shootouts on TV in the past with England and knew I'd feel some nerves. Now I'm in the thick of it and it's 10 times worse. This is it: the responsibility, the carrot dangling of being champions of Europe, maybe a once-in-a-lifetime opportunity. The emotions are unreal. It shows the power of concentration that I'm not bothered by the torrential rain or the atmosphere. I've listened to Lisa talk about Moscow and she mentions the weather and the atmosphere and it being late into the night Moscow time. I'm oblivious to all this. I'm in my own little bubble. Only winning the trophy matters.

The wait for penalties seems to take forever. I never like it when someone takes their shin-pads off or rolls their socks down. Sub-consciously, it gives the wrong vibe, game over, I'm tired. I prefer to stay in the mindset as if the game's still going on. It's easy to switch off and lose that edge in your mentality. These might seem little details that don't mean much in a shootout but it's my way of not giving anything away. I'm in my zone. I don't look for my family or think of the consequences. All I think about is how I'm going to take this penalty. That's all I can control.

As Carlos Tévez goes up to take the first penalty, I partly watch him but mostly I'm thinking, *I'm up next, I'm up next, I'm up next. Focus, focus, focus.* I battle to stay in the right frame of mind. Tévez gets us off to a good start, Michael Ballack scores his penalty, as Germans tend to do, and the spotlight falls on me. No turning back now. I jog quite quickly from the halfway line to collect the ball and place it on the spot. Less time to think the better. Strangely, it is no longer my head and my stomach that are in turmoil, now I feel my heart beating out of my chest. God knows what my heartrate is. I feel I'm losing control of my body. I place the ball on the spot carefully and make sure it's flat and the part where my standing foot will be planted is level. Then I walk backwards. I never take my eyes off the ball as I walk back and as I get in position I glance unintentionally at Petr Čech. Chelsea's keeper looks massive, so I quickly look back at the ball and gather my thoughts. *Focus, just focus.* I pause, take a deep breath. Everything falls silent. There is no noise at all, just the sound of my heart beating. Right now my whole world is me v. Čech. I've taken a penalty against him before in the Community Shield, and I beat him then. *Do I go the same way again? What is Čech thinking? Will he think I'm going to change?* I can almost see his mind ticking. I feel strong standing there because I believe in my technique. All those years kicking around in the garden in Howdon, developing at the Boyza and improving myself with West Ham's youth coaches have led me to this. It's just me and the ball. Now, I'm not even thinking of Čech.

I try to simplify the process, strip it back. All I have to do is pass it hard into the corner, a pass I've done thousands of times before. *Pretend I'm on the training ground with no pressure at all. Forget everything else, relax and believe.* A thought of *dive the wrong way* creeps into the back of my mind as I'm about to start my run-up. The thought about Čech goes as quickly as it came. My last thought is, *Trust yourself, execution plain and simple, side-foot, clean strike.* This is my go-to technique where I feel most comfortable and confident. The whistle blows and I set off for the one kick I know will stay with me for the rest of my life, maybe even define my life.

* * *

Anyone with the great fortune to be involved with Manchester United has a duty to keep alive the memories of those in Red who've gone before. That's not being dramatic or me exaggerating, that's really how you feel when you're at United. As somebody who'd fallen in love with the club, I was committed to cherishing the legacy of the Busby Babes. The club expected that, as did the Boss, the staff and all the supporters. I'd heard about the Babes as Dad told me about them. I learned more about them from the stories on the wall of the Munich Tunnel. I read there about the tragedy that claimed 23 lives on the journey back from a European Cup tie in Belgrade. I'd look at the clock on the corner of K Stand which carries the date 'Feb 6th 1958' and one word 'Munich'. In the changing room at Carrington is a black-and-white photograph of the Babes. Their stature and legacy are everywhere at United; they're still the heartbeat of the club.

Going into that 2007/'08 season, the team knew there were two dates that were set to be full of emotion: the fiftieth anniversary of Munich and the fortieth anniversary of Sir Matt winning the European Cup. I honestly felt the hand of destiny guiding us towards the trophy. 'We'll win the Champions League this year,' I told Tony Strudwick pre-season. I just had a feeling it was our time. We were drawn against Sporting Lisbon, Roma and Dynamo Kiev in the group stage, and we started the campaign strongly, winning our first five games and then drawing at Roma. I understood people talking quietly within the club about the inescapable call of history. The Boss often spoke about Sir Matt and his philosophy that shaped the club. 'This is Manchester United, we've always brought young players through,' the Boss would say. It was obvious how proud Sir Alex was to follow in Sir Matt's footsteps, like it was his privilege to carry the torch for promoting young players and playing attacking football as Sir Matt did.

The week of the fiftieth anniversary of Munich, the Boss invited Sir Bobby Charlton into Carrington to speak to the lads about the disaster. It was so poignant listening to a man of the stature of Sir Bobby – England World Cup-winner, European Cup-winner, Mr Manchester United, one of the greatest players in the history of the game. And here he was, standing in front of us, giving a very personal account of what happened on that tragic day in 1958. It was clearly not easy for Sir Bobby to relive the events. For 45 minutes, he slowly and sorrowfully recalled the aborted take-offs on the snowy runway in Munich, that fateful third attempt, and waking up still strapped in his seat outside the plane. He spoke of the friends he lost. 'Duncan Edwards was the best player I ever saw,' he told us. We listened in total silence, trying to take it all in. It made Munich even more real and tragic hearing it in the words of Sir Bobby, especially for some of the foreign lads who'd not grown up so aware of the disaster.

Three days later, it was the Derby at Old Trafford, which was fitting in a way as it gave Manchester a chance to stand together. Every moment of that day has stayed with me. Each United player wore a replica 1958 shirt with no logos, just the number, and it looked so clean and beautiful. I was sub but watched from the back of the tunnel as the team strode out, each player holding the hand of a mascot who bore the name of someone who died at Munich. I remember the young girl holding Ronaldo's hand had WHALLEY on the back of her shirt, a tribute to Bert Whalley, one of Sir Matt's coaches who'd played for United. I looked at his name, and thought of the terrible loss to his family and friends, as well as to United, and it brought home to me even more the scale of the disaster. As we came out of the tunnel, the teams went straight on to the middle, and I headed right to the bench. As I walked along the touchline, I saw all the names of the 23 on the hoardings and the words FOREVER REMEMBERED. I saw all the fans hold up their red-and-white scarves, some clutched pictures of the Busby Babes and I had goosebumps just taking it all in. Munich is a huge story in the lives of fans who weren't even born at the time, whose parents might not even have been alive at the time. Like me, the fans feel a responsibility to carry on the memory. They've got the banners with 'The Flowers of Manchester' and 'We'll Never Die' and the picture of the Busby Babes. All of it adds to the aura of Manchester United. A lot of families started supporting United because of the wave of sympathy for the club after Munich, and that's been passed down from generation to generation. People are deeply moved by the story of talented young men living the dream but tragically cut down in their prime.

Everyone applauded as Sir Alex and City's manager, Sven-Göran Eriksson, laid wreaths on the centre spot. At the ref's whistle, everyone fell silent and it was utterly still and quiet, not a sound at all. City's fans were impeccable, they really were. They proudly held up their blue-and-white scarves until the ref signalled the end of the minute's silence. This Derby wasn't about the game, it wasn't about football, it wasn't about rivalry. It was much bigger than all of that. City fans recognised that, and I respected them greatly for it. I came on and scored but it meant nothing because we lost and, in truth, the emotion of the occasion was too much. The whole week, and the build-up, just got to us, as the Boss admitted afterwards.

We had to reach Moscow, it felt almost a mission now, so when the Champions League resumed we were even more determined and progressed past Lyon and Roma to reach a semi-final against Barcelona with the Camp Nou first, and we knew our tactics had to be spot-on. We never used to spend a lot of time on tactics. There would always be a theme to sessions, forward runs, forward passes, etc., but not usually a stop-start walk-through of pure tactics. Two days before the first leg against Barcelona we came out to training, did our usual boxes, had a short possession game and then Carlos Queiroz beckoned us across to a pitch set up for a small-sided game with two big blue crash mats from the gym plonked just outside the 18-yard box. The mats were behind me and Scholesy and in front of Rio and Wes, our two centre backs.

'Don't let them get on this crash-mat, that's where Barcelona want to play, so cut that space off,' Carlos instructed us. 'Guard the crash-mats with your life.' This was the area Barcelona looked to penetrate, playing little balls and 1–2s. We had to reinforce this area and defend it with our lives, cutting off angles and passing lines, making Barcelona play wide. Barcelona had small, quick, technical players – Lionel Messi, Andrés Iniesta, Xavi and Deco – who we knew would cause damage in the space where Carlos placed the crash-mats. If we pressed high, Rio and Wes pushed up, filling the crash-mats. If the ball went past me and Scholesy, we dropped deep to close the space on the mats. Barcelona didn't have anyone to attack crosses so we were happy for them to have the ball wide. Our wingers – Rooney and Ji – tucked in, leaving space down the side. Carlos drilled us in the crash-mats, and we took the plan to the Camp Nou. The blue mats were in our minds the whole game. We drew 0–0 – a clean sheet, and Carlo's crash-mat plan proved simple yet very effective. In the second leg, the atmosphere was sensational. Roma 7–1 was special, but this was different. A place in the final was at stake. When Scholesy scored a worldie early, the fans carried us through, but the last 10 minutes seemed to last a lifetime. The tension was unbearable but the feeling when the final whistle blew was something I'll never forget. We'd made the final.

The memory of how emotional Sir Bobby was when he spoke at Carrington added a more historic feel to the trip to Moscow to face Chelsea. A Champions League final is always huge, but even more emotion was riding on this one. Also driving me on was anger at losing the FA Cup final the year before to Chelsea, a horrible feeling I needed to put right. The rivalry with Chelsea was so strong and no way was I going to lose this final. I grew up playing with Cole and Lampard at West Ham and knew John Terry and Ashley Cole from England but friendship disappears out the window on occasions like this. I blanked them in the tunnel. When boxers fight friends, they go in the ring to beat them up. I felt the same here. I've known Lamps since I was 14 and have the utmost respect for him. That's why we wanted to beat each other so much. I'd never, ever try to do him. If the ball was there to be had, I'd go in fullblooded, but always a fair tackle, never dangerous or vindictive. Coley was one of my best mates growing up, but I felt only coldness on match days. I always shake hands after games and say, 'Well played' or 'All the best'. Only a brief exchange, though. When I see players from opposing teams chatting coming off the pitch or in the tunnel, I don't like it. It's about being ruthless, and losing this final was not an option.

Games with Chelsea were always physical, so I anticipated a battle and even when Ronaldo headed us in front, I expected them to hit back. Chelsea wouldn't necessarily play amazing football, but they had talented players like Frank Lampard and Didier Drogba who could make it a physical game, and I was constantly tracking Lampard's runs. As soon as the ball went forward, Lamps was off and I'd just run with him. 'Follow Lampard. Stop Lampard,' was the instruction from the Boss. I'd lean into him when we ran to put him off. He was my man, so when he broke through and equalised just before half-time, I was fuming with myself. I'd stopped on the edge of the D, not thinking the ball would go anywhere near Lamps, but it deflected his way off Vidić, Edwin slipped and Lamps scored. You couldn't blame me for it, really, but Lamps was still my man, and I felt responsible. Typical Lamps, that, give him a yard in the box just once and he'd take it. Up until then we'd played great and should have been two, maybe three, up so the goal came at a bad time, right before half-time. The Boss was calm in the changing room, just determined for us to go back out there and do it again. We knew Chelsea would come at us again, especially Drogba, who was quick and strong and it sometimes took two defenders to cope with him. Vidić's quite aggressive and got into him. From nowhere, Drogba slapped him in the face and got sent off. He was one of Chelsea's main penalty-takers so for Drogba's head to go was very strange, crazy really, especially five minutes from the end of extra time.

From the last few minutes, I started to focus on taking a penalty. I knew I was going to take one. I told myself, *This is the test of how strong you are. Can you handle it? Have you got the bollocks to do it?* I'd always have regretted it if I'd said, *I don't fancy this* and left the responsibility to others. But this was why I came to United, to be the best. So, when the Boss came round asking who wanted to take a penalty, I volunteered for the second or third. We agreed on the second and I focused on grasping the challenge. It was horrendous, really. Just the thought of taking a penalty was terrifying. It is a lonely, scary place. What happened in the next few minutes in Moscow lives with me now.

After Carlos and Ballack scored, it was my turn. My main thought was, *Pretend you're going right but whip it left.* I wasn't thinking about my technique or how to do it. That comes naturally, That's what all the years of practice are for. Thankfully, as it left my foot, I saw Čech dive the other way and the ball nestle in the bottom corner. Wow! What a feeling of relief and satisfaction. I tested myself. I asked the question could I really do it when it's all on the line. I could.

Looking towards United's fans, I clenched both fists and screamed, releasing all that the tension that had built up and up. As I jogged back to the lads on the halfway, I also clenched a fist towards Lisa, Mam and Dad in the stand, as a gesture to say, 'It's OK, don't worry'. I knew how they must've been feeling: more nervous than me and probably fearing the worst. As I reached the lads on the halfway line, I took a deep breath. As I exhaled the realisation hit me of what had just happened.

That passage of play, the most significant of my life, was over. I knew it was down to others now. Looking back, I knew all I could do was encourage the teammates following me from the halfway line. Juliano Belletti made it 2-2 and now it was Ronaldo's turn. Penalties are brutal. Ronnie was our Player of the Year by a country mile, scored penalties all year long and had so much belief in himself, but he missed then. He was obviously devastated and all sorts must have been going through his mind. It happens. I went to Burnley and missed a penalty. I missed one in the fourth round of the EFL Cup against Boro. So, I'm not the expert. Penalties are fine lines, nobody blamed Ronnie and, anyway, it wasn't over. Hargreaves made it 3–3, Ashley Cole gave Chelsea back the edge and then Nani pegged it at 4–4. This was it. John Terry marked the last-chance saloon for us. He scored, we'd lose. I'd watched every penalty so far and it had not gone our way. I needed to do something different, so I decided not to look. As Terry stepped up, Rio stood next to me and pointed to Edwin to dive to his right. I wrapped myself in the protective blanket of my team. I draped my left arm over Rio's shoulders, my right over Vidić's and just looked at the soaked grass as I waited for the reaction to Terry's penalty. I felt completely empty, standing there, not being able to do anything. Seconds felt like minutes but then Rio and Vida leapt into the air, a huge roar sprang from our supporters that could only mean only one thing. John Terry had missed. I didn't have a clue what happened. It didn't matter. We had a lifeline. Suddenly from being dead and buried, we could win it within moments. Later when I found out what had happened, I felt sorry for John Terry, because his planted foot slipped. But there was no sympathy then, no chance.

Shootouts are stressful enough but when they descend into sudden death, it's torture. The more penalties, the more agony. By now, I was even more relieved to have got my penalty out the way early. The antic-ipation of each kick was unbearable. Anderson was up next. Ando had some terrible injuries but what a talented kid he was. The Boss loved him, played him in big games against Steven Gerrard and Liverpool at Anfield in December. Ando stood up to that test, and would surely do the same here, wouldn't he? Ando was fearless and he needed to be now he was facing Čech. I couldn't watch. Only looking at the DVD later did I realise that Ando took his penalty as if he didn't have a care in the world, and smashed it in. At the time, the only thing I was watching was the grass.

When Salomon Kalou put the pressure back on us, Giggsy calmly returned it. Nicolas Anelka went up, and I placed my arms on the boys again and looked back down. Again, the seconds crept past so slowly. Was this the moment? Another second. And another. I stared at the floor. Suddenly, Rio and Vida bolted off in front of me screaming. I was left standing with my arms outstretched but dangling in the air. By the time I looked up they were five yards away. I followed as quickly as I could with my arms in the air just shouting and screaming like I'd never done before, sprinting as fast as I could towards Van der Sar. I was totally lost in the moment. Everything around me was a blur for a split-second before the buzz and adrenaline of emotion took over. Even now, a decade on, when I look back at the tape, and see Van der Sar saving from Anelka, that elation flashes right back through me. I don't really keep memorabilia on show in the house but John Peters, the club photographer, got the picture of me in Moscow. I was standing there with my head down. Then, *bang*, we'd won. I've got that on the wall. Like the picture, the memory and the emotion of Moscow never fade. I remember vividly all the noise in the Luzhniki and yet there was an eerie silence around me as we ran to Edwin. I felt like I was in a film, with all the chaos around, and yet everything was happening in slow motion. As I sprinted behind the lads to Edwin, all the rest of the squad, the subs, coaches, back-room staff charged as well, and I arrived in the six-yard box to a big pile of bodies going crazy. We were jumping on each other, shouting at each other, and I was screaming and hugging as many of the lads as I could – it was the best feeling I've ever had in my life. Everyone was running in all different directions, overcome with emotion. Seeing the sheer joy and happiness on everyone's faces was so special. We were champions of Europe!! Wow!! After that minute or so just losing myself I hit a brick wall. Two hours of exertion, the relief of my penalty and the joy of winning all merged and hit me like the wall in a marathon. The ultimate surge of adrenaline died down and I was gone. I had nothing left.

I walked 10 yards to the side of the pitch towards Mam and Dad and Lisa, and I was a wreck, an emotional wreck. It hit me in a big way.

I didn't know whether to laugh, cry or collapse. I was finished, physically and mentally. I've never cried on a football pitch, but I nearly cried like a baby there and then. Thoughts flooded into my mind of the journey I'd been on from Wallsend, and the sacrifices that everyone in my life had made to help me reach this special place. I saw Mam, Dad and Lisa jumping up and down and going mad in the stands. Graeme unfortunately wasn't there, but I thought of him, and all those years playing football in the garden with him. I thought of Dad and Granddad taking me to the Boyza and starting me on the journey to Moscow. I hoped Granddad was looking down, because my victory was his too.

As it calmed down, I spent the next few minutes going round all the back-room staff, and all their faces were a picture. It seemed to take forever to organise the lifting of the trophy. Slowly, the players gathered at the bottom of the steps leading up to the trophy. Sir Bobby was there and I shook his hand. 'Well done, congratulations, you're champions of Europe,' Sir Bobby said. His eyes filled with pride at another magical, historic moment for his great club, and that made our achievement even more special. Standing alongside Rio Ferdinand, I waited for the nod to go up the steps. 'We've done it!' I said to him, laughing. I still couldn't quite believe it. Being next to Rio made me even happier, a friend who's been there since I set out as a 14-year-old at West Ham.

It was late in the night in Moscow – 1am or 2am – when we finally finished celebrating on the pitch with the trophy. It was pure theatre with dark rain streaming down, creating such beautiful, unforgettable images. For me, one of the many joys of winning a trophy was getting back to the sanctuary of the changing rooms and having a moment with all the lads – those of a similar age: Rio, Fletch, Sheasy, Wes, Wazza; then Ronnie, Tévez, Evra, Vidić, Nani; and the older ones like Giggsy, Scholesy and Van der Sar – we were so close-knit.

I looked round the changing room and smiled. No cliques existed between young and old, British and foreign or different interests, we were just altogether, bonded by a passion to win trophies with Manchester United. We fought alongside each other all season and this was the moment to sit back and give a nod to each other in appreciation and respect of what we achieved and everything we had to come through to do it. We sang and bounced around. It was something quite simple, no glitz or glamour, no outside noise, just us. To see the joy on the faces of the back-room staff, the chefs, the physios, the kit men, the masseurs – it was wonderful. They don't get much recognition but they're with us every step of the way, day in, day out, and most of them are diehard Reds. To give them something back was very satisfying. I saw how much it meant to them that United were the pride of all Europe again.

At the dinner back in the hotel, we got Giggsy up on stage and presented him with a watch for passing Sir Bobby's appearance record. It was not a night for sleep, no chance, and I went straight from the bar to the airport in the morning. I just wanted the night to never end. The announcement that the flight was delayed by five hours was a blow. We just sat there waiting, heads throbbing but still smiling. We eventually landed in Manchester at 9.30pm, and I put my arms around Owen and Vida as I came down the steps at the back of the plane. Fans were patiently waiting for us and we held up the European Cup so they could see it, before we climbed on the bus. The European Cup was back in Manchester. I got up the front on the top deck of the bus with Wazza and Ronnie waving the Cup to the photographers. The smile never left my face.

The bus dropped us at Carrington. Louise was at home, she was just two and a half months old, and I was desperate to cuddle her in my arms, sit back and take it all in. So, we all headed home. We swapped a few shouts of 'Enjoy the summer' and then parted.

A big regret of mine is that we never had a parade in Manchester. The council and police said 'no' after trouble flared up with Rangers fans at the UEFA Cup final at City's ground a week earlier. When I look back now, it seems even more of a pity. We'd won the Premier League and the Champions League. How could the city not celebrate it? That night, I didn't really take it in that we were not going to have a parade. The day was a blur, apart from one thing I remember Sir Alex saying as we got off the bus at Carrington.

'Get yourself ready, lads, we've got the league to win next year.'

10

ROME

Small and frail-looking with long hair, this kid looked like he was about to play in the schoolyard with his mates when I got my first close look at him. He was so casual, he even didn't look old enough to play! But could he play! This kid was the real deal. He lit the place up. He came alive with the ball at his feet, all velvet touch and scuttling away from tacklers with his rapid little legs. He played on the right wing when we beat Barcelona to reach Moscow and now I could see what all the fuss was about. So, this was Lionel Messi.

He was as sharp with the ball as anyone I'd ever seen and changed direction in an instant. A couple of times I thought I had Messi but then, oops, see ya, he was gone. 'Show him on his right, he's all left foot,' people say. Yeah, good one. The way he manipulated the ball in tight areas was incredible and you couldn't get it off him. We managed to keep two clean sheets in the semi-final against Barcelona on the way to Moscow. We won but Messi would come back to haunt us.

Returning for pre-season as champions of England and Europe was great but to prove we were the best we had to do it again. Some teams were happy to win a trophy, sit back, admire the view, take the plaudits, do the nice interviews on the soft sofa and lose their edge. Not us. Not with the Boss. Sir Alex was hungrier than ever and immediately challenged us. Could we make it three titles in a row? Could we take unprecedented back-to-back Champions Leagues? I challenged myself.

Are you willing to keep pushing yourself? Yes. Have you got it in you to climb
Everest and then set off to climb it all over again? Yes. Are you satisfied? No.
The last question was key. Whatever we achieved, it was never enough.

At United, I learned to be ruthless about winning, sacrificing all
things in my life to be the best. June is the only time we get off all year.
For one week max I totally switch off and then this paranoia I cannot
shake off returns, and I tell Lisa, 'I need to go to the gym', 'I can't eat
that' or 'I've let myself go too much'. It happened that summer in 2008.
It happens every summer. Player or coach, I'm driven by winning with
United. I think about it all the time. I get asked about it non-stop.
During the season, it's constant from schoolyard to supermarket to
petrol stations, all the time getting asked about United. Always. I'd go
out for dinner with Lisa and I'd be thinking about training the next
day. There's no escape. I'm proud of how I dedicate myself totally and
I have no regrets at all. As soon as you step through the gates for the
first day of pre-season in the first week of July it doesn't ease up until
the end of May. I'm not chasing sympathy because I've done something
I've loved and reaped the rewards, but for 11 months of the year your
life is not your own. It's mental. The fear of finishing runner-up, the
humiliation of that, never left me. I realised after a while that's what
drove me on, not desire for success but fear of failure.

At United, there was no hanging around and we played our first
game after only four days' training. We weren't exactly match-fit against
Aberdeen on 12 July 2008 and the lads were dying after 20 minutes.
After playing at Pittodrie, we dashed off on a tour to Africa that
touched the realms of insanity when we reached Nigeria. The stop-off
in the capital Abuja was one stop-off too many. Somebody paid United
a good few quid to get us to Abuja. We landed from Cape Town at
3am on the day of an exhibition match against the FA Cup winners,

Portsmouth. 'Shut the curtains and turn the lights off,' security warned us as we boarded the bus to the hotel in Abuja as they were worried about an ambush. When we arrived at the hotel, there were scenes of complete chaos with fans everywhere, wandering corridors and lurking in lifts – they were just mad to see us. We tried to catch a few hours' sleep and then some of us went down for a quiet stroll around the hotel garden, which turned out not to be that peaceful as there were armed police crawling everywhere. As we walked past the swimming pool, this guy from the hotel took a picture of us. That was no problem for us, happens all the time, but it was clearly a problem for the security men. One of them ran over and smashed the camera out of this guy's hand.

'Whoa, what's going on there?' I shouted. They grabbed him, jabbed him in the ribs and dragged him round the back of the hotel. 'Whoa, what's up? It's only a picture,' I yelled after them. We never saw him again. It was all a bit over the top.

Later that afternoon, we drove to the National Stadium and, nearing the ground, I spotted 20 kids on a grass bank, waiting for us. As we got closer, I noticed their legs were tucked underneath them and they shifted themselves up and down this little hill on their arms, really quick. To our horror, we were told later that parents in Nigeria some-times smash their babies' legs so they can send them begging. Could that seriously be true? The kids were everywhere, moving around with just their arms. It was so sad to see.

The whole experience in Abuja was like being trapped in a horror film. Few fans were in the ground because of the cost of tickets. Some tried to break in, but the police forced them back with tear gas. Huge black flies dive-bombed us. You had one eye on the ball and the other on incoming insects. We won 2–1, rushed out the stadium as quick as we could, passing those poor disabled children and raced to the airport.

The trip lasted only 16 hours, but Abuja's effects lasted longer. I vomited for a week, but some lads had it far worse. They were so sick that United sent a sample off to some university and, I'm not kidding, they found monkey and rat shit in the sample. The university docs said they'd never seen anything like it before. So, no, I won't remember Abuja happily and I can't imagine the other lads will either. Those are the type of souvenirs you don't want to bring back from tours abroad.

Far more enjoyable was the trip that December to the Club World Cup in Japan. United qualified as champions of Europe and I felt it was a big deal even if the competition never got much recognition in England. For me it was a massive chance to win another trophy. How many times do you get a shot at becoming world champions? You have to win the Champions League to even have a chance of winning it.

Before going to Japan, we played Spurs at the Lane on 13 December and then our next league game was Stoke away on Boxing Day. Sports scientists at Carrington researched jet lag and how long to stay up after Spurs. Should we sleep straight after the game? Stay awake? Split the time difference? 'Stay up' was the specialist advice so we had a night out in London, a jet-lag remedy greeted with general enthusiasm. We all piled into a casino with the Boss for a bite to eat, and a few of the lads went on to Movida nightclub. When Tony Strudwick and the doc, Steve McNally, tried to get us up in the morning, half the lads didn't turn up! We eventually got on the plane and the sports scientists gave us these little light machines, like headphones, to stick in our ears. They told us that feeding sunlight into the brain tricked the body into thinking it was daytime when it was night. The cunning plan didn't really work. They set the plane up to turn all the lights off at a certain time and gave us different shakes to help us sleep. The ideal scenario was half-and-half, split between Tokyo and Manchester time. We couldn't go full Japanese as we'd have been a write-off for Stoke two days after we got back. On the flight, I noticed Dimitar Berbatov, who'd just joined us from Spurs, wore a big mask because apparently he didn't want to catch anything from the air-con. After we'd checked into our hotel in Yokohama, Berba never came out of his room all week so the chef would knock on his door and leave food outside his room. Berba was the only one who fell ill on the trip. The lads thought it hilarious.

Leaving Berba to suffer on his own, we got on with the tournament. Jet lag was a huge problem and the lads hung around the games room playing pool until 5am, as their body clocks were all over the place. I'd get on the coach for training feeling absolutely dead. Everyone fell asleep in their seats. On the pitch, something triggered in me and I'd feel all right again but when I finished, I'd turn back into a zombie.

Thank God I didn't get many bollockings off the Boss because he could peel paint off a wall from 100 yards, but I did receive a blast in Yokohama. I thought I was playing well against Liga de Quito, the Ecuadorian side, in the final but when I came into the dressing room at half-time, Sir Alex went bananas. He was on my case a lot at that time about my passing. 'Pass forward, pass forward,' he'd shout. When the Boss got something in his head, it stayed there. In that half, all my passes went forward, except one when I turned and passed back to Rio. I remember it so clearly. I wasn't being negative, it was simply the best option, and my only intention was to pass to Rio, get it back and build again. Once Sir Alex saw that one back pass, something flipped and I heard him going mental on the line, 'Fucking hell, will you just fucking pass it forward.'

I snapped, shouting, 'Fucking what?' Not directly at the Boss, I wasn't brave enough for that. Two minutes later, the ref Ravshan Irmatov blew for half-time and I knew what was coming. The moment I entered the changing room, the Boss launched into me. 'Pass the ball fucking forward, I fucking told you,' Sir Alex was raging. When he was like that you had to sit there and take it, let him blow off some steam. On the outside, I was calm, nodding at the Boss's points, hiding my anger. On the inside, I was fuming and saying to myself, 'I must have played 40 passes forward here and he's picked one where I've gone back.' But the Boss was so wound up that I didn't dare voice my defence. 'Fucking hell, a bit harsh, isn't it?' some of the lads said on the way back out.

The Boss didn't take me off, he very rarely did as he always gave players a chance to respond. I think he was picking a fight to keep me on my toes. Early in the second half, Vida got sent off but we ground it out and managed to nick a 1–0 win with Rooney's goal after I'd played the ball to Ronaldo – a bit of a forward pass as well, which was ironic. This was so typical of the team, going down to 10, doing things the hard way. It wasn't the buzz of Moscow but the feeling of being world champions was immense. I was pleased for the fans, too. United supporters were all over Yokohama and fair play to them, considering it was right before Christmas and an expensive trip.

That night, I sat at the bar with Rio Ferdinand and our coach René Meulensteen, having a glass of wine, looking out over Yokohama and just letting it sink in. 'Lads, we're world champions!!' The bar was quiet, nobody really bothered us, and we could briefly savour what we'd done. Having 'World Champion' next to my name was special. But there was no complacency, no time for admiring ourselves as we headed quickly home.

Stoke away was always one of the toughest games of the season and we treated it every bit as important as the final. Tévez scored late on. Job done. It was the sixth Premier League game in succession in which Edwin kept a clean sheet, and our brilliant Dutch keeper eventually went 1,311 minutes without conceding a league goal – a world record. The Premier League gave Edwin an award but there was no tribute from us, no presentation, just a little nod of approval to say, 'Yes, well done.' Edwin got the headlines but I felt they should have mentioned that Rio, Vida and Jonny Evans were in defence. I was in midfield in front of them and we all took pride in shutting the opposition out. Edwin's the keeper so he's got the big responsibility and it was his achievement, but at the same time the record belonged to everyone. It wasn't a big deal in the dressing room anyway. 'This is what we're here for,' as Gary Neville always said.

Anyway, us players didn't need a record to know how valuable Edwin was to United. He'd been at Fulham for four years, surprisingly long, really, because he was a hell of a keeper. He had so many strengths it's difficult to know where to start. Edwin had great distribution, left foot, right foot, he picked people out and I guess that it was no surprise as he came through at Ajax, because they're all about passing and clean distribution. Not only could he command his box, but Edwin was a very good communicator and made sure we were all where he wanted us. He was noisy, but his instructions were clear and calm. I wouldn't have to look at him, just listen in training, then in games it became instinctive as I couldn't hear him as easily on the pitch. Still, when Edwin shouted, I'd do what he said. Ferdinand was the same. In training before someone took a shot, Edwin yelled 'left' or 'right' so I'd block that side, making sure he had only half the goal to protect. He basically moved me around like a shield. Of course, he was gambling because the shot could go through my legs but the number of times it worked was incredible. Edwin's the only keeper I've ever seen do that but then he's smart and what he's doing now as chief executive at Ajax is testament to that.

Soon, our focus returned to the Champions League and we went to the San Siro in February, this time to play Inter Milan. It was a classy side with Javier Zanetti, Dejan Stanković, Adriano and Zlatan Ibrahimovićh, and Mario Balotelli came on. Even though we drew 0–0, it felt like a moral victory and I look back on that Inter game with pride and satisfaction, it was probably one of my best games for United.

Sir Alex was a master at juggling resources and plotting campaigns, and before the League Cup final against Spurs in March, he pulled me, Rooney, Berbatov and Fletcher to one side in the changing room at Wembley and said, 'I'm resting you today, boys.' I half-expected it as he played Darron Gibson most games in the cup, and I had started five days earlier in the San Siro but I was still seething. Silverware was up for grabs, and those are the games you want to play in. As the final headed to penalties, I moved towards the edge of the technical area and stood next to Edwin and Rooney to show my support. Ben Foster and our goalkeeping coach Eric Steele had clips on an iPod of Spurs players taking their kicks and Foster studied them again before the pens. He had a good idea which way Jamie O'Hara was going, stepped to his left and saved. He almost got to Niko Kranjčar's kick and even with David Bentley's miss, he went the right way. Foster mentioned the iPod to the press afterwards and maybe he should have kept quiet as Fifa later banned the use of iPods. Still, what Eric and Ben did just demonstrated United's immense attention to detail.

We got back on the train, somebody casually placed the League Cup on a table and it felt like we were just coming back from a league match in London, all very routine, what's the fuss? It was only the League Cup, middle of the season, and the mood on the train was again not blasé, but it was clear that everyone knew there was more around the corner. We saw off Inter at home, then Porto before we got to play Arsenal in the semi-finals, Ahead of that game, we watched their crazy game against Liverpool. Us and Liverpool were going for the league, it was getting tight, and with it being Liverpool, as ever, the pressure and focus ramped up even more. The Boss had his run-in with Rafa Benítez, who'd gone off on a rant with his 'facts' speech. So, Liverpool's match with Arsenal was huge. We were at the Lowry, staying there the night before our match with Portsmouth, and after dinner we piled into the massage room where they had the Liverpool game on. The massage room was the hanging-out spot, some lads were getting treatment, others were messing about, but all of us were really watching the TV. It was a mad game, one of the classics, and it was as if we were there, supporting our own team. We were rooting for Arsenal 100 per cent! That's the only time in my life I've done that! The game was to and fro and when Andrei Arshavin's fourth goal went in, making it 4–3 to Arsenal in the ninetieth minute, we went absolutely mental. I was getting a massage, lying on my front, and I jumped off the bed, which went flying. Massage beds were thrown around the room. The lads went mad, tearing out of their rooms, running and shouting down the corridor – it was like we'd won the league! Edwin jumped up and down the corridor. I ended up in the bathroom of one of the rooms. It was carnage. It was only when we calmed down a bit did we realise that Yossi Benayoun made it 4–4, but Liverpool still dropped points. Our reaction showed our togetherness, just a bunch of lads loving a crazy game!

It had been Arshavin's best game for Arsenal by a mile. He was ineligible for Arsenal in the Champions League, having played for Zenit St Petersburg earlier in the season. We won the first leg of the semi-final when John O'Shea scored at Old Trafford. Sheasy was a great lad but didn't get the respect he deserved outside United, except in Ireland where he's a legend. That year, Sheasy played right back pretty much every game and was superb. Midfield, left back or centre back, Sheasy would play anywhere for the team. He understood what it meant to play for United, what it took to win and how to act. He was a model pro off the pitch, and I could see why Sir Alex kept Sheasy at United for 12 years because he never had to worry about him, never had to babysit him. The Boss just knew when he needed him that Sheasy was ready.

We won the second leg 3–1, yet our joy at reaching the final was tempered by a terrible decision at the Emirates that meant Fletch was suspended for Rome. Darren Fletch and Cesc Fàbregas were shoulder to shoulder, chasing the ball into our box, and Fletch clearly got the ball first. None of us could believe it when the referee, Roberto Rosetti, sent Fletch off for his challenge and awarded Arsenal a penalty. We pleaded with Rosetti. The game was over. We were through. Don't send him off. I was gutted for Fletch. It was cruel and unfair as it just wasn't a penalty but UEFA wouldn't allow an appeal, even though everyone could see Rosetti had screwed up. Roy Keane and Paul Scholes were banned from the 1999 Champions League final and now it was happening with Darren Fletch a decade later. Fletch took the suspension calmly, but I was devastated for him and for us as he was such a big part of us getting to Rome. Fletch, Anderson and I played 4–5–1 a few times that season, so Fletch was going to be a big loss against Barcelona. We gave a textbook semi-final away performance, hitting Arsenal on the counterattack, it was devastating really, especially Ronaldo's last goal, but everyone was restrained in the dressing room. We had to do it without Fletch. I know you're not exactly weakening your team when you bring Giggs in, but I still felt for Fletch. Finals are the moments you live for and Fletch was denied that chance.

We stayed down in London that night and, back at the Landmark Hotel, we enjoyed one of those rare moments when the crazy schedule slowed and we could pause for breath and reflect. Me, Giggsy, Scholesy and Rio had a few beers in the bar with Bryan Robson. 'I'm in pretty decent company here,' I thought. What an honour! Robbo was a legend.

I remember talking to Steve Bruce once and he said, 'Robbo was streets ahead of anybody. He could do absolutely everything. Up and down, run all day. Good footballer, aggressive, scared the shit out of everyone.' Nev always said to me, 'Robbo was the best player I've played with.' Giggsy and Scholesy always considered Robbo their inspiration. Giggsy told me this story about one of his first games playing left wing. Back then, you got away with all sorts and the full back gave a few verbals to Giggsy like, 'Go past me and I'll break your leg.' So Robbo said to Giggsy, 'Giggsy, swap positions for 10 minutes. Go and play centre midfield.' When the full back got the ball, Robbo went flying through and smashed him with a ridiculous tackle. Robbo got up, dusted himself down, took the yellow card and shouted over to Giggsy, 'You can swap back now.' Giggsy didn't hear a thing from the full back for the rest of the game. Robbo went out of his way to protect those young lads, and that's a tradition passed down at Manchester United. The whole club takes great pride in seeing a young player take the step into the first team. Kiko Macheda came off the bench that April to score winners against Aston Villa and Sunderland, and we looked to have a real star in the making. 'He's the best finisher at the club,' Sir Alex told us. The Boss had massive hopes for Kiko but he drifted, which was really sad. I look at Marcus Rashford now and how he hit the ground running and managed to carry it on, whereas Kiko lost momentum. The ability was there but that's nothing without dedication. It takes commitment to survive at United.

That May, we were drawing 1–1 with four minutes left at Wigan when I managed to score, left-footed too, in one of the best moments of my career. Right in front of our fans, I gave it the big jump and fist pump. Wazza came behind and ended up on my shoulders, toppling over me. At that stage of the season, everything cranked up so much, every goal meant more, every result meant more. Our team had everything, not only the talent and the ability, but also in the way we fought for each other. We never gave up, and we did it again at Wigan. Late winners were ingrained in the club and, believe me, it's the best way to win! Our motivation for giving everything until the death was never fear of the Boss, more a sheer belief we'd get back in the game. As the clock ticked louder, we'd look around at each other as if to say, 'Come on then.' We'd click into a different gear and go marching forward relentlessly, all overlaps and low crosses. I'm not sure people appreciated how much method there was to it. Lumping into the box was never United's style, because that didn't test their defence as they'd all be in position just waiting for the ball. One centre back attacked the high ball, and the rest of them tucked around for the second ball. That's predictable. The Boss never told us to launch it, even with the referee lifting the whistle to his lips. 'Just move the ball around the box, tire them out and the chance will come,' the Boss said. I'd look at Giggsy, Scholesy, Ronnie and Wazza, and they never panicked. They just maintained the pressure with non-stop passing and moving, wearing the opposition out by constantly asking questions. It looked like chaos, but it was organised and controlled. I learned so much in my first season from watching and talking to Solskjaer, who scored so many last-minute goals because his head was never clouded. He always possessed calm in the storm. So did Giggsy, who would go to make that last cross, knowing that it was our last chance in a game but he had the composure to do it properly, coolly and effectively. The Boss wouldn't hesitate to have four centre forwards on the pitch. That was just his philosophy – get as many goalscorers on as he could in the last 10 minutes. It didn't matter who played where, just get Rooney, Ronaldo, Tévez, Solskjaer, Giggs, Scholes and Saha on. I remember chasing the points at Derby County in March 2008, when Sir Alex threw me and

Saha on with Ronnie and Wazza up front and Giggsy getting in there. We attacked more and more, eventually Ronnie volleyed the winner, and that play showed the genius of the Boss.

The intensity of training under Sir Alex also gave us the ability to last until the dying seconds of a game and at that time nobody could match our fitness. So much was talked so widely about our late goals that I could see in our opponents' eyes how much they feared them. Once they sensed our late surge coming, we had them. Villa always seemed to dread it, and I remember Ole, Ronnie, Kiko and Chicharito all scoring late winners against Villa.

The resilience I deeply admired in my teammates brought United a third title in a row with a point at Arsenal on 16 May 2009, although it was a hard, painful affair, which came at a cost to me when I fractured my big toe in a tackle. I didn't notice the discomfort at the time as I was too busy fighting for the draw we needed, and getting my head to clear free kicks from Fàbregas and Robin van Persie. We held on, the celebrations began and ended dead quick as there was something else to prepare for. When the adrenaline wore off, I took in the extent of the damage to my toe and realised there was no chance I could train properly before the Champions League final in 11 days. Three days before the final, I trained to see if the pain-killing injection I'd had worked and just about passed the test. I still stepped gingerly on the plane to Rome for the match with Barcelona. We booked into a hotel on the Piazza della Repubblica which wasn't the best. We ate in the basement and by the time the food came down in the lift it was cold. My toe still killed me so I sat out training in the Stadio Olimpico but nothing would stop me starting the next night. After all, this was the Champions League final. Moscow made me want this moment in Rome even more. One hour before the final, I got an injection off Doc to numb the pain and eased my frozen toe into my boot. The injection did the job. My toe didn't feel 100 per cent but I'd played with plenty of injuries before.

I focused solely on the game, I wasn't distracted by my foot or by the atmosphere, even when Andrea Bocelli sang the theme tune from *Gladiator*. I was more concerned by the heat, as I much prefer to play in colder conditions. Still, my mood was confident. We were unbeaten in the Champions League since the Milan semi two seasons before. We beat Barcelona over two legs the year before. We believed this was ours. 'You can get at Barcelona,' people told us. We had total faith in the Boss' game plan, pressed Barcelona from the off and looked dangerous. Quickly, Ji had one cleared off the line and Ronnie started causing them problems. Then Pep Guardiola made a change. Messi started on the right but swapped with Samuel Eto'o to play as a No. 9, but he was not like a typical centre forward. Messi kept dropping deep, meaning Vida and Rio had no one to mark, and leaving us outnumbered in midfield where we were already up against Xavi, Sergio Busquets and Andrés Iniesta. That's what Barcelona do to you – they overload midfield, getting that extra body or two around the ball and make life so difficult for you. Barcelona dissect the pitch, play in the part where they have more players and that's how they take control. Sir Alex warned us of Barcelona's 'passing carousel' which could make us dizzy, and I soon saw what he meant. Xavi, Busquets, Iniesta and Messi circulated the ball between them, keeping it, hurting us and punishing mistakes. I was loose with a header and Iniesta was on it in a flash, passing to Messi. Barcelona are ruthless in transition. I was close to Messi but couldn't prevent him passing back to Iniesta who got ahead of me and Anderson. Iniesta slipped the ball to Eto'o, who got away from Vidić. I slid in but only got close enough to Eto'o to see him score.

In quiet moments in the weeks to come, that passage of play kept returning to haunt me. I couldn't get it out of my head. It sounds melodramatic, but I've never recovered from it. The memory of conceding such a soft goal is always there in my mind. Giving the ball away to any team was dangerous, but to Barcelona it was suicidal.

I still recall a moment in the first half when Messi took the ball away from Vidić, Wazza and me, and we just couldn't get close. For someone tall like me, it was even harder getting to grips with a player who had such a low centre of gravity. Some players have speed, some a footballing brain and others a velvet touch, but what makes Messi unique is that he possesses all three. He's brave, too, as the way Messi plays, he's going to get kicked, the same goes for Ronaldo. Ronnie always bounced back up and asked for more, just as Messi did. That's the sign of the great players: they keep coming back for more, no matter how hard they're kicked. Messi plays the way you can't teach anyone to play. He's developed his skill, yes, but it doesn't matter how much coaching you gave a player, they couldn't do what Messi does. He's just a genius, and he's so stubborn too. I liken him to Giggsy when he played midfield. Giggsy would give the ball away two or three times, but he's so stubborn and confident in his own ability that he'd just do the same again, and eventually it would work. Similarly, Messi would dribble and dribble, play a 1–2, and it might get cut out but he'd do the same again and again. Lesser players would take an easy option if it didn't work first time, but Messi was relentless. Xavi, Iniesta and Busquets were good, but Messi gave them that extra dimension. I keep coming back to Messi because the ball kept coming back to him, and the story keeps coming back to him and his brilliance. He could beat two players within a blink of an eye and how do you defend against that? You can't. You can go man to man with him, but that doesn't faze him. You can't kick him because he gets back up. We're talking about one of the greatest of all time here.

I often hear the debate about Ronaldo or Messi, but it's so hard to choose because they're so different. I played with Ronnie and witnessed close-up the incredible variety of things he can do. Messi's only predictable at being unpredictable. I got close to him and sometimes I even thought I'd got him, but he was just teasing me and he was off, while I was left challenging thin air. I experienced how rapid he was over those first five yards and where Messi really kills you is in changing direction. His legs are so short and fast, he would have contact with the grass straightaway while I'd still be in the air. By the time I'd put my foot down to change direction, Messi had taken two steps and often shifted tack. Back then, it was not only what Messi did with the ball, but it was also his intelligence that set him apart. He was always passing it for a reason, to ask a question of us. Some players are gifted technically, and you can throw them the ball, they'll juggle away and you can make unbelievable clips of their tricks. Messi doesn't do step-overs or skills. He's direct and dribbles with such speed and purpose. I looked at Messi and saw somebody more than just a brilliant dribbler, more than just a magnificent passer and more than a prolific goalscorer. Messi did the lot but what made Messi even more effective and devastating was that he saw the whole picture in slow motion. Even manipulating the ball at full tilt, Messi was still able to have a clear picture. Genius. He knew everything that was going on around him and that helped him make the right decision on whether to play a little pass over the top or keep dribbling. Everybody else would see a blur of bodies at that speed, but the picture was sharp for Messi. It was a strange feeling playing against him because normally I'd end up disliking who I'm playing against but not him. I had to respect Messi.

Below: I never felt any pressure taking Roy Keane's old shirt.

I played with some great players and loved being involved in amazing games like winning at Anfield *(top right)* and beating Roma 7–1 at Old Trafford *(above and left)*.

Totally United: They were a great bunch of lads, and felt more like brothers to me.

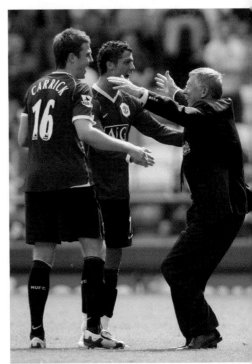

© Alex Livesey/Getty Images

© Matthew Peters/Manchester United/Getty Images

© Matthew Peters/Manchester United/Getty Images

© Matthew Peters/Manchester United/Getty Images

© Alex Livesey/Getty Images

Scoring my penalty in the 2008 Champions League final was the most special moment of my career. Winning was a drug.

Addicted to winning: I loved getting my hands on a trophy... and the party afterwards.

Losing to Barcelona in 2009 was my low point.

Left: Teamwork: Th standard of 'boxes' in training was top drawer, especially with Scholesy, Giggsy and Rio.

© John Peters/Manchester United /Getty Images

Right: Wayne Rooney's penalty against Blackburn that secured the league title in 2011. Wazza played angry, but by playing angry he was devastating.

© Dean Mouhtaropoulos/Getty Images

Left: Celebrating with Lisa, Louise and Jacey made winning even more special.

© AMA/Corbis/Getty Images

I had my best season for the club in 2013, but it was the end of an era.

Left: Playing alongside Scholesy was a privilege.

The Boss: A legend as a manager and as a man, it was an honour to play for Sir Alex.

Playing with footballers similar to his ability and on his wavelength made Messi even more lethal. Could we have man-marked Messi in Rome? The Boss would never have considered that, even if Fletch were available. 'We can score,' Sir Alex told us before kick-off. He wanted to be on the front foot, not cautious and man-marking, which was never the Boss's style. He wanted Ronnie upfront to relieve him of his defensive duties, give him a free role, so he could attack where he wanted but we didn't give him enough of the ball. Rooney sacrificed himself for the team and played on the left. But we just couldn't get enough of a grip on the game. Busquets was in the middle and what he does won't make the highlights reel or get him YouTube views, but I always felt it was pretty special. When Busquets is closed down, he just pops the ball off one touch to diffuse pressure. Barcelona's pivot had this incredible awareness of what was around him and what made Busquets truly special was his belief in his ability to play that way – one touch, pass and move, get the ball back, pass and move. Busquets didn't dribble, he'd have three touches max and just keep the carousel turning. He makes the game look so easy.

Even when the Boss changed it at half-time, sent on Tévez for Anderson, and Giggsy dropped back alongside me, we just couldn't get the ball off Barcelona. Most players I faced in my career, I closed them down and they'd pass it wide to the full back or past me towards the centre forward, but Iniesta and Xavi kept passing to each other, six or seven passes sometimes as if they owned the ball and were playing their own private game. Because they played so close together, when they lost the ball they invariably had three or four players nearby to win it back. On the rare occasions that I got possession, Barcelona swarmed at me, like hornets, and I found myself pressed by three, four or five of Guardiola's players. You didn't have time to breathe against Barcelona. They controlled the final and with 20 minutes left, Messi jumped high to head in. It was over.

That was the worst I've felt on a football pitch after a game by a mile. I was mentally devastated, angry and frustrated by my performance and by United's. We let ourselves down in Rome. Waiting to collect our loser's medals was painful. I just wanted to get the hell out of the Stadio Olimpico. We gathered in a broken line, Sir Alex at the front, followed by Giggsy, Scholesy and Wazza while I stood with Rio. He said a few words to me, but I wasn't taking anything in. We'd been so good for two years, so amazingly consistent, a record 25 games in the Champions League unbeaten – a hell of a run – yet we'd ended up giving our worst display in Rome. The pain in my broken toe was nothing compared to the agony of defeat and underperforming. I was numb, just standing there, staring into space, asking why? Everything I did in the game felt like it was going through my mind on repeat. I was beating myself up, sinking lower and lower, slipping into a depressed state.

After receiving the medal I didn't want, I trudged back to the changing room. I didn't want to speak to anyone. I slumped in my seat and cradled my head in my hands. The Boss was understandably angry and had a go at everyone. 'You need to have a look at yourselves and see if you can play at this level,' he said. Moscow was irrelevant. We were Manchester United and the expectation was relentless. 'You've let a good chance slip away here,' he said. The Boss summed up exactly how I was feeling. After he finished, I just questioned myself again and again. *Am I good enough?*

We sloped back to the Piazza della Repubblica and there was a party for all the families and staff in the rooftop bar. It wasn't a party, really, more a wake and it didn't matter what Lisa, Mam, Dad or Graeme said to take my mind off the game, I just couldn't get the final out of my head. I sat there in silence. There was nothing to say. As the night went on, I had a few beers and livened up a bit, but when I woke in the morning, the heartache was still there. It was like I'd been hit by a bus. I'd never been this low before.

I left Rome but I don't think Rome has ever really left me. When I got home, I sat out in the garden and didn't speak to anyone. I couldn't. I was totally numb. A couple of mates like Bradley, who'd been to Rome, called in the day after the final, but I didn't want to talk about the game, I didn't want to talk about anything really. I went into the garden with Louise and just sat on the grass as she played around me. I hardly moved. I pulled out of the England squad who were due to play in Kazakhstan because of my toe. Fabio Capello still made me meet up with the team and have an X-ray. My toe was clearly fractured. Capello wasn't happy as I hadn't told him before the final. Well, of course, Sir Alex wouldn't let me tell anyone as he wouldn't have trusted them not to let news of my injury slip. He didn't want Barcelona to know I was struggling. Capello was unimpressed. I left England the same day and hurried back home.

I just wanted to be left alone to play with Louise, probably because she was one of the only people who didn't see the game and was far too young to understand. I watched her crawling around at my feet, but my mind was still a thousand miles away, just thinking, *Why?* I thought about my passing in Rome, when I'd tried three or four long passes. One was good, a diagonal to Rooney in the first half, another was a decent pass but it bounced over Ronaldo, and I also over-hit a couple to Ronaldo and Rooney. The one to Ronnie was only a fraction off but in those games, a fraction looks a mile. I sat there thinking, *Was it my broken toe? Nah, that's a shit excuse. Take it like a man.*

My mind was besieged by so many questions, and I just couldn't find any answers. It was a lonely place to be. I had so much support and love from my family but nobody could help me. I had to fight through the depths of depression and that took a long, long time.

I also thought about Ronaldo. Rome was Ronnie's last game for us and he'd always seemed destined for Real Madrid. It was as though there'd been a conversation with the Boss in 2008 to say, 'Give us another year and we won't stand in your way.' In that extra year he was with United, nobody would have guessed Ronnie was thinking about leaving because his performances were phenomenal. Between Ronnie, the Boss and the club they all showed a bit of class in handling the situation. Manchester United kept it quiet that Ronnie was going, and I didn't know for certain until after the final with Barcelona. I was sorry to see him leave but everyone respected what Cristiano Ronaldo had done for Manchester United, and that he was going to a great club in Real, and he left on good terms.

After he'd gone, the Boss offered me Ronnie's shirt. He called me and Michael Owen in the office. 'You can have No. 7 if you want it,' he said to me. No. 7 is a massive number at Manchester United. Best! Robbo! Cantona! Becks! Ronnie! When you look back at the players who have had it, it means a lot. But, as with the No. 16 and the Keane connection, numbers didn't bother me. And Owen said, 'I'll have it!'

'Go ahead!' I said. That's football, though, isn't it? It moves on so quickly. I just wish I could move on from Rome.

We went to Majorca for a couple of weeks to try and recover physically from a long season but more to recover mentally from Rome. Louise was 15 months and just walking so I spent most of the days chasing her around. Not much rest at all! Even though I spent much-needed time with Lou and Lisa, all I could think of was Rome. I just couldn't shake it off. When Lou napped, I just lay there in a daze. Lisa was unbelievably patient. She could see I was suffering but she never told me to snap out of it. Lisa just left me to it, really, and we both hoped the new season would rescue me from my depression.

I I

WEMBLEY

Depression over a game of football sounds extreme, doesn't it? But I genuinely felt in a very dark place. It might sound a crazy exaggeration comparing football to a death but after Rome I felt like I was grieving. Six months earlier we'd been crowned the best in the world and now I tortured myself with questions about why we'd come second in Europe. Everything we did to reach Rome meant nothing to me now.

I'd had a string of massive highs: three league titles and winning a Champions League final, then I just hit rock bottom. I was weak, naïve and insecure enough to think after Rome, *Top players don't lose Champions League finals. If I'm that good then why have we lost?* Looking back at the mess my mind was in, it's crazy really, because Manchester United had still won the Premier League and League Cup in 2009 but, to me, that was totally irrelevant. Rome defeated me.

I've never talked about Rome with the Boss. I can't, it's too painful. Even now, almost a decade on, the gloom from Rome has not completely gone. I returned pre-season, and just couldn't shake the depression off and 2009/'10 was my worst season for United. I'd lost that edge. I had a heavy head and a heavy heart, even my body felt heavier. Nothing came easy. Sir Alex left me in the stands for the first Premier League game of the season – the win over Birmingham, but I started against Burnley, had a penalty saved by Brian Jensen, and we lost 1–0. It felt like I was stuck in a rut, stop-start-stop. I tried but I just couldn't shake myself into life. Confidence is a major part of a sportsman's performance, when it's there you take it for granted and if it disappears, it's desperate. In games, I went from having a calm, clear, sharp mind to a cloudy, slow, uncertain one. I went from seeing the best option without even thinking to seeing six things at once and choosing the worst one at the wrong time. I knew it was all in my head, but I felt that I couldn't turn to anyone for help, I'm too stubborn. I don't find it easy to open up to people, really only Lisa and Graeme, Mam and Dad. That period after Rome was a depression I had to confront on my own. I felt trapped in a vicious circle: my football suffered because of my bleak mood, which made me feel worse, so my mood darkened further.

Could I play my way out of depression? The Boss started me in the Champions League against Beşiktaş in September, and I was grateful and excited because the Inönü was the only stadium I'd been to that rivalled Celtic Park for noise. Surely this experience would jolt me back to my pre-Rome self? When I got there, I was actually afraid that the Inönü would fall down, it shook that much with all those crazy Beşiktaş fans jumping up and down. They tried to intimidate us, which is often the way in countries like Turkey, and Beşiktaş fans hung over the tunnel, threatening to kill us, so I just smiled back which wound them up even more. I loved it. It was a buzz to play in that atmosphere. Maybe I was getting my belief back. Maybe not. I got subbed after an hour in Istanbul and was in and out of the side until October. It's a lonely place when you're not in the team, training and trying to give your best, searching for that feeling, knowing you aren't performing anywhere near the level you can and praying the next session will be the turning point. I looked at my teammates who didn't seem to have a care in the world and were playing great, and I envied them. *When would that be me again?*

When I did play, there was no hiding place. There were times when I was struggling and played safe to get through it. Going back to basics was my way out. The plan was to work hard and defend as well as I could. I actually ended up playing centre half when Gary Neville and Wes Brown got injured against West Ham in December. Sir Alex had eight defenders out for the trip to Wolfsburg three days later, so I knew what was coming. I embraced it. I enjoyed the fresh challenge, it freed me up a little bit. It was me, Darren Fletcher and Pat Evra – not a natural three at the back but we made the best of it. It was tough, I was up against Edin Džeko and suffered some tricky moments. I tackled their midfielder, Makoto Hasebe, from behind and brought him down – a clear pen, but the ref Björn Kuipers didn't give it and I escaped. We won with a Michael Owen hat-trick – a hell of a win that got us top spot in the group and life seemed good again.

Next up was Fulham away. The others still weren't fit so Fletch, Ritchie De Laet and me formed a back three, we only played as a three because none of us were centre backs and we needed that extra body for security. It was a step too far. Up front for Fulham was Bobby Zamora who put himself up against Ritchie, a young kid playing left centre back. Bobby was strong and clever, and it was a disaster of a game, which we lost 3–0. The Boss said a few nice things about me helping out at the back, but he had to praise me because he needed me as we were that short in defence. For a few seasons on the bounce, there was always a spell where I'd play centre back and I enjoyed playing there. I found it easier physically as there was less running, but I definitely felt vulnerable compared to midfield as there was no safety net. If I was left one-on-one or if the ball went down the channel, it was just a race between me and the centre forward. I lost Yakubu for a goal when I played centre back against Blackburn at Old Trafford in 2011. At

Goodison the following season, Marouane Fellaini battered me. I was marking him at a corner, trying to stick close, but he jumped too high for me and Everton won 1–0. That was a brutal experience, really. I never, ever considered a second career as a defender, even though Mick Phelan suggested it once. We thrashed Wigan 5–0 at Old Trafford in 2011 and, as I walked off, Mick said, 'You've just found yourself a new career because you've made it look so easy.' Not for me, thanks!

As we headed into 2010, I still couldn't get going and went off football for a while, just didn't want to know. I was so out of sorts I even got sent off against AC Milan for the first time in my 174 games for United. My disciplinary record was good and I'd been booked only 11 times for United before San Siro. I'll never forget that night on 16 February 2010, and not simply for the red card. Both clubs had special histories and the San Siro had that feeling, that history. It was hostile, loud and aggressive, with loads of whistling and booing. Brilliant. Milan had a hell of a team, with lots of big names. Ronaldinho, Andrea Pirlo and David Beckham played, alongside Alexandre Pato and Massimo Ambrosini. When Ronaldinho's shot deflected in off me early on, I thought, *Could be a long night, this*. Ronaldinho wasn't at his peak but he was still one hell of a player, and he kept managing to pull his tricks off. I've always thought of Ronaldinho as the master of the unexpected and that sort of player is the hardest to play against. I was constantly waiting for him to produce something so I didn't know whether to stand off or get close. In the end, I left Rafael da Silva to deal with Ronaldinho! Rafael was the perfect full back to play against Ronaldinho, as he had a low centre of gravity, which meant he could chop and change direction, and he played with so much emotion. He was so aggressive with a great attitude – Rafael was all heart. Ultimately, he was a typical United full back who loved a tackle.

I was still trying to help out with Ronaldinho and my first booking actually came for a foul on him. My second yellow, right at the death with us leading 3–2, was a bit of a pointless booking, really. Evra fouled Pato, the ball came to me, and I didn't really mean to kick it away but I just flicked it towards Evra and the ref, Olegário Benquerença, booked me again. I couldn't believe it, especially as there were only 60 seconds left of injury time. I felt embarrassed, uncomfortable and a bit shocked. As I walked off, I didn't look at the Boss, I didn't dare. The decision was very petty. I shouldn't have done it, though. Sir Alex never said anything to me. Maybe the Boss knew I hardly ever got booked. I still waited for a letter to drop into my locker telling me how much I'd been fined. I waited and waited, the letter never came and I certainly didn't complain.

I'd never been sent off as a kid, and I like to think I was a clean player. I never dived during almost 20 years as a professional. OK, I've jumped out of a tackle but there's a difference because sometimes I've seen a tackle coming in and thought, *If I leave my leg there I'm going to get hurt.* So I've leapt out the way and it might look like a dive but it's actually self-preservation. I've done it to win free kicks but I'd never roll around feigning injury. I'd never go down if no one's touched me. If someone on a booking flew in on me, took me out and it was a foul, I'd stay down for an extra few seconds, yes, but I wouldn't writhe about. I struggle to get my head round people actually doing that when they're not hurt. My hatred of cheating comes from way back as all that rolling around was not tolerated at Wallsend Boys Club. There's still something of the outraged Boyza kid in me when I see players holding their face or clutching their leg when they haven't been touched. So many players do it now and it's sad, but I also know we have to be careful criticising individuals for simulation too much because it's in some players' culture. It's celebrated as a skill to con the ref, it's almost an art form, particularly in some South American countries. If streetwise teams are winning, who's to say it's wrong? I know the image of the game gets tarnished but they're playing to win, not to make the game look better.

Personally, it's not for me, I'd rather concentrate on my actual job. However, there are tactical fouls, like subtly stopping a counterattack early with a little foul knowing if you bring somebody down 10 yards later when the danger is greater it's an obvious yellow. I have time-wasted by walking to a ball or rolling a ball away from someone. At times, I've felt a nudge and gone down, not hurt, but not rolling around or getting the physio on if there was nothing wrong with me. Unless I'm really struggling, I hate it when the physio comes on. It's pride, I guess. I mean, there are times when you've got a kick and it's sore, but what's the physio going to do for you? I broke my right elbow against Roma at Old Trafford in the Moscow season, when the Brazilian Mancini fell on top of me, and it was painful but I played on and finished the game. Actually, I don't know how I got through it. I had to keep my arm bent as when I tried to straighten it the pain was a joke. I was out for a month. I still can't straighten it now. I'm not trying to make out like I'm a hero, I thought, *I can carry on, do I need to really come off?* If you can get back up and help the team, then do it. I remember the old magic sponge as a kid. Somebody would run on with a bucket and the magic sponge soaked in water, and you'd bounce back up, and think it's magic! It's just cold water! Nowadays, the doctors run on, especially in Europe, in suits, and pull out the magic spray. Really, come on, man, what's that going to do? You know the pain is going to go.

Anyway, Milan was my only red card. Twelve days after the San Siro, before the League Cup final against Villa, Sir Alex hadn't forgotten he rested players the previous year so he went round all of us in training, asking, 'Did you play last year in the final?' 'No, I didn't play, Boss,'

I replied. 'You rested me. It was scandalous!' And laughed. So, the Boss went, 'OK, you can play then.' This was rotation on a grand scale, over 12 months, but I was relieved and delighted to get a shot at another medal. I have to confess we got away with a decision from Phil Dowd at the start. Villa were furious that Vida wasn't shown a red for pulling Gabby Agbonlahor down when he was through on goal. Vida should have been sent off, no doubt. James Milner scored the penalty but so often when we went 1–0 down, even 2–0 down under Sir Alex, I thought, *We're still going to win this*. Owen scored, then ripped his hamstring. He never had any luck with his hamstrings but he was a deadly finisher. Rooney came on and headed the winner. I felt comfortable throughout and the dark cloud was lifting, or so I thought.

My positive mood soon faded, and I struggled to see a way through the gloom. I felt like I was trying to run up a mountain and always slipping back. We went to Molineux and won but I wasn't myself. It was a struggle. I hoped a trip to Munich in the Champions League quarters would lift me from this low. I'm a big fan of the Allianz, a proper football stadium, tight and enclosed, with a great atmosphere, and I prayed this would be the launchpad to get me back to my level. Bayern were Louis van Gaal's team then, a typical van Gaal team – very thoughtful and deliberate in their movements, and all in sync. Bayern had a very dangerous attack with Thomas Müller playing off Ivica Olić and taking up very clever positions behind me. I kept getting dragged really deep. We took an early lead through Wazza's volley but I was crap again, I just couldn't find my rhythm and the Boss took me off with 20 minutes to go. Arjen Robben and Olić turned the game around, but that was nothing to do with subbing me because I was way off. I knew it myself.

Eight days later, the Boss had us absolutely fired up for Bayern at Old Trafford. One of my first chats with Bastian Schweinsteiger when he joined from Bayern in 2015 was about that second leg. 'That first 25 minutes!' Basti said. 'We didn't know what to do.' Darron Gibson's shot and Nani's flick gave us early control, and from then on it was pressure, pressure, pressure, just running forward and passing forward – all very reminiscent of Roma. Nani made it 3–0 and I thought, *Yes, we're back where we belong.* We were heading to the semis. From having such a heavy head and shoulders, the cloud lifted and I felt light and free, but not for long. Again. Stop-start-stop. In the first half, I clashed heads with Basti at a corner. I'd gone to flick the ball on, and Basti got me on the side of my head, and gave me a right big lump. Just before half-time, I tried to be too helpful and over-covered our centre halves. I'm kicking myself now just thinking about how I got trapped between Rio and Vida as I challenged Olić for Müller's header on. As Müller's ball came over me, Olić stood on my Achilles, my boot came off and if that wasn't enough of a foul, he shoved his right arm across me, knocking me over. It looked like Olić shrugged me off easily, and I got slated for weak defending, but the ref Nicola Rizzoli should have blown for a foul. To this day, I maintain it was a 100 per cent foul. Olić slotted the ball in, Edwin gave me a look, and I felt the dark cloud returning. Bayern now had a lifeline and then Rafael got sent off for a second yellow, a stupid yellow, for a foul on Franck Ribéry having earlier fouled Mark van Bommel. Bayern threw bodies forward and we were hanging in there. Bayern got a corner, which Ribéry went over to take. Down to 10, we had one man on the edge of the box against two of theirs, Fletch was split between Basti and Robben. This is how games are decided – on tiny details. I thought, *Robben's furthest away from goal,* so I had an eye on him, but I had my man, Olić, in the box. As soon as I realised Ribéry's corner wasn't going to Olić, and would clear me, I sprinted towards

Robben. I threw my body in front of him but it was too late, and Robben connected. As I twisted, I looked back and saw the ball flying past Edwin. It was a hell of a volley, there was only one place Robben could put it and he did, so that was 3–2 and us out of the Champions League on away goals. It looked like Robben was my man, when he wasn't. *What else could go wrong?* Oh, yes, I got an eye infection, missed Blackburn at the weekend, we drew 0–0, threw the league away, and I sunk even lower.

Every season I'd been at United, when it counted and in all the big games, the Boss started me, until now. For the final four games of the season, I was on the bench with my head in turmoil. We lost the Premier League by a point, which was devastating, and it would have been four on the bounce, which was unheard of. Everybody was in bits and I was distraught as I genuinely feared that all I'd done to get myself into a strong position at the club I loved could now be swept away. Sir Alex hardly spoke to me towards the end of that season. I felt vulnerable. I hadn't played and I was thinking, *Has the manager got his eye on someone else now?* I expected any minute to be hauled into Sir Alex's office and instructed that Manchester United had accepted a bid for me. I had two years left on my contract, and I was just waiting for the Boss to say, 'I'm going to have to let you go.' After having had three great years, it was painful to think I could suddenly be discarded for somebody else. I couldn't bear to think of leaving Manchester United – my home, my love, my addiction. I just knew those who fell below the standards of Manchester United fell by the wayside. And so they should. I feared the worst. Fear filled my life.

There's always that dark side to being a footballer. The best players ride it out, overcoming all the doubts, loss of confidence, lacking sharpness and feeling tired. That's just pure mental strength, really. But back then I felt fragile and vulnerable. Especially playing for United, there's no hiding place whatsoever. There's pressure and expectation, there's the pride you have in yourself, and there's your desire to perform and your desperation not to lose. Throughout my time as a player at United, I struggled to unwind following a game. I would be lying in bed until 4am or 5am, just wide awake and so hot, still, even hours after a match. Before a game, I'd often be cold in the changing room, almost as if I feel a chill. It's like my body is preparing for what's ahead, as if it knows the heat of battle is coming. It's really strange. I'll have an ice bath after the game, but that battle heat just stays. I can be watching TV after a game, late at night, and be boiling up. When I just can't sleep, I go into the spare room or sometimes I've jumped in with the kids at 3am. Other times, I'll sit in front of the TV, trying to nod off on the couch. I've taken sleeping pills the odd time, but I don't like the groggy feeling you get the next day.

I read about Jonny Wilkinson talking about his issues with mental health in the *Daily Express* in January 2018. It just shows that however confident someone may appear, there are more often than not vulnerabilities, fragilities. With kicking in rugby, mentally you've got to be so strong. I've always admired kickers like Jonny, Owen Farrell and Dan Carter, who are carrying the hopes of their team on their shoulders. I always saw Jonny as being the ultimate mentally strong player so to read about how he'd suffered from anxiety struck a chord with me. I felt similar. I doubted myself. Sometimes I had to fight with myself to get in the right frame of mind to be at that top level. I had to keep convincing myself to be positive. I had to keep telling myself that I'd prepared better than the other team, that I'd made more sacrifices than them. But it was a struggle. Talking to friends and family about this darkest period of my life, I don't think I was difficult to be around as

I'm like Dad and I keep my emotions hidden. I bottled that anger and frustration up.

Lisa definitely knew how bad a state I was in, especially during the World Cup in 2010. In South Africa, I was in a really bad way, homesick as well as depressed. Physically, I was in my prime, but emotionally I was a wreck. 'I'm coming home, I've had enough,' I told Lisa. She knew I was in a mess, but then Lisa was having a tough time at home having just had Jacey. Lisa was in a bad way as she'd had problems with her back since giving birth to Louise, and still does, so I felt guilty even moaning to Lisa. Jacey had just arrived and having a son was a blessing, but I was a mess. I reached the stage in 2010 where I thought, *Do you know what? I don't know if I want to do this any more.* I was just so down, so depressed and I didn't want to play. My depression built over the summer of 2010 and infected the next season. After I returned from the World Cup, I drove to Carrington, telling myself over and over, 'I just don't want to play football today. I don't want to go training. I wish I could do something else.' I'd wait for the lights to change on Carrington Lane, turning into Isherwood Lane leading to the training ground, and think, *Hang on a minute. I'm at the best club in the world, working with some of the best players in the world, the best manager in the world, doing all I've ever wanted to do. I've got two kids and a wife, and I'm as happy as I could possibly be at home.* I then started beating myself up about, *What am I getting depressed for?* But I just wasn't enjoying football any more. I wished I could go back to those innocent days when my love of football was just so pure – in the garden at Howdon, at the Boyza and at St James' Park. There was just a void now. If my career had finished in 2010, I wouldn't have been bothered. I questioned myself every day and the only answer I kept coming back to was that I'd had enough. I wanted my mind back. I wanted my life back. I'd been 15 years away from home, on the move, always under pressure but never, ever before had I been depressed like this.

My mood was not helped by my Achilles plaguing me and I'll never forget the indignity of a reserve game against City in the Manchester Senior Cup at Ewen Fields in August 2010. Sir Alex pulled a squad together of lads, who had not been involved in the match 48 hours earlier against Fulham in the Premier League. Wes, Gibbo, Nev, Chris Smalling, me, Ando, Rafael, Tom Cleverley and Kiko were in the squad with some of the usual reserves like Magnus Eikrem, Will Keane, Ben Amos and Joe Dudgeon. Sir Alex told me I was playing as we walked off the pitch after training at Carrington. I was fuming.

'Why the fuck am I playing reserves?'

'You need a game.'

'It's pointless. I might as well train. Reserves is fucking shit, what am I doing?'

'Listen, you're fucking playing. Just get on with it.' And that was it. Sir Alex didn't actually snap. He just spoke in a way that made it very clear there was no room for debate. He could have ripped my head off and gone, 'Who the fuck do you think you are?' But he just told me I was playing and walked off. God knows why I spoke to him like that. I hadn't before and didn't ever again. I shocked myself. The thing is the Boss was very calm with me when he had every right to slaughter me. On another day that could have been the end of me. Maybe he sensed something.

By now, I'd got myself into a frame of mind to get something out of the game. I couldn't toss it off. Pride, I suppose. So I walked out in front of 1,569 people to play City's Elite Development Squad. Gary Neville started and this match summed Nev up. By kick-off, I thought

I'd got all the business about 'I don't want to be here' out of my head. A ball broke loose, the surface was quite wet and this City lad slid in. It was close to the touchline, the ball was going out, so I thought there was no point me sliding really, it's not worth it. I'll just get a throw-in and play on. Nev went nuts, screaming, 'Carras, fucking hell! What you pulling out of tackles for?'

'Fuck off, Nev. Calm down!!'

We had a brief tear-up but I realised, *He's fucking right, pull yourself together and get on with it. Nev is 35, it's a reserve game and he's still on it.* When he was playing, he was all in, Nev. He gave everything. It was an example of his professionalism: 602 appearances for United, 85 England caps yet he played a reserves game like it was an FA Cup final. Respect!

The Boss also played me in a League Cup tie against Wolves on 26 October 2010, the only time I shared a pitch with Ravel Morrison. Ravel was one of the few kids I saw coming into first team training where senior players actually stood off him, scared in case he'd beat them easily. Ravel had this ability to glide past people like they weren't there. He earned respect straightaway. It was like, 'Oh, we've got to be careful here.' When some kids came up, I could just go and take the ball off them, brush them aside, but I was wary of Ravel. Sir Alex told us Ravel was the best player he'd seen as a young kid but his career has gone nowhere, sadly. It's a shame, and I know Sir Alex tried everything to keep Ravel focused. The Boss threatened Ravel with being kicked out of the club, he booted him out of the changing room and ordered him to get changed on his own. The Boss also went the other way, putting an arm around him, putting him in the first team changing room, put him with us as a 16-year-old training with us every day. Nothing worked. Rio Ferdinand and Gary Neville spoke to Ravel a lot and tried to get him to be dedicated. What a waste of talent that was. Ravel could have been great.

I was playing in that Wolves game after I'd had an injection at Carrington to clear up my niggling Achilles. I was out for a couple of weeks, but as soon as I was back training, Sir Alex said, 'That's the best I've seen you looking for a while that. You're moving well there.' The Boss never needed to show his human side towards me, really, as I was pretty low maintenance but that gave me the boost I needed. It also made me realise how much I'd been carrying my Achilles. I felt free again. I had the edge back. All of a sudden, something clicked and I just felt at home again. It coincided with starting talks about a new contract in November and agreeing it in March and almost being at peace again. I felt United wanted me, they believed in me and I believed in myself again. Fans look at well-paid pros and don't understand loss of form but we're humans and we have our fears and our lows. Footballers are not robots.

I've been mentally stronger ever since, and haven't doubted myself in the same way again, though I still had the odd blip. I got pulled into the Boss' office after we played Marseille away in February 2011, it was a horrendous game, a bobbly pitch, 0–0 – completely forgettable. Back at Carrington, I discovered somebody hadn't forgotten. Sir Alex called me in and he didn't dish out a grilling as such, more a 'Come on, Michael, you need to liven yourself up.' Work harder, I told myself. I thought of Granddad and how hard he'd worked, Mam and Dad too. So I got into Carrington early, left late, and spent longer hours in the gym. I gave every last drop of sweat in training, craving to be at my best again.

My recovery was helped by a change in midfield, which made me take more responsibility. Scholesy had injured his groin so he was out and Fletch was badly ill with colitis. I didn't want to bother Fletch too much, so I sent him texts, just wishing him the best, and let him be. It was something he'd battled for some time but kept quiet from us. I've so much respect for Fletch. How he came back from that was amazing. So at that point, Giggsy and I played together in midfield and we started both legs against Chelsea in the quarter-final of the Champions League. The partnership with Giggsy was, obviously, different to the one with Scholesy. Scholesy was more controlled, more of a passer. Giggsy was a dribbler, and you don't get many dribblers in midfield. But Giggsy was so forward-thinking, so direct, and if he saw a space, Giggsy ran into it or passed through it. I really enjoyed those few months, playing with Giggsy. Yes, he was getting older, but nobody would have guessed he was 37. He played every minute of those two Chelsea games, he was that fit. I played more of a defensive role, which made it easier for Giggsy. It was such a pleasure, in the same way that it was to play alongside Scholesy. I was more than happy to sacrifice my game to help them perform to their best.

I'm really conscious of who I'm playing with and how I play to make the best of us playing together. I might not necessarily play my normal way, but if that's going to benefit us as a pairing, surely that's what I'm there for, isn't it? It's no good me thinking, *I'm doing great*, when really as a team we aren't achieving as much. It might enhance my reputation but I'm there to win and the way I play the game is focused on helping the team achieve that goal.

This leads into how I see the game in general. I really enjoy thinking two or three steps ahead about how to drag the opposition out of position. It's like a game of chess where you're trying to open up your opponent. For example, a lot of the time, a midfielder will pass it to a full back and the whole stadium claps and goes 'Good pass'. I'll be thinking, *Actually, it was pointless*. The full back's on his own, he's just going to pass it straight back into midfield. Whereas, I prefer to keep hold of it, and by the time someone moves, I'll play it forward. I'll try to control the opposition sometimes with a soft or fast pass. Instead of passing fast directly into a player's feet, I might pass it softly on an angle, forcing the receiving player to come off sideways for the ball, posing a question for the defender about whether or not to follow. If the defender doesn't follow then the receiver can turn. If the defender is attracted to the receiver, I can get it back with the passing line I originally wanted now open as the defender's been moved out of position. The key isn't only in executing the technique but in the thinking.

I'll occasionally play it short, bring the pressure on to me, drag the defender across, suck them in and find the opposite winger, one on one. I see so many players make a big switch, that big diagonal pass, everyone applauds, but it's quite an obvious pass. The player receiving might be in a space, the pass might look beautiful and it might get there, but if the defence is all set, ready for it, then the defence hasn't moved. It's about trying to move the opposition about.

That unbelievable 60-yard pass to the winger, might be easy for the defence to deal with. Whereas a five-yard pass through their two midfielders can suddenly put their whole defensive shape in a mess, asking questions, like does the centre half come out or does he not? Passing forwards between the defensive lines has always been my biggest skill. A lot of it is down to timing and disguise. It's not a highlight and it's not glamorous. People won't necessarily think, 'What a pass that was!' But it can be the most effective pass. I've never played a pass for applause.

Sir Alex would always tell me 'get on the ball', to take it off the centre halves even if we had somebody tight to me. Other managers don't do that so much. If I had somebody tight up my arse, they'd say, 'It's a risky pass, don't give it.' Because Sir Alex trusted me and Scholesy a lot, he'd be like, 'Play. Bring them on to you.' I'm under pressure but I want my opponent to come and mark me. I'm trying to play a game with him, like, 'All right then, are you going to come or not?' I've just got the bigger picture of where the space is or who we're trying to get on the ball. Then all of a sudden if it's Rooney, Giggs or Ronaldo coming in on that space, I'll pass it. Sometimes I'd come short and if the opponent didn't come with us then I'd get the ball and turn, constantly asking them a question. When I played with Scholesy, we'd pass to each other an awful lot instead of playing it to the full back. If I pass to the full back, the man marking me can switch off, and think 'My job is done.' When Scholesy and I passed it between us, the marker didn't know what to do. Has he got to close me down? That's working him overtime. Without ever discussing it, it was almost like me and Scholesy were playing a little two on two in the middle of the park. We played an extra three or four passes just to work them, basically. A little game within a big game. We might not get any joy from that, but five minutes later the opponent might think, 'My legs are tired' or switch off completely. Then, it becomes a psychological game as well as a physical one. I'm testing, testing and testing them. Graeme and I talk about it a lot. It's about thinking, technique and vision.

On the morning of the game at Stamford Bridge, me and Tony Strudwick, Rio Ferdinand and Eric Steele left the Corinthia Hotel for a little wander, round past the London Eye and enjoyed a bit of a chat. It was a ritual at away games. I was relaxed. Driving to the game, I felt confident and excited. I did the warm-up and felt light, sharp and quick. I got a few shouts from Chelsea fans, the usual 'West Ham reject', 'Tottenham scum', 'dirty Northern bastard', and I laughed at them as usual. My mood was so positive now and I was right up for this.

The pressure was massive, playing an English club in the Champions League. I found it easier facing Real or Milan because we just didn't want to give Chelsea anything. If Real or Milan beat us, and went on to win the Champions League, we wouldn't see them again for a while. If Chelsea knocked us out, and went on to be champions, disaster. I'd be thinking, *That should be us.* It's a healthy rivalry. These rivalries change over the years. Liverpool are always there, that's an eternal battle; Chelsea were there from the start of that great period of English competition; Arsenal were there for a bit, one or two years where they got close, then they'd fall away; Tottenham were never really like that and then City came into it. I observed Sir Alex over the years and noticed which managers he took on and it was only those who threatened him, like Benítez, that he feuded with. Sir Alex never bothered going head to head with managers who weren't challenging him on the pitch. No need, I suppose, it would have been a waste of time and energy.

That quarter-final at the Bridge was momentous for me because it was when I felt I finally conquered my Rome depression. The game happened in my head at a slower pace. I was calm. This was the feeling I'd been searching for. I felt in complete control, and I played the pass to Giggsy to set up Rooney's goal. Finally, thank God, I was back to my best level on the stages where the big questions are asked. I couldn't wait to get back to Old Trafford to finish it off. We won 2–1 and playing Schalke away in the semi-final was one of my very best performances. Raúl played for Schalke that night and fortunately for us he never really had a chance. We should have had five or six, but Manuel Neuer was on fire. It didn't feel like a Champions League semi-final at all. No disrespect to Schalke but they weren't a massive team and we came away with a 2–0 victory and for the home leg, Sir Alex sat me in the stand. I was loving football again but I sort of understood the Boss's thinking as we had Chelsea at home on the Sunday for the Premier League.

'I'm making a lot of changes for Schalke,' the Boss said. When we were alone, the players were like, 'What the hell is the Boss doing? It's the Champions League semi-final. If they get an early goal, it's game on, this.' Sir Alex must be the only manager in history to rest players for a Champions League semi-final. We trusted him. It was moments like this when I admired the Boss even more because he was just a born risk-taker, wasn't he? The lads won convincingly, we all came back in for Chelsea, fresh and ready for business, beat them and the Boss's selection was again vindicated, as if anybody could have doubted his judgement.

I only had a brief celebration upon winning my fourth Premier League medal. We had 20 days to 28 May and the Champions League final repeat against Barcelona, and I just couldn't wait. I'd never watched the 2009 final back, as I'd tried to erase the negative thoughts, but now I needed to understand where we went wrong against Barcelona so I went downstairs into the TV room at home with Graeme. I sat back to analyse a game I'd beaten myself up over for two years and found the 2009 final actually wasn't as bad as I thought. Some of the darkness I'd fought came from a negative perception of the game that wasn't entirely true.

Reviewing Rome brought hope, but the problem with facing Barcelona in 2011 was that they were now a couple of levels above their heights of 2009. Everyone was talking about Barcelona by then: 'They're special.' 'Messi's a genius.' 'Guardiola's a visionary.' I heard so much praise for Barcelona in the build-up to the final at Wembley. Of course, we knew we were going in against a team at their peak. Barcelona destroyed Real Madrid in the semis, playing some unbelievable football, and in my heart I knew we had been stronger in Rome when we had Ronaldo. We were still confident as I felt we'd learned lessons from Rome. Barcelona's passing carousel was not an unknown weapon to us this time. Messi as a deep No. 9 was not going to be a shock. We all felt this was our chance to put Rome right. There was a definite sense of unfinished business. We had this long preparation period and worked every day on our tactics, particularly pressing Barcelona before they could get their carousel turning. We knew Messi would drop in and the wingers, David Villa and Pedro, would stay really high.

Knowing is one thing, combating it is another test entirely. Do you press really high and take that risk of them passing through you, and then you're open? Sir Alex would not waver from his philosophy. 'We are Manchester United, we play this way, we're playing to attack,' he told us. His team talk at Wembley was split into three messages: 'get in their faces', 'press them high up the field' and 'play through their press'. Some people urged caution but we went for teams and we had no fear of Barcelona, just respect. Our team picked itself really with the main decision being who to put at right back as Rafael was injured, so Fábio, his twin brother, came in. The twins were great lads and the Boss always messed about with them, saying in the early days he was going to sub one for the other at half-time without telling the ref and see if anyone noticed. My heart went out to Rafael for missing the final as he was a true United player who wore his heart on his sleeve, ran up and down without pausing, took risks and gave everything. Rafael was respectful but he hated losing. Some lads hide their feelings, like me, but Rafael was all in on the pitch and in training. He brought emotion to the game, which the Boss liked, and which maybe Louis van Gaal didn't like so much and that's why Rafael left, I guess.

Chicharito had scored against Chelsea and played against Schalke, so he started. Whenever I look back on that team and think of Chicharito, one word springs to mind – goals. They weren't necessarily clean finishes, and quite a lot of them were actually scuffed, but Chicha came alive in the box and he'd be on to any little ricochet in a flash. He was always on the move in the box, always on the prowl and when the defender stood still, Chicha stole away into a space and gambled on a ball falling his way. He wasn't as good as Wayne Rooney, Louis Saha or Dimitar Berbatov at holding the ball up and bringing others into play but what he gave us was goals, energy and speed.

Sir Alex had to tell Berba he was not in the match-day squad, and Owen was on the bench. I remember the Boss saying it was one of the most horrible parts of his job to leave lads out of the squad. He did it to Ji in Moscow. I sympathised with the boys who missed out as these were the games we lived for.

We didn't change our set-up. Wayne Rooney played off Chicharito and the plan was for him to look after Sergio Busquets and break forward off him when we won possession back to beat their press. That position the Boss gave Wayne off Chicha was perfect for him. Wazza was so unselfish and went out of his way to help the team which he never got enough credit for. His goals record at United speaks for itself but that doesn't tell half the story. People never fully grasped how good Wazza was or how raw, fast and strong he was, but what I really loved about Wazza was that he was never about personal glory, never. He was never in the gym but he'd be incredible in training, working his nuts off, and then practising shooting for an extra half an hour most days at Carrington. Wazza was a beast, blessed with that mad strength and speed that meant he didn't need the gym. He was horrible to play against and the word 'aggressive' doesn't really do him justice. He was on the brink of being genuinely frightening and I always sensed some fury there. Wazza played angry, but by playing angry, he was devastating. Yes, he got sent off a couple of times but that hatred of losing was the flip side of being a winner. He possessed such a high level of football intelligence and the timing of his movement when I had the ball was the best I've played with and made my job so much easier. He had the right to stay in the No. 10 position and just shout, 'Give me the ball.' Many 10s would have stood there waiting for the ball. Not Wayne Rooney. He always wanted to help out. He always listened. I'd give him simple information, 'left', 'right', getting him to cover in front of me, and he did it instantly. We had a great understanding.

At Wembley, Barcelona had so much of the ball that Rooney dropped into midfield more and more to help us because we were being overrun. Guardiola's whole team created space for Messi, Xavi and Iniesta through their centre backs Javier Mascherano and Gerard Piqué dropping deep and their wingers standing high on the touchline to occupy Fábio and Evra with Ferdinand and Vida covering across. Wembley's huge pitch got stretched, more space opened for Messi, Xavi and Iniesta, and they were constantly asking questions of us. I looked at Xavi. He was slight, not quick or muscly, but guarded the ball with his life. I hoped old-school physicality would overpower him but it was tough to get close. Xavi's so intelligent and his appreciation of the space and angles around him and others on the pitch was so impressive. Barcelona keep probing and prodding you to find a weak spot, and create space, then, *boom*, they change the speed of the ball. It's like they're using scalpels the way Barcelona open you up. Pedro scored but we fought back. Giggsy played centre midfield alongside me, and he brought that attacking mindset. He got in the box and set up Wazza for one of his great goals, 15 yards, top corner. We were back in it. It felt like a merciful relief getting into the changing rooms level because those first 45 minutes were so sapping. We all knew we were in a serious fight with Barcelona constantly stretching us and tempers ran high. Vida tore into me because he felt the midfielders weren't protecting the defence enough.

'Messi's getting behind you, Carras, drop off, you're too high,' Vida screamed at me.

I'm not that vocal in the changing room but I shouted back, 'Well, you've got to press on him, Vida. I can't do both.' Vida was an absolute pleasure to play with and this was the only time we had words. We knew we had to solve the problem of Messi's movement somehow. Messi was effectively Barcelona's centre forward. I understood Vida and Rio also had the problem of David Villa and Pedro making diagonal runs from outside to in and behind them. That's why Barcelona were so devilish to deal with and Guardiola so clever. But what do you do? Do you take the risk and put a centre half right in on Messi but leave space in behind for their wingers to fly into? Guardiola played this game of dare to lure you out of position. I know coaches study Barcelona and fans talk incessantly about them, but nothing prepares you for actually being in there against them because they're so elusive. Guardiola's style was imprinted deep on this Barcelona team.

Arguing with Vida, I mentioned an instance where we pressed high and Messi ran behind me. Barcelona got the ball into him, Vida wasn't quite up on Messi, who turned Vida, and they counterattacked. The ball came across the face of the six-yard box and I ended up getting back just in time to clear. Vida's problem was Messi getting the ball, turning and running at them.

'You have to cover, Carras,' Vida said again.

'If I stand on Messi, Giggsy's got Xavi, Wazza's got Busquets but Iniesta's on his own,' I replied. 'So, we've got no chance. I'm trying to push on Iniesta. I can't do Messi as well.'

My problem was that, as our midfield and forwards pressed high up, if I didn't go with them then Iniesta was free all day. Vida's problem was he didn't want to leave a big hole in the back four by coming in to press Messi dropping deep. In other teams, less strong ones, arguments like this might be divisive. Not with this United team. Rio, Vida and I were on the same wavelength, we were good friends off the pitch and worked well on it. I'll give you an example: Rio, often Vida, screamed at me 'Carras, LEFT' or 'Carras, RIGHT'. I wouldn't even look over my shoulder, I'd automatically step to my left or right, knowing Rio was telling me someone's behind me, usually Messi at Wembley, so I could block the pass. In basic terms, Rio operated like my radar towards incoming threat. It made Rio's job easier, but I never thought, *He's taking the piss out of me, making me run more.* I trusted him. It made my job simpler as I didn't have to look. I just listened for the call. Rio was the best all-round centre half I've played with, against or ever seen – an unbelievable player. He made the game so easy. As a professional, Rio had everything: a winning mentality, commitment to training and great communication with everyone. As a player, Rio also had everything: speed, strength, presence, aerial ability, intelligence, knowledge of the game and he could take the ball anywhere. From the moment I saw him at West Ham, I knew Rio Ferdinand was special. Yes, Rio had his interests outside football, like restaurants and fashion, but no one was more dedicated in training and I could tell from the way he spoke about the game how passionate he was about football. It doesn't surprise me one bit that Rio now makes such an insightful pundit on TV.

I've so much respect for Vida too. If you had to pick one man to defend your life that man would be Vida. He was so imposing and aggressive, and hated losing. You'd take Vida in your team any day of the week because he put fear in to the opposition. He was just a magnet for the ball in the box. He had that Serbian aggression and played on the edge, sometimes straying over into that red mist. Vida trained like that as well and if something upset him, he wouldn't hide it, he'd tell us.

If someone kicked him, Vida would go after them and say something back or give them a boot in return.

I defy anyone to name a greater defensive partnership of the past couple of decades than Vida and Rio. They brought out the best in each other and had an unbelievable understanding. I watched them play, and saw the balance in their partnership. Vida read the game as well as anyone, but he was more forceful with his defending, whereas Rio was more thoughtful. Rio never got dirty as a centre half because he anticipated danger early so he wouldn't find himself forced into making last-ditch tackles. I loved the way Rio put the fire out before the sparks started. I see some defenders throwing themselves into tackles, putting their body on the line, when they could have avoided the situation by reading the game better. My one frustration was the way that the press and fans took Rio for granted, and didn't realise quite how good he was, because he never did these dramatic, saving challenges. Defensively and on the ball, Rio gave off this aura of confidence, arrogance even, and that composure rubbed off on the rest of the team. He was very vocal and let everyone know what he thought of them and what they should be doing. The only player he wouldn't say anything to was Scholes, but nobody said anything to Scholesy. But Wazza was a different story! I couldn't keep count of the times Rio and Wazza screamed at each other from either end of the pitch. Rio was on about Wazza stopping the other team playing from the back. Wazza shouted at Rio, 'Get higher up the pitch. PUSH UP!!' And waved his arms about. It was very entertaining to listen to these verbal volleys flying past and I'd have a little chuckle to myself. Rio and Wayne were good mates, and after the game they might have a little debrief, like a discussion of what each one was doing. That shouting was Rio's way of leading. They'd end up always laughing about it. It was a good sign when they argued. They wound each other up and it was their way of firing themselves up as much as each other. Their will to win was incredible. That wasn't just in games, though, quite often in training too.

Vida was vocal too, especially during that half-time at Wembley, and it was unlike me to bite back. Eventually, the Boss got us together again and said, 'Look, we're in the game. Calm down. It's 1–1. It's all to play for, let's go again, and really press them.' Just as we tried to get going again, Messi scored with a low shot from the edge of the box. You can't give Messi chances like that, to shoot from 20 yards. Messi strikes a ball with very little backlift, which makes it even harder for a keeper to anticipate his intentions. Messi played a part in Barcelona's third goal, which killed the final. Again, we could have avoided it. I blocked the cutback from Messi, gave it to Nani, but Busquets took it off him, and David Villa finished with a brilliant strike. Mistake, *bang*, goal; that's how Barcelona can punish you. I struggle to take any satisfaction from this but I have to state that on 28 May 2011 at Wembley, Barcelona gave the most complete performance I've ever seen. That team of Guardiola's with Xavi, Busquets and Iniesta at their peak in 2011, and Messi sensational, was the best side I ever faced by some distance. I watched the last 13 minutes from the bench when the Boss put Scholesy on, typically trying to get another goalscorer on the pitch but like in Rome it was a slow, painful end.

As I walked up the tunnel, I was met by an official and escorted straight to the little doping control room tucked away in a corridor round the back of the changing rooms. I wasn't allowed to go into ours to see the lads or the Boss. Doping instantly after the game is frustrating. I understand all the reasons why they do it, of course I do, and I agree with testing because football must be kept clean.

However, after a final that you've won and all your teammates are celebrating together then surely you have to be allowed to be part of it? These are the very best moments of your life and to have that taken away doesn't seem right to me. Similarly for me at Wembley, I was stuck in this room, not able to leave after losing one of the biggest games of my life. Again, that is when you should be together as a team. All I had was the doc coming in and out, organising the process to make sure we played by the rules. If you're a sub it's not such a big deal as you're still hydrated so it's a quicker process. If you've played through, the process of producing a sample is painfully slow and I was there ages, sitting and staring into space. It's not a time for chit-chat, the last thing I want is a guy I don't know trying to ask me about the game two minutes after I'd just lost the Champions League final. That was a killer as I sat in silence, stewing and reliving the game over and over in my mind.

I totally get the fight against doping. I'd be very, very surprised if any player of any significance at a good level was trying to get away with taking something. You've got that much chance of getting caught, it's just not worth it. I've never taken any medication unless I've got it off Doc and it's been cleared. It's not worth the risk. I don't take any other supplements or any remedies unless I've got it off Doc. I've never been tested at home but often at Carrington and after games. I got tested six, seven, eight times a year. The testers target certain players who have to constantly give, but I've never been one of them. Some lads were tested relentlessly. It's supposed to be random but it's funny how the same names keep coming out every time. It seems to be the biggest players and target testing.

What frustrates players is the inconsistency. There's the FA, there's UEFA and they've all got different rules with doping control, it's crazy.

Sometimes it's blood, sometimes it's urine, sometimes it's saliva. It depends which agency is doing the doping control. Sometimes you can't go in the changing room, sometimes you can. Sometimes you can have a shower, sometimes you can't.

At Wembley, I was taken straight to doping. When I'd finally supplied the sample, I got on a very quiet coach and went back to the Landmark Hotel. I saw the family at the party afterwards, they came in and had a couple of drinks. They just said, 'Unlucky.' What more could they say? I was a different person after Wembley than I had been after Rome, thankfully, I had learned how to handle it better. I just said to them, 'Do you know what? I've given my best. It wasn't good enough tonight.' I wasn't accepting defeat, I'd never do that, but there was a sense of reality about Wembley and it didn't hurt as much as Rome. We let ourselves down in Rome. We hadn't at Wembley. Barcelona and Messi were simply better.

12

ENGLAND

England, England, England – that's what all football-mad kids dream about, and normally it's something you can never achieve, it's so far away from where you are that it's impossible, or so it seems. My ultimate dream as a kid was to run on to that famous pitch at Wembley in front of a full house and represent my country. Italia '90 was my inspiration. I was hooked watching Gazza and the lads. I had the 19 on my back with the red numbers, I was just a young boy swept along by the hurricane only a World Cup can bring. The whole country was lit up by Bobby Robson and his heroes. I remember thinking, *These weren't ordinary people, they couldn't be. They were footballers playing at a World Cup. Normal people don't get a chance to do that, just imagine what it must feel like?* I'd be out in the garden with Graeme with my Gazza kit on and my Quaser Lineker boots copying every move and getting shouted at for churning up the grass because I had studs on.

Eleven years on and I was one of the lucky few to realise my dream. It was the proudest day of my life. I later went on to play at Wembley in front of a full house and even played in a World Cup. What more could a boy want? Living the dream, right? Well, some of it was the dream but unfortunately some of it wasn't what I'd hoped it would be. I have so many mixed emotions about my time with England. As I've grown older and finished my playing career, I can strip it all back and feel immense pride to have been selected to pull on an England shirt.

I've always felt proud to play for England, I just didn't always enjoy it. It's sad. I wish it was the fairy tale and I could paint a pretty picture, but unfortunately that's not how my story goes.

I never really got to grips with England squad, never felt comfortable. It was always a bit of a struggle. You're probably saying, that's a bit weak, a bit spoilt; get on with it, cheer up, grow up. Believe me, I've told myself all that a thousand times. The more I asked the questions of myself, the worst I felt. I beat myself up for feeling like this and the more I did that the worse the feeling became. I was trapped in a vicious circle. I was battling with myself. I was desperate to play and play well but I never got a run of games. I was in 87 squads and got 34 caps, but only seven were competitive starts.

A lot of it was my fault. I've always questioned myself first before looking elsewhere and maybe criticised myself too much, but that's my nature. There were games when I didn't play well enough but there were also certainly games when I played well and then, *boom*, next game I was sub again. During the tournaments that I've missed, like Euro 2012 and the 2014 World Cup, I've heard people saying, 'We need Michael to play to keep the ball.' However, when I did play, those same people were saying all I do is pass sideways. They demand eye-catching actions and moan when you keep the ball for a spell because 'it's not the English way'. We played in straight lines over the years – 4–4–2 with no fluidity – and found it very difficult to control games in possession. We were outnumbered in midfield and were expected to press to get the ball back. Very basic. 'Play like you do in the Premier League,' people said. I'm sorry, but you can't. It's not as simple as that. We were getting left behind in playing out from the back in possession with the fear of giving the ball away. As soon as we were half-pressed high it was a case of go long, no risk. Other countries see it as 'if we have the ball then you can't score'. 'Careful you don't lose it there' was the message to us, not 'let's dominate on the ball and keep it'. We had a totally different mindset to other countries. That was the English culture, giving us no rhythm so we were constantly fighting against the game, struggling, using up more energy and never being in control. Basically, we were just living in hope.

Fortunately, England's style has changed over the last year or two and I have to admit I'd have liked to have been given a chance in Gareth Southgate's side, but my time was up by then. If only I was a couple of years younger! As you saw in the World Cup in Russia, we now have players in between the lines, they are less rigid, look more relaxed, composed and confident, and are more energy-efficient and able to control a game for longer periods, which is vital to compete with the best. There's an aura about England now. I've admired from a distance what Gareth has achieved with the squad, and the way he has the boys enjoying it. There is a clear happiness shining through the squad which rubs off on everyone else. The spirit seems fantastic. It's such a shame, and it pains me to say it, but I can't say I've been involved in England set-ups with a spirit like they have. If only.

I played twice in the same England side as Gareth in 2001 and could see he was a strong person. As England manager, Gareth has done it his way and ignored all the fuss from press and public to pick this or that player, and that's exactly how it should be. What's the point of being England manager if you're just going to be swayed by public opinion? That strength of mind has been lacking at certain times over the years. As England manager there is enormous scrutiny on you and constant calls for change, the extremes from game to game are huge but that can't and shouldn't influence the manager surely? I've never seen Sir Alex or José pick a team because of that, not a chance!

With England, there has always been a culture of shouting 'PICK HIM' after a player has played three or four good games for their club, then people start saying, 'He deserves it, he's in form.' How can you find a settled team if you chop and change every single squad? It's impossible to make any progress without consistency as a group. I've always looked at how our rugby team do this and to be selected you have to have proven you can play at a high level for months, even a year or two, before you can get in. Then when you get in there is room for ups and downs in form, we all suffer from it, but that then breeds an identity and a spirit to move forward. As a manager, you have to be decisive enough to have a plan and stick to it, tweaking it along the way. This gives players a much better chance of performing over a period of time.

It will be interesting to see how England move forward and what the next campaign brings. After reaching the semi-finals of the World Cup, they've raised the bar and that brings extra pressure. It's also refreshing to see a connection between the squad and the public, which has been sadly lacking for too long. Let's hope it lasts.

My England journey started at Chadwell Heath when I took a step closer to living my dream. It was around 9.30am on Friday, 23 February 2001, when I had a shout from Harry to go into the office. As I went in he was standing with a fax from the FA in his hand. 'Congratulations, Michael, you've been called up to the England squad.' I couldn't ring my family quick enough, what a moment that was telling them the news! I was as proud as I could ever be. It was Sven-Göran Eriksson's first squad as the new manager, the match was a friendly against Spain at Villa Park, and I was in it! I played against Bradford the following day feeling 10 feet tall, the only problem being I slightly felt my hamstring tighten towards the end.

Normally, I'd have been pulled out of the squad, but Harry let me go to meet up. I was picked up by a chauffeur-driven car and taken up to New Hall Hotel near Birmingham where I was met by Michelle Farrer. Michelle had the tough job of keeping all the lads in line and organising everything, making sure we were all on time for meals and meetings, and that we were wearing the correct clothes. She briefly explained the itinerary and where to go.

It felt like walking into the reception of a new school halfway through term, only that my fellow students happened to be some of my idols I'd been watching on TV. I was there with my bags, checking in, staring at them as they walked past – Beckham, Scholes, Owen, Fowler, Campbell. They were superstars. *What was I doing here?* I was very shy back then and I just nodded and said hello, before shuffling away to dinner.

I met Sven, who was polite and welcoming. He didn't say an awful lot really but at least I'd broken the ice. Picking a seat for dinner was daunting, as I was walking into a room full of stars not knowing who usually sat where. I just wanted to get in and out without drawing any attention. Luckily, I had Lamps, Rio and Coley from West Ham to lean on. I got through unscathed and left the next day to go back to West Ham for treatment. I missed the game, but I got a taste of what to expect, if there was to be a next time.

Thankfully, Sven didn't forget me and called me up for the next games, the World Cup qualifiers against Finland and Albania in March. Training with the lads for the first time was a real 'pinch yourself' moment. I was excited, nervous and desperate to do well. It was as if I'd won a competition to come and join in for a day.

The squad at that time was full of big characters and they all had a touch of class. They seemed like real men compared to me. I noticed a clear divide at the dinner tables, a United table with the Class of '92 on, who understandably all never left each other's side. Why would they? They were best mates – Becks, Butty, Scholesy, Phil Neville and usually Gary Neville, but he was injured. The same as the Liverpool lads on their table: Jamie Carragher, Owen, Gerrard, Robbie Fowler and Steve McManaman, who'd moved to Real Madrid.

I studied their every move. What did they eat? How did they behave? What were their attitudes like? I felt a bit out of place and I knew I had to prove myself. Sven gave me my first chance on 25 May in the friendly against Mexico at Pride Park. Sven would have a meeting at the hotel just before we left for the game and always had a small tactics board that he would hold up himself, resting it on a table and against his chest while looking over the top and moving the red or blue markers around the board to show what he expected of us and the opposition. He always kept it very simple and put a lot of trust in the players.

I'll never forget my England debut, it was the proudest day of my life. It's the little things I remember, the police escort with their flashing lights, sitting next to Coley on the bus and the sheer excitement of preparing for what was to come. Coley was more confident than me, more sure of himself and a bit more streetwise. My personality was very different, more reserved and I was a bit unsure of myself back then. Even though I was on my way to play for England I was still awkward in the company I was with on the coach. I didn't feel anywhere near their level yet.

By kick-off I was sitting on the bench and after belting out the National Anthem and seeing the mosaic of the flag of St George behind the goal I had goosebumps. *Was this really happening?* I couldn't help but think of Mam, Dad, Graeme and Lisa in the stand. This was a special night for all our family as well as every coach, teacher and friend who had played any part in helping me get to this point.

Wembley was being rebuilt and the England roadshow was in full swing, travelling to various grounds around the country. It created an extra buzz and made for a better atmosphere at England games as people who wouldn't normally get to see the games came along to support the lads.

I watched the first half, but it was all a bit of a blur. Becks unveiled his Mohican as only Becks can. He had been elevated to superstar status by now but what shone through for me was his hunger to win. Becks trained his nuts off and his attitude was top drawer. He was by far the main man, Sven trusted him and Becks was a huge influence on the squad. He scored a trademark free kick that night. He had a poise when he passed the ball like no one else. I could watch him pass a ball all day long – it was beautiful. Between him and Scholesy they were as good as you could get at picking somebody out over 40/50/60 yards, although they had very different techniques they were both just as effective. Becks was more side on as he struck the ball like a golf shot creating backspin whereas Scholesy would have his toe down and slap the back of the ball as if he was shooting, sending the ball flying like an arrow with no spin on it at all. Scholesy's ankles were solid. I wish I could strike a ball like that, but I couldn't with my weak ankles. They're too stiff and I couldn't dip my toe enough, I had to go more side on. Scholesy scored one of his thunderbolts that night.

As the half-time whistle went I got the nod I was going on, this was it. Coley got the nod too for his debut and we stayed out on the pitch with a few others to warm up for five minutes. I went back to the changing rooms for final instructions on set plays and to finish getting ready, put my shirt on and shin-pads in. That's when it hit me the most. My mind raced. My whole journey flashed before my eyes. As I stood on the touchline ready for the linesman to let me on, I thought about Granddad and hoped he was looking down on me, I knew he'd be proud of me. He was there for me when it all started, I would have loved for him to see me out on the pitch now.

My number went up and that was it, I'd made it: a gangly kid from Wallsend playing for England. I glanced around at the other players, trying to take it in, I was playing alongside Butty. I have very clear images from the game, like getting the ball from the right-hand side, turning out to Chris Powell on the left. It was one of those switches where you get a clap from the crowd. I don't know why, really, it's a nothing pass, but you get applause. I was quickly brought down to earth. Teddy Sheringham had a right pop at me, 'Give me the ball, pass it forward!' Teddy had dropped in, as Teddy does, playing in the 10 role. It's a vivid memory I'll never forget. I raised my hand in apology. It was that extra edge, that level up where those details count. I played quite well, we'd won 4–0, and I left the field hoping it was the first cap of many.

Sven was very consistent with his squad and team selection, maybe too loyal, but I respected him for that. This was the era of the so-called 'Golden Generation'. Regardless of who we were playing or how our lads were playing we all knew what the team would be. We were blessed with some of the best players in the world, all at a good age. One of my frustrations though was that Scholesy was having to play tucked in off the left wing for a spell to fit all these great players into the XI. The genius that he is, that's not Scholesy's game and it would have been great if we could have utilised players better, not necessarily playing them all at once. It's about creating the best team not about the best 11 individuals. What a group of players, though! Sol, Rio, John Terry, Nev, Ashley Cole, Becks, Lamps, Gerrard, Owen, and eventually Wazza. Throw some other lads into the mix, like Coley, Ledley King and Owen Hargreaves, and England should have been unstoppable.

They were a special crop. I say 'they' because I wasn't part of it. I'd loved to have played more. I played against Holland at the start of the next season but didn't play again for four years. I didn't deserve to. I suffered a dip in form mainly because of the groin and pelvic problems I've mentioned, as well as being part of the team at West Ham that got relegated.

I still played for the Under-21s, when I first got to know 'Eggyboff'. It's a game that started at Spurs with their youth team where if someone calls something like 'next person to stand up is Eggyboff', you mustn't do it. If you do, you're Eggyboff and nobody can talk to you. Basic, and childish right? Well, word spread and one day in 2002 when I was in the England Under-21s with David Platt as manager, we were pulling up to the training pitch and someone called 'first one off the coach is Eggyboff'. 'Uh, oh,' was the immediate response of all the players because it was a battle of wits. Who was going to blink first and get off the coach? Nobody did. Two minutes went past, then five flew by and one of the England staff gave us a little 'come on, lads!' Some lads got up to go and walked down the bus but then sat down again at another seat. I'm not proud of this at all. It was so disrespectful but actually it showed the spirit and togetherness in a way that nobody budged. By now, Platty had been standing in the middle of the pitch for 15 minutes. He then came marching on to drag us off. He stood there at the front until every player walked past him.

I eventually managed to get back in the senior squad after I had been at Spurs for a season, and in some ways it meant more than the first time because it had been a tough few years, watching and wondering if my time would ever come again. I was proud to be back in the squad for the tour of America in the summer of 2005 and starting against the USA and Colombia was a massive boost. For a lot of the lads these were meaningless friendlies, not for me, though. This was my big chance. I took it and managed to show Sven I deserved a place in the World Cup squad to go to Germany in 2006.

I was on a high heading to Germany on the back of having my best season and playing by far my best football. I was in a good place. In March I got another chance for 90 minutes and played well against Uruguay in a friendly at Anfield.

The excitement and the anticipation in the build up to the World Cup was unreal, given I'd dreamed of this for so long. Organising hotel rooms and flights for family to come over was all part of the buzz. I was like a kid on Christmas Eve waiting on Santa Claus to deliver his goodies.

We arrived at our base, the Schlosshotel Bühlerhöhe in Baden-Baden, sweating on the fitness of Wazza who was recovering from breaking his foot at the end of April. He was our go-to guy and from watching the Euros in 2004 I could see how England relied on him even then at such a young age. When he played in Portugal he was only 18, but my goodness, what a player! He went into a team full of world stars in 2004 and took over to become the main man. Wazza could do absolutely everything. In full flow he was an awesome sight – so fast, strong, aggressive and with a will to win to match anyone. If you were to clone a footballer, it would be Wazza at that stage. The build-up was all about would he be fit in time, and he went back and forth to England for tests and checks, and Sir Alex was concerned, understandably. Wazza was his player and he had a responsibility to have him ready for the following season at United. He was announced fit and it was a relief to have him back. He wasn't fully ready for a World Cup, as that was impossible in that time frame, but we needed him.

I was there with nothing to lose and everything to gain. I knew I wasn't one of the first-choice starters, but I threw myself into training and was determined to make the most of it. Steve McClaren was a terrific coach and it was all I hoped for. I had fellow Spurs lads Jermaine Jenas and Aaron Lennon alongside me living the dream. I didn't have a care in the world, trained every day like a free spirit and soaked it all up hoping I would get a chance.

The families of the players stayed in Brenners Park, and Lisa was there with my family. I wanted them to soak up the experience. It was a once-in-a-lifetime opportunity. 'I'm just going to enjoy it,' she said. But it was madness. There were photographers outside, reporters inside. Lisa suddenly found herself on the front page of *The Sun*. They were in this bar called Garibaldi's and Lisa was pictured lifting up the World Cup with Neville Neville. Somebody had passed the World Cup to them, and set them up, so it seems. There were these guys who said they were from the hotel, but they took a picture of them and then it all blew up in the media. Perhaps Lisa was a bit naïve, but I can't blame her for it. I saw a few of the pictures and it didn't look good, but they weren't doing any harm. It was blown up by the papers and people say, 'Ah, it's a disgrace. They've taken the players' concentration away.' It didn't take my concentration away. But I think Lisa struggled with it. We were always low-key. I think it helped her understand the scrutiny that came with my world a little more. All of a sudden, they couldn't leave the hotel. It was horrible for them. Lisa, Mam and Dad and Graeme were frightened to enjoy themselves. There were pictures every time they did anything. Lisa went to play tennis one day, and there were photos of that. They had to put screens up around the hotel. It was quite sad, really, because going to the World Cup should have been the best thing in the world for my family.

On the pitch I got my chance. Gary Neville pulled his calf in the group games. Hargreaves slotted in at right back for the round of 16 game against Ecuador in Stuttgart on 25 June, and I got the nod in midfield behind Lamps and Gerrard. It was my first competitive appearance for England, no pressure then. Sven told me the day before and I couldn't wait to tell Mam, Dad, Lisa and Graeme. I was quite calm though, not as crazy and excited as I thought I'd be. I look back at photos and see all my family in the hotel wearing my unused England shirts from the group games, jumping on the beds dancing around their room having a right sing-song. I was hugely proud and excited but I had to keep a lid on it and do my job. It wasn't the same as the euphoria you get down the pub or having a barbeque in the garden with all your mates, watching the game with a few beers. I was distanced from all that. It's an emotional rollercoaster for everyone else but as a player I was cold and calculated. It's not as enjoyable as you might think. Once you win then the elation is extra special but until that point it's like living in a bubble.

There were a few England fans singing in the street outside our hotel in Stuttgart the night before the game and that's when the feelings ramped up. When we were in Baden-Baden stuck on top of a hill in the middle of nowhere, there was no big World Cup buzz. We didn't see anyone, it was a routine of coach to training and back, coach to training and back, and pop down to see the families for an hour or two every three to four days. It's surreal as you know what's going on, and experience it via the news on TV, but you aren't actually part of it constantly. Back home, the fever takes over the whole country, all the flags on cars, draped on houses and hanging out of pubs. The night before the Ecuador game was the first time I felt any of that buzz and hence the sleepless night. My phone started going mental as word spread that I was starting and I was getting messages from all sorts of people from the past, and that's when it hits home the impact the World Cup has on everybody. This shit just got real!

We had the usual meeting with Sven just before we left on the coach to the stadium, nice and calm and quiet with very simple instructions. I was just doing my normal job, nothing different, feeding the lads in front as much as I could while protecting the back four. We arrived at the Gottlieb-Daimler stadium and the usual playlist was playing. All the lads picked one song to play and it was on random, David James was in charge. I chose Byron Stingily 'Get Up (Everybody)', and it ended up being the song we always played last as a little boost before we bounced out of the changing room ready to go. Picking the song was my biggest contribution to the tournament apart from the Ecuador game.

It was roasting out on the pitch, so we warmed up in the shade of the corner to try and conserve some energy. I saw my family in the stand, gave them one quick wave, then that was it. Game face on, I could have been playing anywhere. Singing the anthem was the only time I let myself soak up the occasion, however I wasn't there as a tourist and all I was thinking about was the first few minutes – first pass, first tackle, my positioning, trying to create little pictures in my mind of what I would be facing. All that mattered was that we won. Not about how well we played, just that we won. Thankfully we did as Becks caressed one of his free kicks into the bottom corner and we were through, job done. I felt relief, as there was huge pressure on my shoulders. I played OK but nothing special, and this is where you sample the extremes. All of a sudden on TV Alan Hansen and Alan Shearer said I played well then everyone jumped on it. 'Masterclass', 'Man of the match', ' You can't leave him out now', 'Why has it taken so long for him to play', etc. It was as though I'd saved the world.

I understood Sven not playing me in the quarter-final against Portugal, as much as I was disappointed, Nev was fit and came back in and Owen went into midfield. It was what Sven trusted and I could accept that. I couldn't argue that you need to prove yourself over time and then expect after one game to be in for the biggest game. I'd be contradicting myself but there is a case for taking your chance and I felt I'd done that. Sven walked over as we were about to do the team shape in training the day before the quarter-final and said, 'You're not playing tomorrow, Michael.' Plain and simple. I was gutted.

Wazza was getting back towards full fitness but Ricardo Carvalho was nibbling away at him as you'd expect. During one challenge, Wazza reacted and had a bigger nibble back, standing on his leg, nothing major but enough for Carvalho to roll over and Wayne to get sent off. It was all very reminiscent of Becks against Argentina at France '98. Ronnie gave the Portugal bench a wink as if to say *job done*, and our fans and the press jumped all over it, crucifying him in the weeks and months after. We do love a scapegoat. Ronnie was there to win and you have to understand in the heat of the moment he wasn't bothered if it was Wazza, Rio or anyone else. It gave Portugal a better chance to win. I didn't really have a problem with it. That's sport at the highest level, trying to snatch that extra inch whenever you can.

We were up against it but played very well with 10 men and took it to penalties. Jamie Carragher came on for the last two minutes for Aaron Lennon to be one of the penalty takers. Carra had been the best taker in training for weeks, every time we practised them he never missed. We re-enacted the walk from halfway, trying to replicate the scenario. It's impossible to imitate the pressure but you can hone your technique and mentally prepare. Carra unfortunately missed, as did Gerrard and Lamps who are both up there with the best penalty takers around. There's a huge focus on England and penalties and rightly so for the amount of times we come up short, six times in eight shootouts. Thankfully, Gareth Southgate's side won theirs against Colombia. I'm no expert. I've missed one or two myself, but the fear of missing takes over and it's easy for your mind to wander to *What if?* Negative thoughts creep in and it becomes so much more difficult. I'm lucky enough to have scored when it mattered most in Moscow but I ask myself, 'Why was I at that moment able to compose myself and deal with it and then miss one at Burnley a year later and then against Middlesbrough at Old Trafford in 2015?' The answer having focus, positivity and clarity in my thoughts. I felt more comfortable over the ball in Moscow than I did at Turf Moor.

Back then, there was always an underlying negative feeling surrounding the England team, especially from the outside. The downs were always highlighted and it seemed to me that people took pleasure in homing in on or predicting failure. Then when we did lose or failed to perform there was a mass 'I told you so'. It's a pity the culture was like this, and it definitely affected all the squads I was in, from the managers to the players. We couldn't shake it off. The shirt weighed heavy, and that was obvious for everyone to see. The dressing room was full of winners and yet England were seen as a losing team, who were always coming up short. We struggled to mould a team and create an environment where the players thrived. The culture of happily highlighting underachievement felt to us like people were constantly waiting for England to fail. I was always having to defend myself and the team. With United the press was never spoken about, we didn't care one bit. With England it was there and you could see the effect it had on the whole set-up.

This only got worse when Steve McClaren took over from Sven. Steve was a very good coach and took all the sessions with Sven, so it felt like a natural progression and I thought it was a good appointment at the time. It's a huge transition from coach to manager, particularly in balancing the shift in the friendships and relationships that you've created with the players. Stepping away from the day-to-day interaction and becoming the boss is a whole new ball game.

There were some tough times ahead and I played in Croatia when we lost 2–0 in October 2006, with Paul Robinson conceding a back pass from Gary Neville. I was on the bench when we played against Andorra in Barcelona and the England fans were ruthless, they slaughtered Steve McClaren. I felt for Steve, we were 3–0 up and they were still calling for his head. Steve didn't pick me much and a lot of the time I wasn't even on the bench, but I still wouldn't wish that abuse on anyone. The England manager's job is one of the best jobs in football but facing abuse from your own supporters like that was brutal. This was the most frustrating time in my England career as I was playing some of my best football for United but Alan Smith and Phil Neville were being selected in front of me and they weren't even midfielders really. That's nothing against the lads at all, I have a lot of respect for both of them. Estonia away in June 2007 was one of the low points when I was left in the stand by Steve. I'd just won the league, got to the semi-final of the Champions League and played in the FA Cup final. I wasn't sure what else I could do.

Steve was replaced by Fabio Capello not long after that in 2007. Fabio came in and certainly made an impression. He was a strict, imposing figure. He would push and pull players into positions in training if he wasn't happy with what they were doing. He was very matter of fact. He changed the environment and suddenly it went from being quite relaxed to becoming rigid and serious. He changed the food and cut out all sorts of things, plain pasta with no sauce before a game was now routine as well as no butter with bread. This change of diet didn't make sense to me. We all performed for our clubs week in, week out and looked after ourselves so to change our diet drastically for a few days surely did more harm than good.

Even so, I was hoping under this new manager that I might get more of a chance. It wasn't to be. Again, I was playing in big games for United and winning leagues as well as the Champions League but I still only played in eight of Capello's 42 games. I'm not full of myself and I don't have a big ego, I'm not here trying to tell you I was brilliant and I deserve this or that. Not at all. But I do believe I should have been more involved and could have offered more. I also respected the manager had a job to do and I just had to live with it.

I didn't live with it very well though and I gradually fell out of love with England. I have to admit shamefully to dreading going away with England at that time. When I was away I was desperate to get back to United and the environment I loved. England was suffocating. I felt that I could only breathe freely when I got back to Carrington. Before the 2010 World Cup I'd been going away and not playing, 10-day trips, double-headers, and I was not even close to playing and I hated it. I was a nightmare on the phone to Lisa, just miserable all the time I was away. It was dragging me down. I can understand you reading this and saying, 'You're going away with England, man, cheer up, you're living a dream.' Believe me, I also told myself over and over, 'Pull yourself together, man, this is ridiculous, get on with it!' I just couldn't shake it off. Even when I did play the odd game I still felt the same. It got to the stage where I really didn't want to go to the World Cup in South Africa. Jacey was born on 30 April so leaving him after only a couple of weeks or so only made it worse. I was down and also not in a great place with United, fearing I could be out the door at any minute.

I started against Mexico at Wembley on 24 May but I was terrible and got subbed for Tom Huddlestone. Six days later, I sat on the bench against Japan in Graz thinking there's no way I'm going to get picked to go now. There was Huddlestone, Scott Parker and me vying for the last place as Gareth Barry was first choice with Gerrard and Lamps.

In the past people have tried to create a rivalry between me and Lampard and Gerrard. Why? I never had a rivalry with Scholesy, Fletch or Ando at United. We're playing for the same team, not against each other! I did a press conference with England when I was asked whether I believed I was good enough to play for England. I replied that I'd played in big games and managed to win some trophies so, yes, I felt I was. All I meant was that I thought I was capable of playing at this level. I wasn't comparing myself to Lamps and Gerrard. The next day the headlines read 'Put your medals on the table' as if I were challenging Lamps and Gerrard, saying I had more medals than them. I'd never do that. I respect them too much. It was this sort of classic twisting of quotes that summed up the press culture around England, this taking pleasure in creating negative stories. All I meant was that my experiences would help me. That's the problem with England – everything has to be a drama. If there's not one, then create one. A lot of people say it's wrong, but then love the circus. It was like we were always fighting fires with England.

When we landed back in England from Austria, Capello informed us that we would get a phone call the next day to announce the squad. I went straight up to Newcastle to see Lisa and the kids, who were staying at our apartment. Lisa wasn't in great shape as she was suffering from her back problem that had been caused by the pregnancy. She was struggling to cope with no sleep, a baby and Louise who was two. It was when I saw her that I thought, *I don't want to leave her like this, I can't go to the World Cup.*

When Capello's assistant, Franco Baldini, called, I was ready for him to say, 'Well, I'm sorry…' But he said, 'Congratulations, see you in a couple of days.' I genuinely believed I wouldn't get picked. It was a bizarre feeling. It caught me by surprise. I told Lisa and it was like we'd received some bad news. I know it's madness, right? It was playing in the World Cup for England – an honour, an amazing experience. Even now I can't understand how I got in that squad. I didn't deserve to.

So, I packed my bags and headed off to South Africa. Our hotel in Rustenburg seemed ideal as it had our training pitches on site but it was stuck in the middle of nowhere. There wasn't anywhere to walk to for a change of scenery for an hour or so. There was no escape, mentally. The FA understandably were wary of the circus from Baden-Baden but this was the other end of the scale and it wasn't healthy. It was miles away from a productive environment and it dragged us down, me more than most.

There's an argument for concentrating on the job, and I hear people saying, 'You're only there for a few weeks and surely you can sacrifice yourself for that?' Yes, I agree to a point. The fact is that intense isolation didn't suit us. There was no release. At home there were other things to help us switch off between games and training, like school runs, kids' activities, dinner with friends or just seeing different faces. These all keep you refreshed. In Rustenburg, we went stale.

During one of the first training sessions we lost Rio to injury, which was a big blow, for us and for him. I felt for him as it was going to be his last time at a tournament with England. I felt very detached even from early on in the camp. I tried to give my all but I had nothing to give, there was no spark. I'd spend long days in my room counting down the hours to the next thing on the schedule, whether it was dinner or a meeting. The longer I was there, the deeper I fell into a state of depression. I was so down and had no energy or enthusiasm to do anything. It was a weird time for me. There were some good days, when

I'd be playing snooker with Coley, JT and Ash or managing to get a few holes of golf. We even squeezed in a safari but ended up seeing more photographers than elephants. It doesn't sound that bad when I'm talking about golf, snooker and safari, but believe me it was. 'I just want to come home,' I said to Lisa on the phone. 'I'm really struggling here.'

It should have been the best moment of my career, unfortunately it was the complete opposite. I felt lost and lonely. Looking at the other lads in training I'd think, *He's playing well, he looks happy. I wish I was like him.* At one point, I thought about coming home. I'd never have actually done it, no way, but it was on my mind.

The atmosphere in the camp was terrible and after a disappointing draw with the US we headed to Cape Town to play Algeria. I was sitting on the bench watching one of the worst games I can remember, thinking there's no chance I'll be coming on. It wasn't a nice atmosphere in the stadium either the longer the game went on and it ended up a very boring 0–0 draw.

We stayed in Cape Town for an extra day and enjoyed a rare day off. I couldn't get away quick enough to go and see Mam and Dad who were staying in Camps Bay. We had a bit of lunch and just sat on the balcony on the sea front. I hardly said a word. They knew I wasn't happy but I didn't let on to them how bad I was. I didn't want to spoil their trip.

I knew I wasn't right when, on the way to the Slovenia game, on the coach, I was sitting with my headphones on and I nearly started crying. From nowhere. This wave of emotion hit me. I felt like I could just bawl my eyes out there and then. Quickly I had to pull myself together.

It was a weird camp with stories leaking on a daily basis into the papers. It was a mess. But I just felt detached from all this and detached from the starting XI. One day in the middle of a training session, Fabio called the starting XI plus a couple of extras who had a sniff of playing over to do some team shape and set pieces into the goal at one end. The rest of us were left on the halfway line. Five minutes went past, then 10 and we had nothing to do and no one said a word to us. Peter Crouch, Shaun Wright-Phillips and Stephen Warnock drifted down the other end of the pitch and started messing about with a ball. It was a farce really and we all just started laughing. It was laugh or cry. I sat down on the grass at the edge of the box and watched while the lads were lashing balls at Crouchy who had gone into goal. This went on for about 15 minutes with the lads laughing, shouting, doing overhead kicks, celebrations and all sorts. Becks, who was one of Fabio's coaches, saw what was happening and came over to put some finishing on properly. It summed up how far away we were from the team.

We beat Slovenia and were now into the knockout round of the last 16 with Germany up next in Bloemfontein, it was set to be a huge game full of history. Lamps had a good goal ruled out for not crossing the line when it was clear for everyone to see that it was a perfectly good goal. We never recovered. We were out and heading for home. I finally arrived back to Newcastle and I was wiped out for four days with a virus. Welcome home! During the three weeks I was given off, I headed to Ibiza with the family. One of the best holidays I've ever had and a chance to reboot the system. As they all went into town to watch the final in a bar, I stayed in the house, putting the kids to bed. I couldn't face it. I wanted to get away from football and totally switch off.

When the new season got underway, I sat on the bench at Wembley again against Bulgaria and then in Basel, still with the same feeling of depression I had in South Africa. Towards the end of the season, I pulled out of a couple of squads with injury. I had to confront the problem. I had a chat with David Geiss and told him what I was thinking and how I was feeling. In the early part of the 2011/12 season he spoke to

Adrian Bevington from the FA at a coffee shop in Bishop's Stortford and explained my situation. I didn't even get to speak to Fabio, that's how disengaged I felt.

Fabio then left England in February 2012 and Stuart Pearce took over as caretaker manager for a friendly against Holland. I knew and respected Pearcey from West Ham, and he wanted to involve me in the squad. The Euros were around the corner and the truth is I just couldn't face going away to a tournament again. South Africa had affected me that badly and it had taken me a long time to get over it. Pearcey wanted me to play in the Holland game. I could have gone and played but I took the tough decision to stay away, and it wasn't easy as I was turning down what I had dreamed of as a child. I battled with myself for a few days because I understood exactly what I was giving up on. But I had to make the best decision for myself.

Looking back now, the decision to turn down England still doesn't sit comfortably with me at all but that was my state of mind at the time. Once I made the decision, though, I was different man, I felt a sense of release and relief to be out of it. I didn't let on to Pearcey the extent of my feelings, only a handful of people knew, and I'm sure he couldn't believe it when I told him but he accepted it and we moved on.

Roy Hodgson was appointed to take the squad to the Euros and beyond. Then word came through asking if I would go on standby but again I needed to get away from it all. My focus needed to be on my own well-being.

Coming back from the holidays I was refreshed, and did an interview in which I spoke about how I'd not given up on England. Nev, who was now Roy's assistant, rang me to see how keen I was. I was in a much better place and I was excited at the thought of making up for lost time. 'I don't expect to play every game but as long as I can make a contribution in some way then great,' I told Nev. I started England's next game after the Euros, against Italy in Berne, and loved it, it felt exactly how it should feel to represent your country. I then went on the tour to Rio in 2013 and played against Brazil in the historic Maracanã, as well as being in the side to play Poland at Wembley in a must-win game to qualify for the World Cup. As the season went on, I had the sense that I wouldn't get picked for Brazil. We had a rough year with United and it slipped away. It was Giggsy's last game as United's caretaker manager and we'd just flown back from Southampton. As I was getting into my car at the airport, Roy rang me to tell me that I was on standby. There was nothing for me to say to him apart from wishing him and the boys all the best. Ranting and raving would have been a waste of time. I respected Roy had a decision to make and it must have been a tough phone call for him to make. I was disappointed, but I wouldn't say I was devastated. My England experiences had taken their toll by then and I'd learned to come to terms with it.

My playing style probably counted against me over the years with England. I often heard people talking about being bold and getting on the ball, but when it came to the crunch and teams pressed us a little then it was all about no risk. Playing out from the back into midfield was seen as dangerous. Not any more! Gareth has changed the culture. Over recent years, there's been a change in the style of football we have in the Premier League and I think that's educating more people. It's much more tactical and less gung ho. Counterattacking is still used but now it's a lot more measured and deliberate. Counterattacking can be tough in the heat if you're constantly chasing the ball, especially after the long slog of an English season. I think the winter break will help a little with this, preserving the energy for summer tournaments.

Still, missing out on Brazil hurt. I was enjoying myself under Roy more than I had before. There was a shift in the structure too and Roy brought in psychologist Dr Steve Peters as part of his back-room team. Together, they tried to get players to take more responsibility and have more player-led meetings, encouraging more input and welcoming feedback. I remember standing in the middle of the training pitch at St George's Park a few months before the 2016 Euros in France and Roy said to us all, 'I want you to go away this afternoon and think about how we are going to win the Euros, come back later and tell me because I don't know!' I appreciated what Roy was trying to achieve but I was a little surprised by what he said.

My last cap came against Spain in Alicante in November 2015. Friday 13th – I should have guessed. I limped off towards the end having twisted my ankle after a late challenge on me. I never got picked again. Even after the frustrated journey I'd been on with England, I was so grateful for the opportunity I'd had.

England also made me realise how good we had it at Manchester United, where there was none of the noise, dramas and agendas that I encountered with England. Nevertheless, despite it all, I'm still proud that I was able to realise my childhood dream. I'm one of the lucky few.

13

END OF AN ERA

I've experienced some incredible highs but also some sickening lows. The emotions are extreme but the margins between them are fine. Football can be so brutal and it was for me on Sunday, 13 May 2012 – a day that pains me even now. That Premier League season went right down to the wire, which was thrilling for fans. Everyone remembers the maths: we were level on points with City, but they had the edge on goal difference. We were at Sunderland and City were at home to QPR, so I told myself, 'Ah, there's no chance.' I never thought for one second City would draw. Going into this last game it was all about winning and finishing on a high. Suddenly, we had a chance. We led 1–0 with 20 minutes to go at the Stadium of Light when our fans started cheering. What was going on? Jonny Evans came up and said, 'City are losing!' I learned later that Jamie Mackie had given QPR the lead, so as it stood we were champions for a fifth time in six years. That's not only Manchester United's twentieth league, but that's also two more than Liverpool. But I didn't want to hear anything from the Etihad, I just wanted to focus on our game, so I just zoned out, ignoring it. There's no way City won't win, I told myself. United fans were still celebrating. One minute to go, Sunderland had a goal kick, the clock ran down, and suddenly it hit me fully, *We could win the league here.*

Howard Webb blew the whistle for full-time, and we hung around on the pitch, waiting for news from the Etihad. The very first time I let myself think we had a chance, *boom*, it began to get ripped away.

'City have scored,' Howard said. I didn't really know what was going on. What was the score? Had it finished? Dzeko equalised, apparently, but City still needed a winner and our dream was still alive. Sunderland fans celebrated City's goal loudly. This had nothing to do with Sunderland, but they stayed on in their thousands as the title drama played out. We walked towards the tunnel, where the Boss was standing and Phil Jones was already there, stripped to the waist, listening to somebody's radio. And then it came, the hammer blow.

'City have scored again,' Jones said.

Agüero. City were champions. We now just wanted to get out of the Stadium of Light as fast as possible.

'Clap the fans,' Sir Alex reminded us. Even in this moment of disappointment, the Boss made sure we were dignified. That was class from the Boss. So, we went over to thank our amazing fans, who'd briefly believed the title was ours. Sunderland supporters showed no sympathy or mercy to our misery. They taunted us as we crossed the field, and absolutely loved it that the trophy was snatched away from United at the death.

I wasn't surprised by Sunderland fans' lack of class. Wherever I go with United, I'm always reminded how popular we are and can sense the colossal jealousy others have towards England's biggest club. That's the culture we're in nowadays – people are happy to see someone successful suffer. I guess it was a compliment to United in a way. As Ashley Young and I walked back from our fans, Mick Phelan tried to console us, but it was difficult to hear anything because of the gloating Sunderland fans.

'Who are ya?' they chanted as we trudged towards the tunnel. 'Who are ya?' I glanced back and saw thousands of them in one corner doing the Poznan – the celebration that City took from a Polish club where they jump up and down with their backs to the pitch. They must have looked at themselves afterwards and thought, 'What were we doing? What's it got to do with us?' You'd think they'd won the league. Very strange! Confirmation of the City score came up on the electronic board and the gale of delight from Sunderland fans almost blew us down the tunnel.

In the changing room, it was dead silent, nobody was moving, we were just frozen in frustration. We could have been champions. How fickle was football that a whole season comes down to one touch? On the bus outside the Stadium of Light I fell back sighing in my seat, reflecting on what might have been. The Boss walked up and down the aisle, telling all of us, 'Don't you EVER forget what this feels like.' His emphasis was powerfully on EVER. His message was mainly to the young players because the Boss knew the senior ones were smarting and already counting down to next season. 'Don't you EVER forget what this feels like,' he repeated. 'Let this motivate you to win the league next year.' The Boss didn't go mad, he didn't shout, he just rammed home the message.

We were not only angry at losing out on the title, but also at the crowing of the Sunderland fans. Every time we played Sunderland after that, their joy at our pain in 2012 was remembered. The Boss certainly mentioned it the following December in his team talk before we met them at Old Trafford and again at the Stadium of Light in March. It's not something you forget easily. In the coach on the way home it started to sink in how close we had been but all I could think about was drawing with Everton then losing out to Wigan. We threw it away. I can't shake off that disappointment to this day.

The end to 2011/'12 left a bitter taste also because QPR knew they were safe in the final minutes at the Etihad as Bolton drew with Stoke and couldn't catch QPR in 17th. I'm not saying QPR gave up, but they had their safety net and during injury time when Agüero scored, QPR weren't fighting for their lives. They switched off. If they hadn't, they'd have defended harder against Agüero, and we'd have been champions. You don't forget things like that.

I reflected with some pride that in the six years I'd been at United, I'd won four leagues, and lost one on goal difference and one by a point but events that season hurt. Occasionally, the sports channels show the Agüero goal and I look away. To this day, I've not watched City lift that trophy.

That was a difficult season from the very beginning. I always had one persistent fear, and that was the ruthlessness of Sir Alex. The Boss subbed me off at half-time of the 2011 Community Shield, put Tom Cleverley on and I remember sitting there the second half, going, *It's a bit strong, that. I wonder why he's done that?* Then, Clevs and Ando started the Premier League, and I was thinking, *Is this the changing of the guard? Is this the Boss trying to put the young blood in?* I fought back from sinking into depression. My track record at United was good, really successful actually, and I never gave them any grief. I knew I had to prove myself every day, and fight off the challenge of younger men.

Looking back on my career, I fully see the pattern of my seasons and it gives me insight I hope to use now I'm coaching. Each player is different and some start the season strongly, like Ando, and others, like me, take time to get into their stride. It was often not until September or October that I nailed down a starting place, when my form was sharp, and then I usually maintained it all the way through until May. Some of the delayed starts were due to injuries or niggles but more it was because the Boss said, 'You start playing well when it starts raining.' I thought Sir Alex was joking, and he was to a point, but there was science to his argument. He believed softer pitches suited me. I hear many debates about players' form, and there were plenty about mine, and nobody really thinks it could be to do with the going underfoot. We're like racehorses in a way, and I was better on softer grounds as harder surfaces made my Achilles problems flare up. It sounds a weird excuse, but slow, dry pitches also didn't suit my passing. I preferred them well-watered, so the ball moved faster. It meant my passes got there a fraction quicker and I could pass it from further away and it wouldn't slow down on the grass. If there was a gap, then I could get it through. When it's dry the the ball sits in the grass. These are the fine margins that matter. I liked hitting side-foot through the lines from a distance into the front men and that was easier on a slicker pitch.

I was still easing my way into that season and on the bench at Anfield in October when Luis Suárez made a racist remark to Pat Evra. United were immediately very strong in backing Pat, as we all were, big-time. Abuse like that was absolutely disgusting. We wanted to protect Pat, who was obviously really hurt. Pat was one of us, and we all felt real anger towards Suárez. He got punished for his racism. Banned for eight games. Of course, Suárez's first game back had to be at Old Trafford, and when we lined up, he ignored Pat's handshake. It wasn't a great situation and it could, and should, have been handled better. I shook his hand, yes. Pat knew everyone was behind him and the whole situation didn't need any more fuel on the fire by me snubbing Suárez. We had a game to play and it was not worth intensifying the tension. It kicked off briefly in the tunnel at half-time when Pat sprinted past Suárez, a couple of lads ran towards them, but nothing really happened, just tension spilling over. We won, and that was our way of saying, 'We support you, Pat.'

That season was full of shocks and surprises, and I'll never forget the moment at Carrington before we played City in the Cup when

Scholesy came over to our pitch with a couple of the younger lads from the reserves. Since he'd retired, Scholesy did some work with the reserves, coaching them with Warren Joyce as well as keeping himself fit. Scholesy joining in with our 10 v. 10 created a real buzz. I just thought, *He's making the numbers up just to have a game.* When I got to the Lowry Hotel that night, Scholesy was there. Again, I thought, *Oh, he must be coming to the game to keep an eye on some of the young lads.* He sat on the coaches' table, not where he used to be with us, so I didn't think any more of it. On the bus to the game, Scholesy sat in his old seat. The funny thing about the coach is there was an unwritten rule that we each had our own seat. Scholesy jumped straight back into his as if it was normal procedure. Nobody had taken over his yet. When I got down to the dressing room at the Etihad, I saw the kit man hang Scholesy's shirt on a peg, and he was there, calmly getting changed. What is going on here? Is Scholesy back?! The Boss interrupted our thoughts, 'Oh, Scholesy's on the bench today.' We all started laughing. Wow! One of the true Manchester United greats was back. I thought my days playing with Scholesy were gone! We all got a massive lift. Scholesy was just in the corner, putting his boots on, having a little chuckle. Typical Scholesy, as if he was tipping up for a kickabout with his mates. Coming out the tunnel to warm up, I had to laugh when the United fans saw Scholesy. It was like Christmas for them, especially when the Boss put him on for Nani in the second half.

We won that Cup tie, but to our eternal frustration, City still had the last laugh in the Premier League. Let's not make any bones about it, we messed up with the title within touching distance: 4–2 up against Everton, Pat hit the post, and we drew 4–4, our points had been thrown away. We then went to Wigan where victory would put us eight points clear of City with five games left, one of them at the Etihad. Wigan was a nightmare for me as Albert, the kit man, forgot my special orthotic insoles for my boots. My left leg is slightly longer than the right, so my orthotics are built to balance this out. Albert hadn't transferred my orthotics from my training boots to my match boots. It was a weird feeling to put boots on without my insoles that have a higher arch. Albert forgot Giggsy's insoles as well and kept saying 'Sorry, son' to the pair of us. I'm not using that as an excuse for us losing to Wigan, we just weren't right, and more points thrown away. The Boss was absolutely fuming. He'd prepared us to peak at the end of the season, not to lose against a side struggling to avoid relegation, and throw away an eight-point lead. We'd been so ruthless in recent years come the end of the season. We then lost to City 1–0 and that was game over.

I headed off into the summer still hurting. It was the Euros, I wasn't involved, and I had the longest holiday since I'd turned professional, seven to eight weeks, and that totally refreshed me. United is my life and it's intense, relentless and unforgiving. I love the feeling of dedication and making the sacrifices and always pushing to be better but come the summer holidays it's vital to switch off. I was so selfish during the season. It was frustrating for Lisa because I'd say, 'I'm not coming to that party' or 'I'm not going to your friend's wedding, it gets in the way of my football.' Our whole life was wrapped around me and my football, something I feel guilty about now actually. Sitting at home or playing with the kids, I was thinking about having to perform at my best either the next day at training or the next game or two coming up. I couldn't help it. I always had a routine and a plan. Yoga, Monday and Thursday. Core – upper body. Legs – strength, power. Runs – what did I need to top up? Speed? Endurance?

If someone rang or texted me on the day of the game, I'd think, *Are you taking the piss? That's disrespectful. What are you texting at 4pm for?*

I'm playing at 8pm. Do you not realise I've got a game? Why are you bothering us now? I'd text Lisa at 1pm, 'I'm going for a lie-down now. Don't ring me. I'll see you after the game.' You might think it's an obsession and, yes, it is. When the season's done and the summer comes, Lisa says, 'I've got Michael back.' I'll have a right blow-out in the summer and in those few weeks, I am a different person. 'Fun-time Michael', Lisa calls it. I restrict myself so much through the season, not drinking, sleeping long, and training hard that at some point something has to give and I need my release. A couple of nights a year the lads come down from Newcastle and we'll have a few beers. You'd go mad if you didn't have a release. Food-wise, I'm sensible. I don't eat fast food and rarely drink. I've got a sweet tooth. If you offered me a glass of wine, beer or champagne or ice cream, I'd go for the ice cream all day long. Sometimes Lisa will sit and have a glass of wine, while I'll be eating my Dairy Milk and Galaxy.

This obsession of mine doesn't just affect me, it massively impacts on Lisa, Lou and Jace. In June, I'm free and this time is so special, quality time around the pool or on the beach, and I'm there for them. Only when I'm on holiday do I look back at how much football takes its toll mentally and physically. At times, I need to take a step back and think about other people, the people most important to me, my family. At home, it can be difficult to go out with the kids. It can be relentless with people asking for autographs. If I'm with the kids or we're eating, I want some peace. But then I see what Louise and Jacey are like when we go to the wrestling, and they see the wrestlers and it's, like, 'Oh my God, it's the best thing ever!' They want autographs and pictures, so I get that. But people can be rude. Quite often they come over, and go, 'Carrick, sign this.' So, I say, 'Any chance of saying "please"?' And they look at me as if I've got two heads. Louise has said a good few times, 'Dad, I can't wait until you retire, so people don't bother you.' That gets me a little bit. She used to love going to the Trafford Centre. Once, I took her shopping to River Island for a little time out, quality time together, but she ended up standing there a lot of the time while I was signing autographs. Another day, I said, 'Do you want to go to the Trafford Centre, and we'll get you some bits and stuff?' She went, 'Oh, no, Dad, I don't want to because you just get bothered and I don't really see you.' It's sad and made me feel so guilty.

First thing we did that summer was go to Barbados with all our family – Lisa's parents, her brother Glen and Jasmine, his wife-to-be, and my mam and dad, Graeme and Kay. For the first time in a long while, I could leave my phone in the room and enjoy what the day brought with Lisa and the kids. It's so rare and beautiful having that freedom, waking and deciding where I wanted to go that day, what I wanted to do. I know how lucky I am, but football's so regimented. From 1 July until the end of May, my life belonged to Manchester United, and still does. I love United but it's good not being under orders for a week or two, just belonging to Lisa, Lou and Jacey again. That summer was magical. After two weeks in Barbados of doing nothing I've got to admit I started getting twitchy as I always do. *Get me in the gym, get me working out now.* I always stay fit even when I'm not in formal training.

After Barbados, Lisa and I went to Ibiza, getting the boat across to Formentera and having a bit of lunch there. Just us, perfect. We had Jacey's christening back in Newcastle. Over the rest of the summer, I went to Grands Prix and weddings, and returned to Carrington *thinking, That's me fully refreshed. I can't wait to go again.* I was ready. I had reached that stage in my career where I naturally took more responsibility, and was feeling at my peak. My Achilles held up, and the scenes at Sunderland stayed with me. 'We're not letting that happen again,' I kept telling myself as we started the season.

I was fascinated by who the Boss would buy. He signed Robin van Persie and that intrigued me as Robin wasn't a typical Sir Alex signing in age or cost. The Boss paid a lot of money for a ready-made player in Robin, which he rarely did, but I never suspected that meant the Boss was thinking short-term because he was considering leaving. A big signing like Robin gave everyone a lift. Robin was a hell of a finisher with that Dutch single-mindedness, but he fitted in really well and totally embraced Manchester United. He understood the tradition of the club and the strong characters in that squad helped him settle in. The first training session, we looked at Robin as if to say, 'All right, what are you going to bring us?' His first touch was so good, we knew he'd do. I recall being 1–0 down against Fulham when Robin popped up with a fabulous volley that lit the place up, and he then scored a hat-trick against South-ampton, bagging two of the goals really late on. I remember thinking, *He'd definitely do for us.* The Boss also signed Shinji Kagawa, the Bundes-sliga Player of the Year, and I remember the first week of pre-season watching Shinji and listening to Scholesy saying, 'He's a player, him.' That's the ultimate seal of approval if Scholesy rates you. Shinji was a gifted footballer, always wanting the ball and happy to be a link man, it was a shame he didn't really fulfil his expectations with us.

At United, the very best players were not only driven but also incred-ibly original, almost revolutionary, in their thinking. One incident that season particularly stood out for me. Picture the scene: 0–0 just before half-time at Anfield on 23 September 2012, Giggsy gets the ball and runs down the left wing, targeting Martin Kelly, the 22-year-old playing right back for Liverpool. Giggsy turns back, and I'm there, in space, for the pass, it's made for me, so I scream, 'Giggsy!' He turns back again. 'Giggsy! Yes! Giggsy! Any chance?' I shout again. He keeps turning, short and sharp, chopping again and again, constantly moving the ball, taking Kelly one way and the other, but not passing. 'For fuck's sake, Giggsy!' Chop, chop, chop, get to the byeline, chop again, and he ends up getting a corner. United fans are going, 'Fucking cross it.' The ref blows for half-time after the corner and as we go to the tunnel, I say, 'Giggsy?!' He smiles, gives me a little pat on the back and goes, 'His thighs will be burning. His legs have gone now.' 'Fucking hell, so that's what you're doing it for.' Genius! Giggsy never let Kelly settle. He kept him on the move constantly, threatening inside, outside, coming short, going long. For big lads it was tough to keep quickly changing direction. Giggsy was more direct against smaller full backs. He'd hug the touchline and go straight at them. The variety Giggsy had in his game was outrageous. He didn't just play his own game, doing what he wanted to do, he did what he *needed* to do – there's a big difference. He put so much thought behind it, his football intelligence was amazing. Giggsy was like a boxer, wearing an opponent out. He inflicted the same treatment on Micah Richards at City. Bearing in mind Micah could outrun him and bench-press him in the air if he wanted to, Giggsy tired him out with small movements, jinking away. No one watching the game would know what he was up to. He would get his joy later on. He slotted Michael Owen in for the winner against City at Old Trafford in the sixth minute of stoppage time in September 2009 when Micah should have been there, tracking Owen's run but he was finished. When I spoke about it with people at United, they mentioned how Solskjaer played right wing against Arsenal at Highbury and tore Ashley Cole to bits. Solskjaer kept moving Ash inside, then outside, taking him out of his comfort zone. Sir Alex always gathered players who thought deeply about the game.

We hunted the title again, as we always did under Sir Alex, and one game that really sticks out in my memory was Newcastle on Boxing Day 2012. It was an absolute battle on a bog of a pitch at Old Trafford, it was a real storm and rained non-stop, making it even more of a crazy game. In a way, it was a classic Sir Alex match as we kept fighting, coming from behind three times, I assisted Robin's equaliser for 3–3, and then we went for Newcastle even more. The seconds were running out when Rio Ferdinand slipped me the ball. I wasn't as good as Giggs, Scholes or Rooney at winning a game late on but this was a slow-motion, clear-as-day moment for me. *That's what these great players must feel all the time*, I thought. I took a little look up and saw Chicharito on the move, and knew this was it – our one chance of victory. *We always get one chance.* I lifted the ball in, Chicha slid in and it was mayhem. He jumped into my arms, the Boss hugged Mick and gave high fives to fans by the dugout as everybody celebrated us going seven points clear.

I look back on that Newcastle match and see it as testament to how I'd matured into this player, who was happy to lead more. United fans also embraced me fully and 23 February 2013 at Loftus Road is a day I'll never forget as I became aware of them singing, 'It's Carrick, you know; It's hard to believe it's not Scholes.' I'm not exaggerating, for 25 minutes they sang my song – and it meant so much to me. Apparently, the song was around a while – Pete Boyle, a diehard Red, came up with it – but that QPR game was a big moment for me. We were in control, the game was dying and the whole end was singing my name. Loftus Road's a small, tight ground and the song was really clear to hear. It had a huge effect on me, giving me extra energy and confidence. Nothing was really sung about me before, not like this, so to go to this extreme was like, *Whoa, this is nice!* Fair play to the fans for coming up with that. Not a lot rhymes with Carrick! I didn't acknowledge the fans during the game but, at the end, I gave them a little clap of appreciation. I always do, but it felt even more personal and special at Loftus Road that day. I'm not one for googling myself, but I did go on social media that night and saw a load of videos going round of fans singing that song even after the game, down the back stairs and out into the street.

The Stretford End sang my song after Loftus Road and it took off. Even now, people come up to me and say, 'I was at QPR that day, and everyone was singing.' I thank them because it meant so much that day, and still does. Until Loftus Road, I often felt that players appreciated me more than supporters. That didn't bother me, but this was special. The fact that it was away fans singing made it even more special. That's the greatest compliment you can be paid when 4,000 people are singing your name away from home. I hear them singing about Cantona, Butty, Wes, Scholesy and Georgie Best. Sheasy's song is a classic. So, hearing my name in there was incredible. United's away fans feel they're defending their club, and they'll start reeling off all the old songs. It's like they're showing pride that this is what we've achieved, this is the history we've got, and look who's played for us. There's pride in making a noise, creating an impression, and saying, 'We are here, in your front room and we're louder than you.' I know the sacrifices they've made in time and money to get there. That's true dedication. I've noticed our away fans stand the whole game, and that attracts a different type of person. The fan who wants a nice, comfortable afternoon out does not necessarily want to go with away fans and stand for 90 minutes, and might not want that more raucous atmosphere. United's away fans are the best, real hardcore. Sometimes, we forget that Manchester United takes over people's lives, and it's madness really but that's the beauty of it. Manchester United is a religion to millions. I find it quite scary to think I wasn't just going out to win a game of football, but I was actually representing these people's lives. I understand that to some people United simply means everything.

As that season went on, questions were asked about Sir Alex leaving but they were asked every year and I never thought there was much to it. With hindsight, I guess when David Gill announced in February that he was standing down in June that really posed the question about Sir Alex. David had worked so closely with the Boss for a decade, and I always felt one was the left arm and the other the right. They were on the same wavelength, and I saw how much that brought stability and calmness to Old Trafford. If David got on the bus after an away game, you'd hear the Boss on the table behind us hammering David about the refs, 'David, we should be doing something about these refs.' David was on the board of the FA who were in charge of refs. David had a skilful way of dealing with the Boss in situations like this. David would sit there, taking in all the Boss's complaints, listen patiently and then go, 'Right, Alex, that's enough.' It wasn't in a bad way, it was just David saying he'd heard the Boss's point and it was time to drop the subject. The huge respect they had for each other was obvious. I watched David with Sir Alex and felt he was probably the only one who could keep the Boss in hand. David had this aura that commanded respect from everybody and he always seemed calmly in charge. He'd come in the changing room after a win, draw or loss and be exactly the same, chatting to the back-room staff, asking after their families, just being a decent guy. David still comes in now, has a chat, and says, 'How are you doing?' I've always found him easy to talk to. He'll have a laugh and a joke, shake everyone's hand and make a few comments on the game. He'd never intrude, really. I'd be sitting there, taking off my boots, look up and there was this man with great presence. David was an authority figure but very likeable with it. He did things with a touch of class, whether it was small talk after a game or sorting out contracts and, most importantly, he loved United with the passion of a fan.

Even with David's announcement, I still had no inkling of the Boss's plans. I've looked back, searching for any clues at the time, and I probably should have read more into the Boss's reaction to going out of the Champions League to Real Madrid in March. I mean, Nani getting sent off at Old Trafford wrecked our chances. 1–0 up, second leg and cruising, then Nani collides with Álvaro Arbeloa and catches him with a raised boot. Nani's not looking at him, and everybody can see it's a pure accident except the ref, Cüneyt Çakir, who unbelievably brings out a red card. OK, a yellow, fair enough, but come on, mate! Red? It killed us. We felt we had a sniff of going all the way again and defeat hit the Boss really hard. Champions League was the one he was desperate for, and he was raging on the touchline. Normally after a loss like that, it's silent in the dressing room, but the Boss was still on about the decision and he was so angry he didn't do the press afterwards. Sir Alex must have known his last shot at the Champions League had gone.

I don't pay much attention to refs usually. They're doing their job. But Pierluigi Collina stood out as an iconic referee, a big presence. I remember the picture of him going head to head with Tomás Repka when Collina refereed the Czech Republic against Holland at Euro 2000. The veins were bulging in Collina's neck and his eyes were staring. He almost played up to that image as well. I know Mark Clattenburg from the north-east. He refereed me in local cup finals when I was growing up. He was young, only six years older than me. He was a good ref, had a dip, then came back. You could talk to Mark. But what I really can't stand is when you try and talk to a ref and he's just dismissive, almost rude like a schoolmaster. Generally, I'm going up to them because something's happened. If the ball's gone out, and there's a goal kick, I'll jog slowly over to the ref. I'll go up and say, calmly, 'Oh, by the way, how did you not see that?' But some refs don't want to know. Surely there's got to be a little bit of a conversation. 'No. Go away. Get out of my face.' 'I'm just trying to understand why you're not…' 'No! Go away!' They wave you away, and there's a barrier straightaway and that bugs me. I'm not saying the ref has to explain every decision, but some communication would be good. I'm just trying to understand the rationale behind their decision. Some will have a chat but others don't give you the time of day. Back at Old Trafford that day, Çakir wouldn't listen – Nani was off and we were out.

We still had the Premier League to fight for, and I took consolation and pride from playing the best football of my career. I was pleasantly surprised on hearing I'd been shortlisted for PFA Player of the Year on 19 April. The award was voted for by the players, and the others short-listed were Robin van Persie, Luis Suárez, Eden Hazard, Juan Mata and the eventual winner, Gareth Bale. It was a tough list to get on. Winning United's Players' Player of the Year that season was one of my proudest moments. To fight alongside the boys all season and for them to then award me the honour of their own choice, well, I could die happy! Trust and respect from my teammates meant the world. You can't kid your teammates, they see everything. But what I cared about most was winning, and Robin's hat-trick against Villa in April brought us the title, my fifth. Even now, just thinking of Robin's second goal, an unbelievable volley, takes my breath away. It was just perfection. The ball from Rooney was right on Robin's toe. Everything about it was special – the delivery, the finish, *bang*, it was just a hell of a goal and the keeper Brad Guzan couldn't do anything. Robin had that swagger and belief that marks out top players.

Six days later, Arsenal fans hurled abuse at Robin when we went to the Emirates but he wasn't bothered, and we didn't care. I wouldn't say we were at our best physically, and I wasn't exactly feeling my freshest, because we played on the Monday night against Villa, went straight into town and had three days celebrating the league. It was a weird one, that, as I had this very strong feeling that we were marking the end of an era as well as celebrating a title. Even though we didn't know the Boss's intentions yet, I sensed a curtain falling on a long-running show and some instinct made me soak the moment up and enjoy it as much as possible. Scholesy was finishing for good, and that added to the sense that it was a time for goodbyes. As we had a few drinks after the title, I looked at all my United mates, and just understood, *Actually, this is not going to last forever.*

I tried to shake off my foreboding that something was coming to an end when we had our golf day at Dunham Forest, near Altrincham, on Tuesday, 7 May 2013. The day followed the Ryder Cup format, players v. staff, 12 v. 12, there were 18 holes in the morning then nine in the afternoon with all the shots and slices shown on MUTV. I noticed as we teed off that Sir Alex wasn't there but then that wasn't unusual. He had so much to do, so I just focused on enjoying the day, well, until 7pm anyway. Somehow, as we walked back to the clubhouse, news started filtering out that the Boss was leaving. I didn't really believe it or didn't want to believe it. Some of the lads were trying to work out if it was true. None of us knew but I drove home hoping it was a big mistake. *Surely, he can't be, can he??* I flicked on the TV and there it was magnified, 'BREAKING NEWS' and 'Sources saying Sir Alex is leaving'. The leak was disappointing but the news was devastating. Sir Alex meant so much to us. There'd been no hint of anything in his demeanour. I racked my brain to think if I'd missed something but, no, the Boss looked fit, healthy and hungry. His anger at going out of the Champions League seemed to show how much he wanted to win it again. I didn't understand.

I got in early to Carrington the next day, and found many of the other players already there, reading the newspapers. It was all over the papers, saying Sir Alex was leaving. Was leaving, was leaving, those words thumped through my head. It must be true, then. The Boss was already in the building, but we didn't see him until we all got called into a meeting in our changing room for 9.45am.

The Boss walked in and it's strange the things you remember, like exactly what he wore. Sir Alex was really casual, just a polo shirt, chinos, loafers and some bright socks. It was like he was dressed for going away on holiday. I was thinking, *Where did you get those socks from, Boss?* They were almost luminous. It sounds trivial but I knew how important this meeting was, so I took in every detail. The Boss began speaking and became quite emotional.

'Look, boys, I didn't want to do it this way. I wanted yous to be the first to know. I'm really disappointed how it's come out. I really did want to be telling you first, but I've been forced to tell you now because it's come out last night. Someone's leaked it.' He was fuming about that. There couldn't have been many people who knew. Sir Alex went on, 'Look, boys, this is not something I've taken lightly.' He mentioned Lady Cathy's sister passing away. 'I feel that I owe it to my wife to be with her and look after her. It's been unbelievable and thanks for everything, I've loved every minute. I don't really want to go, but I've got to take this decision.' You could see it was hard for him to finally say, 'This is it, boys.'

Sitting there was such a weird feeling, hearing all these things that were going to change my life. This was a huge moment in the history of football. Everyone was silent. Everyone was in shock. It wasn't a time for anybody else to speak. Nobody talked, just Sir Alex. This was a man for whom words came so easily, whose team talks were like verbal fireworks that lit up your imagination and yet he struggled to find the words to say goodbye. This was a great man, as tough as they come, and here he was leaving the club he loves and players who were like sons to him. He finally said, 'Look, lads, I'll be supporting you. I'll be your biggest supporter. I'll come to as many games as I can, but I'll never come in the changing room or round the tunnel because it's not fair on the new manager.' He paused and added, 'I've known some of you a long time, some of you not so long. Thanks for everything.' With that, Sir Alex walked out the room and a door closed on Manchester United's greatest era.

None of us moved for what seemed like ages but was probably only 50–60 seconds. Nobody said a word. It felt like a minute's silence, almost a period of mourning which it was in a way. It was as though someone had told us of a death in the family. We were rooted to the spot. The first to react was Giggsy, who was sitting next to me. I watched Giggsy stand up and just head off to the bikes to get warmed up for training. Giggsy was the longest-serving player, a club legend who set the tone and he was always the man who thought about Manchester United and the team and the right way forward. Giggsy stayed silent but he got on with the day. We all slowly followed him, wandering down the corridor like a string of zombies. The world turned, life went on, it was time for training, but the silence persisted. Even as we headed back to work, nobody uttered a word, because that was the shock we all felt and the respect we had for Sir Alex. My mind was all over the place, leaping from one thought to another and from one memory to another – all the amazing events and trophies I'd shared with the Boss. I understood his reasons for retiring, of course, but I worried what it meant. I could see the huge significance for Manchester United and he told us just before the club made the announcement to the Stock Exchange at 10am. 'The consequences of this are huge,' I said to myself as I worked on the bike. Scholesy was retiring for good which was a big enough loss. The leader who everybody at the club looked to for guidance, the man who brought me to United, who led me to five titles and the Champions League was leaving too. I was a ghost as I drifted through training, on the bikes, then outside, into the famous boxes, which were a subdued affair, and on to a bit of preparation before the game with Swansea on Sunday. After training, we all went to Chester races. The Boss had a horse running but he didn't turn up as he continued saying his goodbyes at Carrington. Cameras followed us everywhere at Chester. It was a good job some of the guys had upgraded and bought some new suits. Looking at the pictures, there's some that wished they had!

The rest of the week was about getting ready for the Swansea game, Sir Alex's last at Old Trafford. It was a strange mood as on one hand we looked forward to collecting the trophy and on the other it would be one of the biggest goodbyes of all time. The night before Sir Alex's last game at Old Trafford, we met at the ground and got on the coach to the Lowry. Wigan were playing City in the FA Cup final and the game was on TV. When you started driving the bus the TV reception was rubbish, so we shut the door and sat and watched the last 10–15 minutes of the game in the car park. Ben Watson scored for Wigan in the last minute and the bus went mental, with all of us jumping up and down, banging on the windows. It was just mad! It was just because it was City, it was a last-minute goal and we're all watching it together that we celebrated crazily. Fifty United fans were standing outside, staring at us, thinking, *What's going on on that bus?!* The next day, that crazy Watford v. Leicester Championship semi-final play-off was on in the changing room as we got ready to take on Swansea. We were screaming and shouting as we watched it, and the noise kept building as Manuel Almunia saved Anthony Knockaert's penalty for Leiccster, more cheering, then quiet, there was the Watford counterattack and the lads were going 'hang on, hang on' and then Troy Deeney scored, and we just totally lost it. It was bizarre. It had nothing to do with us whatsoever. After we'd calmed down, I waited for the Boss to announce the team, almost pleading to myself, *Please, Boss, just let me play with Scholesy one more time.* It sounds almost pathetic, doesn't it? I was so happy when he started us!

His team talk was normal, really, with his message being 'business as usual'. The emotion inside Old Trafford was, as you'd expect, absolutely incredible. Everyone in the stadium felt privileged to be there to witness such a historic occasion. Fans waved 70,000 red flags and the speakers played two of Sir Alex's favourite songs, Frank Sinatra's 'My Way' and Nat King Cole's 'Unforgettable'. What perfect choices! We formed a Guard of Honour for Sir Alex and as he walked out, he was greeted by the stadium announcer Alan Keegan with, 'The man who made the impossible dream possible.' That summed the Boss up. When he took over, no one could've predicted what he went on to do. I looked up and saw two numbers on the scoreboard: 26, 38. We all knew what they meant: 26 years, 38 trophies. I felt it was equally fitting that the Boss's final game at Old Trafford should also be memorable for him collecting the league trophy, his thirteenth, with a winner from Rio Ferdinand late on. Sir Alex couldn't have scripted it better himself.

For me, well, I spent most of the game passing to Scholesy until he went off. And perhaps the greatest tribute to the Boss was that we'd bounced back from the Stadium of Light and honoured his demand of 'don't you EVER forget what this feels like'. We'd not let the Boss down. Sir Alex took the microphone afterwards and delivered one of his epic speeches. I don't think he ever really prepared a speech. He was just a natural orator and effortlessly commanded his audience. I encountered his verbal powers from the very start of my time at United, when we'd do a dinner and he had to say a few words. I always respected how the Boss would get up there and deliver his speech with such presence, and it would just be on point. Even UNICEF dinners, he'd get up there and speak about the charity, the kids and the importance of raising money. No notes, just him talking. Sir Alex always struck me as so much more than just a football manager. He was a great man, a leader, and he'd stand up and deliver a speech and have everyone on a bit of string. People followed him and bought into everything he said. It was amazing to see. We were like that when he spoke to us; we'd run through brick walls for him. He created a culture where each and every player wanted to please him, didn't want to let him down, and that's very hard to come by now with egos and a squad of world stars. That's the mark of how much respect we had for the Boss.

With that final speech at Old Trafford, we felt even more how Sir Alex loved the players and loved Manchester United. It was like how he told the fans, 'You've stood by me, now it's time to stand by the next manager.' He didn't strike me as that emotional that day. The Boss looked more content to me, just satisfied that he'd gone out on a high, and it was as if he were thinking, *It's time*. The Boss achieved far more than he set out to do, all that stuff about 'knocking Liverpool off their f***ing perch'. He'd done that. He'd overtaken Liverpool's 19 titles. He deserved to finish on top. For me, it was special that Louise and Jacey were old enough to come on the pitch for the lap of honour so they could understand some of what was going on. I also felt proud that I'd played such a big part in winning the league, and that I'd played my best for the Boss.

Before our final game of the season at West Brom, Sir Alex called me into his office. 'Thanks for everything,' he said. We chatted about coaching and managing, and he asked, 'What do you want to do?'

'I wouldn't mind going into coaching.'

'When you do, make sure you take a step back, observe people, don't be stuck in the middle where you miss anything.'

He just offered me a few bits of genuine advice. It wasn't an emotional farewell, no tears or hugs, but it was clear to both of us how much our working relationship had meant. It was all about respect. Our respect for each other didn't need putting into words. There was a very British handshake as I got up to leave. 'Thanks for everything and good luck in the future,' Sir Alex said. 'Stay in touch.'

The night before his last game at The Hawthorns, we had a special meal at the Hyatt in Birmingham and there was a presentation to the Boss. Me and Rio know the watch-dealer Tom Bolt, who found us this watch from 1941, the year Sir Alex was born. So, we presented it to the Boss with an album of photographs of his career from the players. Rio made the presentation and the Boss was speechless, for once. I'd never seen him not know what to do or say. He was always this figure of invincibility and yet, for a brief moment, we glimpsed a more sensitive side to the Boss. He was genuinely touched by the watch and the book. They weren't the grandest gifts but it was the respect attached to them that moved Sir Alex. It was just us, his grateful players, saying thanks to the Boss. He thanked us, but was otherwise lost for words.

We then had that crazy send-off for him at West Brom. Sir Alex made me captain, and I was bowled over by the honour of leading United out in the Boss's last game. I've still got the armband. His final team talk was about working hard. The Boss was full-on right to the end of his time as manager of Manchester United. Even at 71, for that last game against West Brom, he could instil fear in lads aged 20, 30. He never lost that incredible fire from that working man's upbringing, that ethos of graft for everything you can get, and then work harder. It would have been nice to have won the Boss's last game 5–4 but 5–5 was fitting in a way, as a crazy scoreline was one of those 'football, bloody hell' moments that Sir Alex made famous.

We drove back up the M6 to Carrington and there was Jonny Evans, me, Giggsy and Tony Strudwick around the table. It was Sunday evening, not even 7pm, and somebody went, 'Do you fancy going out for a beer?'

I went, 'one hundred per cent.' Then I shouted to Scholesy, 'Come on, Scholesy. You having it?'

'Go on, then,' Scholesy said.

'Yes, yes. I'll come,' Rio said. Strudders, Mike the chef, Mick Phelan and Simon Wells, the analyst, were up for it too. Somebody suggested the Barton Arms in Worsley so we left our cars at Carrington and all piled into Giggsy's car because he lives in Worsley. I ended up squashed in the boot. There were probably too many in the car but it wasn't far to the Barton Arms. We had a few beers there, and then went into town for a last night out with Scholesy, having a drink and soaking it all in, the whole season and his wonderful career. Scholesy was packing up, the Boss was retiring and that was Mick's last day as well so the evening felt like the Last Supper, just with a few beers.

We didn't have any presentation for Scholesy. He wouldn't have wanted anything like that. The next day we had the parade, and there had been plenty of time to plan it as we'd won the league two weeks before. We met at Old Trafford, boarded the bus and all the families gathered to watch us leave. We were on the bus for two hours getting into town, going that slow from Old Trafford all the way along the dual carriageway and up into Deansgate. My voice had gone by the time we got on to Deansgate, because I'd been singing at the top of my voice all the way – it was one of the best experiences of my life. The turnout was out of this world. I had my video camera tied round my neck as well as my phone, so I could capture the moment. Turning down Deansgate, it blew me away. There was a building on Deansgate, maybe five, six storeys high, with scaffolding on the front. The builders put a sheet across it as protection but somebody pulled that down and every level of the scaffolding was crammed with people cheering us and I filmed it. God knows how no one fell off. I saw them clinging to scaffolding with one hand and waving to us with the other. They were going mad. It was mind-blowing, and just reminded me again of Manchester United's emotional impact on people's lives. Turning into Albert Square was a sight I'll never forget. It was rammed and the Courteneers were playing on the stage, the noise levels were insane and they must have been waiting ages for us to turn up. Every single one of us on that bus just couldn't believe what was in front of us. This party made up for no parade after Moscow!

We stood on the stage and started bouncing. We didn't want to leave but were told we better as it was almost falling down. In the end, some players left and the staff said their goodbyes from the town hall. Some of us didn't want the night to end and we went to Rosso, Rio's place, to carry on the party. When I'm out, I'm out and can't leave a party early. I'm either not in or all in, and this was a time for going all in – the last big hurrah before trying to do it all again the next season.

14

DAVID MOYES

Sir Alex left a legacy we had to carry on and we owed it to the Boss to continue the success with David Moyes. Even though he wasn't our manager any more, I still wanted to make Sir Alex proud of us. I was desperate to make it work and knew it was a huge responsibility. David was United's new manager, and deserved our respect, but making it work with him was also motivated by respect for Sir Alex. I saw how other clubs dealt with managerial changes and they lacked dignity. We're Manchester United, I'd like to think we have class and we behave with integrity. And that meant greeting David Moyes with enthusiasm and a resolve to give everything for him.

I got on fine with David, never had a bad word with him, never fell out with him. He arrived full of energy and ideas for how to improve us. I remember at one of his first meetings, David said to us, 'I believe I can make you better. I know you won the league last year and I've obviously been watching you. I can make you run more.' Being fair to David, he was looking for a chink, like what needed improving and where we were weak, so that he could take us to another level. I just think what he said didn't come across the right way. We'd just won the Premier League by 11 points, scored 11 goals more than anybody else, and won a lot of games well, with scores like 3–0, 4–0. Our running stats were never that big anyway but we came from behind to claim 29 points that season so we must have been fairly fit, as well as committed. Our capacity for late goals under Sir Alex showed our endurance physically as well as mentally. David was right that in terms of 'distance covered' we weren't one of the top sides in the Premier League. But if you look back over the years, all the good years, teams might come to Old Trafford and run a lot more than us, but quite often we ended up winning 2–0, 3–0 or 4–0. Under Sir Alex, we were very efficient with the ball.

It can't have been easy for David Moyes coming into Carrington where there were so many unwritten rules that had been there for years dictating how everything was done, how to behave, timings, and how you were expected to play. We had to get used to new faces at Carrington. We lost Mick Phelan, Eric Steele and René Meulensteen; in came Steve Round, Chris Woods, Jimmy Lumsden and Phil Neville. We lost good friends and experience. David did appoint Giggsy as player-coach, but it still felt like Giggsy was more of a player. He still got changed next to me and never really went over to being a proper full-on coach until he'd actually finished playing. I was surprised David let Mick leave, he didn't need him to tell him how to do the job, just to guide him and to bounce ideas off. This is not me being disrespectful to David, a manager I admire, I just felt it would have been a good idea to have somebody in the background to lean on at times and get advice from. Being manager of Manchester United is a daunting job with so much to stay on top of.

Training was good and intense under David. He was very hands-on in his approach and his energy and enthusiasm were to be admired. It was a real contrast to before when the Boss never, ever took training as he'd just be on the sidelines, assessing us. David was certainly thorough in his preparation for games, and we did far more work on set-plays than before and he went into far more detail on the opposition. That sort of training was something we'd never really done week to week, normally only for the bigger games.

David was aware that he was surrounded by big characters and experienced winners, and he kept saying, 'You know better than me.' He was almost eager to please us. David wanted to be liked and to gain the trust and respect of the lads. It must be tough to get the balance right between what worked for the players before and making your own mark as a manager. There's a crossover somewhere. It felt like we were all searching between the past and the present, trying to get the right blend to enable us to move forward. And there was suddenly all this talk of new signings and names being thrown about. We were not used to this. The longer the transfer window went on the pressure seemed to build to bring players in. It became a big issue, all this uncertainty.

It was a horrendous season, but I'd never just blame David for our troubles. The other players and I had to accept our share of responsibility for United's worst season in a long, long time. We needed to be better. If we'd been used to a change in managers every few years, like other clubs, it wouldn't have been such a big deal. But it was natural for us to look back to better days. When I wasn't playing so well, I'd think, *Right, in the good times, what was I doing? How was I thinking? What do I need to be playing at my best again?* I knew I had to play better.

In November, I signed a new contract to 2015 with an option to extend for a further year. I didn't have any big conversation with David. It was a no-brainer to sign as I loved United and could never see myself playing anywhere else. I knew I had plenty to offer but it was a struggle that season. It makes you realise how hard it is to be on top. We'd been there for so long. It was a case of fighting to get back there and it was a real fight. If David had taken over a team that was struggling, he'd have had a clean slate to go, 'Right. This is what I'm doing now, because whatever you've been doing hasn't been working.' But he'd have been stupid to change everything because clearly it had been working.

When Sir Alex left it was never going to be easy for anyone at Manchester United. The unknown was an issue. Unfortunately, none of us were able to deal with it well enough. It was difficult for David. Sir Alex was a risk-taker, that was his personality and not many people are risk-takers. You can't escape the fact that David was more cautious. This was a strength of his over the years and proved to be successful at Everton.

A lot of people have talked a lot about that season with the benefit of hindsight. It's easy to say what to do after the event. That's life, ups and downs. Unfortunately for all of us it was a big down. We suffered a few bad results and all of a sudden the slide snowballed and the criticism mounted. I remember thinking, *At some point it's going to click, and we'll be fine.* But we just couldn't snap out of it and the pressure on the manager was relentless. David had come from the comfort of Everton where if he had the odd bad period he could ride that out, no problem. It wouldn't even enter his mind to worry, whereas now everything blew up quickly and he was under the cosh after one or two losses. Questions weren't asked at Everton because everyone knew David had done such a good job, proved himself there and given himself time. At United, because it was new, and no one knew what the answers were, all those questions were getting asked.

I could see David was suffering. March was brutal in the Premier League as we lost to Liverpool at home and City at home. Our biggest rivals strolling into Old Trafford and strutting away with 3–0 wins was, for me, utterly unacceptable. You just can't let that happen. But it did. I've got to say that inside Old Trafford there wasn't really a bad atmosphere. I heard the odd grumble, sure, but there was no mutiny, nothing like that. That showed the pride our fans had in their club, and spoke volumes for their class, as if they were making a statement that, 'We don't have a go at our managers like other clubs. We're better than that. We're not just going to turn on a new manager and behave like spoilt supporters because we've had so much success for 20, 30 years.' It was outside Old Trafford where the pressure got cranked up on David – on social media, in the press and in the TV studios.

We were still in the Champions League – our one flickering candle of hope. The night before we played Olympiakos in Athens on 25 February 2014, I dreamed we'd lose 2–0. And we did. Sometimes, I have really strong dreams. I had a phase a few years ago when I'd dream about the score in our match the next day. The dreams came true a few times, including that one about Olympiakos.

I gave an interview after the game. Speaking after we've lost doesn't bother me. It's easy if you've scored a couple of goals and won, then players queue up to speak. We'd just been beaten by Olympiakos away, 2–0, in the Champions League last 16. It was never going to be a good interview. There was nothing I could say, really. I just had to get through it. Roy Keane said something on TV about the interview being flat and criticised the performance, which was fine. Lisa took it to heart. She thought, *Michael's come out and spoke again, after they've lost.* So, she leapt to my defence and tweeted angrily at Roy. The reaction was unbelievable. Lisa felt the power of social media and it can be brutal. I get that all the time, but it was new to Lisa. I was on the coach, and Lisa was on the phone, crying her eyes out, 'I'm so sorry. I can't believe I've done this, and put you in this position.' Lisa worried it would come back on me. It didn't bother me one bit. I was just thinking about the game. That was my main thing. In some ways Lisa's reaction made me smile. Now we laugh about it. I'm sure Roy didn't lose sleep over it.

Thank God, Robin van Persie rescued us at Old Trafford to take us to a quarter-final against Bayern Munich. After drawing at Old Trafford, we had the poignant visit to Munich on 9 April. We went to the Munich memorial at the German airfield and laid a wreath of 58 red roses and 23 white roses for each person who died in the Munich Disaster. I'll never forget there was a group of about 20 United fans there, singing, 'We'll never die, we'll never die, Man United will never die…' I had a lump in my throat. I've still got a couple of pictures that I took on my phone. It felt very intimate, and it was more powerful with 20 stood there singing in some ways than it would have been if there'd been 20,000.

Bayern were too strong for us in the Allianz. Europe had been our saving grace and now that was gone. We lost at Everton, which must have been particularly painful for David, and the following after-noon, Easter Monday, all these reports suddenly came out that he was going. So many people were saying it that I guessed it had to be true. I wouldn't say I was shocked in the end, not really. I wish I was. But the build-up over a period of months made David's sacking seemed inevi-table, unfortunately.

The next day, Ed Woodward, who'd basically succeeded David Gill, came in to Carrington at 8am to see David and tell him it was over. David then came into the changing room where we were getting ready for training, told us he was leaving and went round shaking the boys' hands. He probably thought he'd been let down. I did feel for him, yes, and I did feel a responsibility. I could have played better. Had I not trained properly or eased up in games that would have been letting David down, but I gave everything. I know I made mistakes, and I beat myself up about them. *Why did I miss that tackle? Why didn't I make that pass. What am I doing? I let that runner go.*

Everyone was disappointed it hadn't worked out for David. I don't think our dressing room was split and there was certainly no rebellion against him. We were far too professional and too loyal to Manchester United for that. We'd all achieved so much together, and we all knew that that season wasn't good enough, in fact it was terrible, and our pride was hurt. I felt sorry for David losing his job, and what he endured because it was a horrible situation. Manchester United is a global beast – hungry, huge and unrelenting. When that merciless pressure comes at the manager, it must be such a lonely place. Not even a year had passed since we lifted the title and now we were all working out what to do next. *How could we turn this round?* We knew we needed to be better. I questioned myself and searched for answers. It was an awful period. How far off were we? We were miles off.

15

LOUIS

I was intrigued by the appointment of Louis van Gaal, a big name and a very successful coach who came with a pedigree not many could match. Louis had coached some great teams as well as having a reputation for developing players. He won the European Cup with an Ajax team full of superstars-to-be, coached Barcelona and also knocked us out of the Champions League with Bayern in 2010. I knew he had presence and a big personality. I was also interested in Louis's arrival because I've always respected Dutch football and style of play. I had good experiences with Martin Jol and René Meulensteen and the way they approached the game suited me. I learned from a young age on that Wallsend Boys Club trip to Holland how different their football culture is to that in England, their style of play is very technical, methodical with more conscious thought than intuition. By nature, English play is more blood and thunder and driven by emotion. So, I was very much looking forward to seeing how Louis worked.

Louis was still at the World Cup with Holland when we returned for pre-season so his coaches Albert Stuivenberg and Marcel Bout, along with Giggsy, took up the reins and set the tone for training. Under Louis, things were different to what I'd seen before – the approach was very structured, very serious. The Dutch were all about the small details being correct – no bounces in a pass, hold your position – every movement had a meaning. It was very thoughtful and less instinctive and took a lot of getting used to as whenever we wavered from what Louis and his coaches wanted they'd stop and highlight it.

I'll never forget Louis sitting me down in his office at Carrington and asking, 'Where do you feel you can play?' I sensed he knew in advance, and was locked in to where I should play but at least he asked. Louis was quite intense when he talked to you and sat really close. He was very imposing. I was determined to remain open-minded and he definitely changed how I played. As a midfielder under Sir Alex, I'd constantly drop into space in front, inbetween or either side of the centre halves to get on the ball. Under Louis, I was told to hold my position in the middle in front of the centre halves and wait for the ball to get to me.

Louis was obsessed with creating overloads – three against two, two against one – and to get that right, meant practice, practice, practice. Training changed and became less physical and more technical, more about patterns and repetitive actions. It was relentless under Louis and he demanded clinical training every day. He didn't really like smiling or laughing in training. I accept this relentless drilling worked a lot of the time as other teams couldn't get the ball off us but I also saw that because it was so structured, we struggled to be creative and look as dangerous. Sir Alex's sessions used to flow whereas Louis's were stop-start. Louis was on at us all the time, and that was tough for the lads to cope with.

'Why did you do that?' Louis kept asking players in sessions. We'd stop, listen to him, listen to him some more, and then start again. This approach took its toll on me mentally, but I must stress I picked up ideas listening to Louis. A lot of the information was very good and it opened my eyes to the effect this kind of coaching can have. Louis made players much more aware of why they did certain movements, and gave them a better understanding of the overall position. This training approach drilled down to the finest detail, but the flip side was that it was frustrating not being able to play with more freedom.

There was a high turnover of players and the stability of the squad suffered. I appreciated that changes had to be made and that we had to move on under Louis, but we lost lads who understood the emotional dimension of representing Manchester United, and the responsibilities and mentality the team required. At that time, playing for Manchester United became a bit more of a job than a passion. With Louis, we had the same routine for each match: meetings to prepare for games and then an evaluation the day after. Those meetings were very good, informative and clear and I learned a lot but the constant repetition meant some of the really good stuff got lost on the players. The rigidity of this routine was mentally draining. Even Louis himself has spoken about how tough it is to play for him as he is so intense and demanding. That was true, it was hard, yet so much of the work was top drawer. We just couldn't get the balance right under Louis of when to be intense and absorb all the information, and when to relax a little.

Louis was very matter-of-fact when assessing a mistake. 'This is not necessary,' he'd say if someone gave the ball away. 'Why didn't you shoot it to the other side?' He'd always want to know if a player had missed a chance. He was very black or white. I was used to Sir Alex demanding a forward run or pass, anything to break up the pattern of the game and make it structurally messy to create indecision in the opposition. 'Penetration, penetration,' Sir Alex would constantly say. Louis had a totally different style, he was measured and controlled, so we had to adjust. Louis was manager, the main man, and if that's what the leader wants then as a player it's your job to do that as best as you can. It doesn't mean it's right or wrong.

I could clearly see the benefits of Louis's coaching and in some areas we improved significantly. The big games in particular were the ones Louis was fantastic at with his tactical changes and tweaks to nullify the opposition's threat. However, Louis took the same approach for a game at home against a much lesser team. That was frustrating. I remember watching from the stands at Old Trafford when Sheffield United, a League One side then, came for an FA Cup third-round tie. Louis changed our formation to a back three because that's how Sheffield United played. We ended up winning with a last-minute penalty from Rooney but it was the disappointment of us changing for the opposition that hit me the most. I'm not showing any disrespect to Sheffield United when I say this but I cried out for us to play our own game and to have the belief we'd win doing so. In the past, it was all about us. That wasn't necessarily the case under Louis.

Louis taught me another way of football, especially how to set up the team defensively, how to squeeze the pitch and suffocate a team. Louis went into so much detail and was so particular that we were difficult to play against when we got it right. The period when it looked like we were making strong progress was in March and April 2015. We played Spurs, Liverpool and City and beat them all comfortably. When we went to Anfield, Brendan Rodgers had Liverpool playing this box in midfield, with Adam Lallana and Philippe Coutinho coming in off the sides. To combat that, Louis instructed me to play midfield when we got the ball and centre half when we didn't, dropping between Chris Smalling and Phil Jones so we'd always have this overload. It allowed one of them to push all the way in on their side and I just dropped a little deeper, which saved me from running from one side to the other. I just moved up and back instead of across the pitch. We tried it in a practice match at Carrington against Giggsy's side. Giggsy always took the opposition the day before the game, 11 v. 11, and we were all over the place. Giggsy's players kept getting through. I remember saying to Chris and Phil, 'Oh, we're getting pulled all over the place here.' Louis walked past me with a smile on his face, going, 'I've made it easy for you tomorrow!'

'What do you mean?'

'I've made it easy. Look, Chris there, Phil there. You don't have to do anything. You have them all around you. Just read it.' Louis showed me my position between them, creating the overload, and supposedly blocking out the space that Liverpool could use. In the end, it was the best performance I've seen from us at Anfield by a mile. All of Louis's details stayed in my mind, like knowing when to drop back, and, yes, it worked.

This was Louis at his best. Juan Mata won the game with an incredible scissor kick, and our changing room was rocking afterwards. The lads all took pictures, as lads do nowadays. When I started at United, the changing room was totally different to now. No chance you could take a picture or have Twitter or Instagram in there. I think Rio Ferdinand was the first to do it and even then he was careful what he posted. Social media has exploded over the last five years or so. It's just accepted now, and I find it hard really. I understand it's a different generation, the lads post their every move on social media. One of the worst things I've done came at Anfield that day and I'm almost ashamed to recall it. One of the staff took a picture with everyone together. I was in the toilets, walked back in, saw the lads gathering for the picture and joined in, against what I believed in. The picture got blown up and sent everywhere. Around the world in one click. *What are you doing here?* I asked myself, *You're dead against all that.* When I spotted other teams posting celebration pictures from the changing room, I didn't agree. Maybe

I'm too traditional. Lisa tells me to move with the times. At Anfield, it should have been a case of soaking it up and moving on quickly. Don't get me wrong, we enjoyed it, especially beating Liverpool, but it was more of an inner satisfaction. We didn't need to show the world. I know this was Anfield but what's the big deal about one win? Celebrate when you've won a trophy. Under the Boss, all we said to each other was, 'Well done, lads. Brilliant. Move on to next week.' I left Anfield disappointed with myself. I was so dead against such displays, yet I'd joined in. I knew deep down it was wrong, immediately.

The day after Anfield, we had one of the evaluations loved by Louis. I do believe there's a place for them but not after every game. Louis's assistant, Albert, took us through the video, again giving us good information, but every game it was exhausting. Me and Wazza went to see the manager to ask, 'Is there a way of lightening it up a little bit?' Credit to Louis, he changed things and there weren't as many evaluations after that. Instead, the manager sent us all emails, so at least it wasn't monotonous meeting after meeting. Louis had a tracker on the emails to see whether we'd opened them, just to know who took in information that way, or who needed a different route like face to face. Some lads don't want to look back at the game because they believe too much analysis clouds their instinct. I'd take a cluster of Louis's emails after three or four games, and go through them altogether, so it wasn't as relentless.

I actually found Louis quite warm, and I certainly never fell out with him. Louis had a funny side, like when he threw himself to the ground because he wanted to mock Arsenal's diving. At our Christmas party in 2014, Louis was brilliant. We had all the wives there at The Place in Manchester for a dinner with music afterwards. Who got the party started? Louis van Gaal. He was up there, dancing and singing, getting everyone on the dance floor. He was flying. So make no mistake, there was that fun side to Louis but come match day, he sat in the changing room forensically studying the opposition like a professor and was never, ever emotional. Louis never talked about the significance or emotion of the occasion. It was, 'This is your job today, this is how the game's going to go...' Louis wanted to take the emotion out of it to enable us to see clearer. I kind of understood that but then emotion is so important, feeding off the atmosphere in the stadium and riding the fans' passion. Football's an emotional game, and that's why we all love it so much.

We managed to finish fourth in the league that year under Louis. We got back in the Champions League, but I couldn't celebrate that. It wasn't good enough. The next season, Louis started by playing me for an hour, then Bastian Schweinsteiger for half an hour and vice versa. We knew this was planned before the game. I wanted to play with Basti because we were on a similar wavelength, passing to each other. His intelligence created a feeling of control over the game. When we beat Liverpool 3–1 on 12 September 2015, Basti and I played well together, and I thought, yes, we can strike up a proper partnership here. Then we got battered by Arsenal, and Louis never played us together after that. The timing was wrong for us, I guess. I'd have liked to have played with Basti three or four years earlier.

In between those Liverpool and Arsenal games, we played PSV Eindhoven in the Champions League when Luke Shaw had his leg snapped in that tackle off Héctor Moreno. I feel sick just recalling it. I was delighted when we signed him, because when I saw him play for England, I thought, *Wow, he can do everything. He's got something really special.* We'd lost Pat Evra, so I was thinking, *There you go, Luke's our left back now for the next 10, 15 years if he wants it.* When Luke arrived in the summer of 2014, he'd come off the World Cup, and wasn't in great shape. Luke took a bit of stick for his weight, fitness and attitude but he was still a teenager, and we all knew he'd learn. Anyway, Luke survived that tricky start, pulled himself right and was absolutely flying by the time we went to PSV. So, I was devastated for him. I was on the bench, and we knew it was a bad injury by the urgency of the medical staff as they scrambled from their positions to rush to Luke. He was in such pain, poor kid. Football's so cruel at times. I'd been around the game long enough to know that with really bad injuries, like Luke's, it can take a year or two to recover and some players don't ever get over them, so we were all praying that Luke would get back. He did eventually, thank God.

We had so many injuries and young boys were making debuts all over the place. It's not ideal for young lads to come into a struggling team, it's so much harder for them. We had a shocking run over that Christmas. When we lost to Bournemouth, Norwich City and Stoke that December, I heard people saying, 'This the worst Manchester United team I've seen for years.' The low point was Midtjylland, a fiercely cold Danish outpost, on 18 February 2016. Having been knocked out of the Champions League, we'd fallen into the Europa League and were now losing 2–1 at a club formed the year United did the Treble. I fronted up for TV afterwards and got hammered. 'Michael Carrick needs to shut up with his usual depressing interviews.' Yes, that was probably a fair comment by one United fan. We'd just got beat and beaten badly. We cared, we hurt and you should have seen the changing room afterwards, seen me sitting in the corner, staring into space; nothing else mattered, it was like the world had ended. That was one of the worst feelings I've ever had and took days to move on from. Defeat was unacceptable, I knew that. I sat there for 20 minutes, running the game over in my head, thinking about what I could have done better. I was gutted for the fans. I knew 800 had travelled out, forking out £71 each for a ticket, and had then had that crap served up to them. Fair play to them, they were bloody brilliant and defiant, and I heard them singing a version of the Ole song, 'Oh what a night / Freezing cold on a Thursday night / And we're playing fucking shite / What a feeling, what a night.' How they kept their spirits up, I don't know. We made amends in the home leg when Marcus Rashford made his debut. That was a shock, that. Marcus trained with us a few times that year, but not regularly by any means. When we did 11 v. 11 the day before, Marcus came over and played for Giggsy's team but, at that stage, I never thought he looked ready for the first team. He showed plenty of promise, but it was early days. Still he grasped his chance brilliantly against Midtjylland and has never looked back.

Just to wreck our season even further, we got knocked out of the Europa League by Liverpool – of all people – and our only chance of any gaining any respectability lay in the FA Cup. West Ham stood in our way in the quarter-finals, and I remember saying in the changing room, 'Look lads, I've been here 10 years and I've never won the FA Cup. Don't keep just thinking you'll get more chances. This could be our chance. Let's take it.' I felt momentum building as we got past West Ham in the replay, and then Anthony Martial scored in injury time to take us past Everton at Wembley. It was one of those special feelings we hadn't had for so long. I still don't agree with semi-finals at Wembley. I'm old school. The FA Cup stands for history and tradition so why not take the semis back to places like Villa Park? I remember playing Watford there in 2007 and the atmosphere was electric. Wembley should be precious, a destination to aspire to, not a stop on the way.

Anyway, we'd got to the final, but the day before our league match against Villa at Old Trafford, I feared I might miss Wembley. United's sports scientists gave us these recovery tights and I was at home, I'd just got out of the shower and was standing on one foot pulling these tights on. They're super-tight, full length, and tricky to get on. I did one leg, went to pull the other one up, and my back just popped. The pain was so excruciating, I thought, *Oh my God, I've done something ridiculous here.* It was like a scene from a comedy sketch. I froze. I couldn't move anything, I just toppled over and was lucky the bed was there to soften the fall. I struggled to get my breath for a minute or so. I shouted for Ann, our housekeeper, who rushed upstairs and saw me lying there in my underpants, one leg in these tights, one leg out. Thank God for Ann. She's worked for us since we moved to Manchester and is part of the family. She does so much for the kids, and keeps us all ticking over really. She rescued me here.

'Oh my God! What have you done?' she said. Ann helped me get the tights off. I knew I had to get to Carrington to see the doc so Ann helped me into a tracksuit, I hobbled downstairs and tried to blank out the pain as I eased myself into my car. During the drive to Carrington, I started welling up, thinking, *I'm going to miss the Cup final.* Every season I dreamed of winning the Cup. I'd waited so long. I felt the tears coming, so I took deep breaths to stop myself crying. I started telling myself, 'Come on man, pull yourself together.' Doc checked me over and said my back had gone into spasm and locked. He gave me tablets to relax the muscles and, thankfully, the pain slowly subsided within a couple of days. I could sleep again and dream of the Cup final.

I was back playing after two games, but bad news kept coming. 10 May 2016 was an absolutely mental, hideous day. We were staying at the Radisson, Canary Wharf before our match with West Ham and had just finished lunch. As we dispersed, Louis said, 'Oh, I just want to speak to Michael.' We went out of the room and found a quiet corner.

The manager said, 'You're not starting tonight.' Fair enough. It was what Louis said next that cut me open. 'You'll play the next two games, Bournemouth and the Cup final. But they'll be your last two games, Michael.' Wow. Louis was very forthright and didn't sugar-coat his decision, 'We're not keeping you on.' I guessed I was half-teed up for it. David Geiss had talked to Ed Woodward about a new contract but Ed kept delaying, saying, 'End of the season, end of the season.' I'd talked to Ed, 'Look, just tell me either way. I could do with knowing so I can try and plan what's happening with kids and schools if we're going to move.' Ed didn't answer, so the longer it went on, the more I thought, *Something's not right here.* But when the news finally came from Louis, it still hit me hard. 'Two weeks,' Louis told me. He'd called time on my career at Manchester United and the clock was ticking.

In one sense, I was glad Louis told me so I could enjoy what time I had left. On the other hand, it was over, my dream was ending and I wasn't ready for it. I respected Louis's decision and it can't have been easy for him to tell me. Only when I got back to the privacy of my room, and lay on my bed staring at the ceiling did it really sink in. My head was spinning. Here I was getting ready for the last ever game at Upton Park, the place where my career had started and I'd just been told my career at United was finishing. My time at the club I love. Over. Emotionally, I was a wreck. I spent the afternoon battling two thoughts: *I'm so sad this is the end* and *Come on, enjoy the last games and finish with a Cup final.* I wanted to be proud of what I'd done. I tried desperately to put the sadness to one side and make the most of the games left.

I called Lisa. 'That's it, babes, it's over.'

Lisa was so calm. She must have been thinking all sorts of things, where will we move to? How will our lives change? How will the kids cope with missing school and leaving their friends? Lisa's always given me incredible support, now more than ever. She just said, 'Wherever you want to go, we'll be with you.' It was so typical of her. She just knows how to deal with these big situations, and how to manage my mood. I don't know if it's deliberate or just instinctive. I didn't want to go anywhere for myself. It was all about Lisa, Lou and Jace and what would be best for our little family. I didn't want to play for anyone else in England. Maybe we'd move abroad for the lifestyle. I asked myself, 'Would it help or hinder the kids?' I thought now was the time to give something back to them. We even toyed with the idea of moving back to Newcastle to be close to friends and family. Over the next few days Lisa was as solid as a rock for me, even though I knew deep down it was very hard for her. She craved stability. These testing times made me realise even more how lucky I am to have such an amazing woman as my wife. I can honestly say I don't think I would have done all of this without her.

I phoned my family to let them know. Graeme, Mam and Dad were going that night with it being the last one at Upton Park. They always had a soft spot for the place. It was such a big part of all of our lives.

Going to the game on the coach, I sat upstairs, looking out and trying not to think of the symbolism – the end for Upton Park and the end for me. It was an emotional night and, sadly, a violent one. We got slaughtered by the press for turning up late at Upton Park which was rubbish, as we actually we left the Radisson 10 minutes earlier than advised and were 50 yards behind West Ham's bus. We were going fine along Barking Road until we reached the turn left up Green Street, 200 yards from the ground. It was then that I saw them: thousands of West Ham fans in the road, and their own bus only just managed to squeeze through. Police boarded our coach, talked to the driver and explained they were creating a path for us through this angry sea of claret and blue. We waited half an hour and then, suddenly, two police vans sped along on our right, the fans leapt back but we got stopped again in the worst possible place right in the middle of the traffic lights, we were blocked and surrounded. It felt like an ambush. West Ham fans swarmed everywhere, outside the Boleyn Tavern, on the Bobby Moore statue and I even saw one standing on top of a police van.

'Have you seen this bloke?!' Giggsy shouted. I rushed down and couldn't believe what I saw. One fella, I kid you not, kept running up to the bus, off his nut, eyes gone, screaming right in the window, 'Come on then, come on then', which we thought funny at first. Police just stood there, ignoring him, even when he started head-butting the glass. The glass was tinted but he saw inside and knew we were laughing at him. Me, Wazza and Giggsy were laughing so much the other players came to see. 'Look at this guy!' I said. 'What does he think he's doing!?' That's what you're up against, people like that. He head-butted the window again, properly nutted it.

I looked at the fans spilling off the pavement and knew we were in serious trouble. Tension was building and I could sense something was about to happen. West Ham fans hate Manchester United and our bus was a sitting duck, totally vulnerable. A couple of police horses reared and I worried that if a fan got trampled on, it would kick off even more. Talking with the players, we said once one thing was thrown it would all go off. Then wallop! One pint glass was launched from way back in the crowd. 'Everyone upstairs,' a policeman shouted. 'Stay away from the windows. Get on the floor.' It was mayhem. Police with riot shields appeared along the side of the bus but West Ham fans pushed in, right up to the glass. A bottle came through the air, smashing against the bus. Then another. All of a sudden, bottles and cans rained down from everywhere. We were trapped and the bus was getting smashed to bits. I heard the thud as another can hit the bus. I heard bottles break on the side of the bus. I heard all their chants, 'Irons' and 'Who the fucking hell are you?' It was a throwback to the bad old days. Some fans gave us the finger, others were too busy holding their phones up, filming everything, and getting a souvenir the modern way. By then, I was lying across the floor. A lot of the players took shelter in the aisle in case the windows got smashed in. Jesse Lingard and a few of the lads had their phones out. Footage from inside the bus got out, which it shouldn't have done. I took a couple of pictures, not to post on social media, just to show Lisa like, 'Have you seen what happened here?!' We finally got safely inside Upton Park at 7.10pm, with kick-off delayed to 8.30. I laughed at David Sullivan's claim that we should have got there at 4pm. What?! Hang around the away changing room for almost four hours? West Ham's co-owner also claimed no damage would be found on our bus. Well, we couldn't leave after the game because the bus was smashed to bits and we had to wait for a replacement. What a bad day, I thought, a day I couldn't wait to end. We also lost and that severely dented our hopes of making the Champions League.

The Bournemouth game the following weekend was an emotional day after Louis ruled it was my final match at Old Trafford. Not many people knew it was my last game. I tried to keep it quiet. I sorted Louise and Jacey as mascots and they were in the tunnel, as we warmed up, when there was an announcement to leave the stadium. My first thought was it was nothing. It was all very calm at first, then it came through that security found a mobile phone taped to a gas pipe and I realised this was serious. Louise and Jacey were still in the tunnel, and I thought the rest of the family were upstairs in the box. I got a bit frantic, and was ringing them, 'Where are you?' They were in the car park and, by then, the kids were too. Anyway, it turned out to be a false alarm as the 'bomb' was a dummy device left over from a training drill and somebody hadn't cleared up properly afterwards. As everyone had left the stadium it was impossible to get the game played. I'd gone through all the build-up of emotion for my final game at Old Trafford and it fizzled out.

The game was rescheduled for the Tuesday, four days before the Cup final, so this wasn't time for going through the motions. I was aware of keeping that edge to take into the final. I focused on the game but with five minutes to go, we led 3–0 and it hit me. I looked around Old Trafford thinking, *This is it. I'm leaving.* I had a lump in my throat, and said to myself, 'Right, this really is it now. This is never again.' Louise and Jacey were again mascots and they ran on at the end and joined me as I walked around with the other players, thanking the fans. It was the saddest lap of honour I've ever been on. Heading up the tunnel, I said to the stewards and security staff, people I've known for years, 'That's me finished now.'

'Thanks for what you've done, Michael, we'll miss you.'

'See you later,' I said. And headed out of Old Trafford.

My whole focus was the FA Cup final. The night before the final, we sat on the roof-top terrace of the Hilton opposite Wembley and just chatted, all of us pretty chilled really. I thought back to when I was a kid and FA Cup final day was the biggest day of the year, because there wasn't that much football on TV then. Memories came back of being five and watching Keith Houchen's diving header for Coventry against Spurs in '87. I remember growing up and Dad telling me about Ronnie Radford when Hereford beat Newcastle in the third round in '72. The Cup took hold of my imagination from an early age. I loved all the build-up to finals as the TV crews seemed to be everywhere, in the hotel and on the coaches, and it was like you invited into places you were never allowed into, and got see the players close-up. I couldn't get enough of that. I'll never forget in '90 and all the talk about the Boss replacing Jim Leighton with Les Sealey before the Palace-United replay. That was huge! So, no, I don't buy the argument that the FA Cup has lost its shine. I know the Champions League is so big now but players still love the Cup. I always found talking to the foreign lads at United, they all knew about the FA Cup. The Cup's famous throughout the world.

We had to win. Not being blasé or taking anything for granted at all, but this was Palace we were up against, it wasn't like my first FA Cup final when we faced Chelsea – that was a massive battle. I lined up behind Wazza and David de Gea in the tunnel and it was so quiet in there, just a few 'come on, lads', and then we strode out into the sunshine to be greeted by an incredible roar. Even when Jason Puncheon scored, I never thought United would lose, never, I just knew we'd win. I felt so calm and, no, I didn't see Alan Pardew's dance! I was too focused on the game. We got back at Palace immediately, going for them and Juan Mata equalised. Juan's so clever, very technical, smooth and tidy, and it was a good finish. Chris got sent off in extra time, but even when we were down to 10, I always believed we'd win. I could have scored the winner, too! I wouldn't normally be up there, but as we were down to 10 and it was the FA Cup final, I gambled. There are days when I look back and think, *Oh, that would've been nice if that header had nestled in the bottom corner!* But seconds later, Jesse Lingard hit an absolute screamer and all my fatigue left me as we chased him, going mad, jumping around in the corner.

The FA Cup makes heroes, and Jesse fitted the bill perfectly. He's United through and through, he's been at the club since he was six and he plays with that attacking hunger the fans love. I loved hearing Tony Whelan at the academy talking about his pride at Jesse scoring that iconic goal. The staff nurtured Jesse. Clare Nicholas and Marie Beckley organised his lifts. Dave Price drove him from school. Everyone played a part in Jesse's development to get to that Wembley goal so it was an unbelievable feeling for them, too. It's all about respect at the academy and Jesse recognises the work they put in. Seeing Paul Pogba, Marcus Rashford and Jesse Lingard always going up and shaking the hands of the academy staff shows the respect. It's a family.

One picture from Wembley is particularly special to me. It was taken at the final whistle when I knew I'd won the FA Cup at last. I'm just standing on my own, bending backwards with my arms in the air, looking at the sky, enjoying a private moment telling myself, 'Well done, you've done it.' The player closest to me was Wayne Rooney and it was brilliant and fitting that it was Wazza I celebrated with first. We'd played together for so long, been through so much together, and waited so long to win the FA Cup.

'Do you want to lift the Cup with us?' Wazza asked. I was stunned. What an honour! My mind went back to all the legendary scenes of heroes lifting the FA Cup when I was a kid.

'Are you sure, Wazza?'

'Yes!!' I still hesitated. This was Wazza's first trophy as United captain so he was well within his rights to want it for himself. I couldn't ever thank him enough for his generosity. That's the mark of the man. Should I have just said 'no' and let him do it? But he was adamant. I followed Wazza up the 107 steps, not the old 39. I was too caught up in the emotion to count but, looking back, it was a shame it wasn't the old Wembley. I grew up with that, and there was something unique and romantic about the 39 steps and the Twin Towers. With the climb to the Royal Box, you disappear from view at one point, it's quite dark back there and very quiet, before you turn a quick left, go up a few more steps and emerge on the balcony. All the way up, I had my back to the pitch and then suddenly it's there, the whole stadium in front of you. What a sight!

Wazza and I waited for everybody to collect their medals before we took a handle of the trophy each. We waited a few seconds longer, looked around all the players, and everybody nodded in a quiet acknowledgement at each other as if to say, 'We've done it.' I kissed the Cup and heard the announcer going, 'The winners of the 135th FA Cup…' The rest of his words were drowned in the roar as Wazza and I lifted the Cup, and we raised it so fast the lid flew up and over the ledge, and it was lucky it didn't hit anyone in the tier below. I didn't know we'd lost the lid until we got back down on to the pitch. I was lost in my own world. It's just magical lifting the FA Cup. It all happens in a split second, but in that time my mind played what I can only describe as a showreel of past captains lifting the trophy – Gary Mabbutt, Steve Bruce and Dennis Wise. I knew as I held the Cup, this was history in the making and one of those amazing life moments.

I waved the Cup towards the box. Everyone was there and they were going crazy: Lisa, Lou, Jacey, Mam, Dad, Graeme, Kay, June, Doug, Glen, Jaz, Bradley, Hoody, Rutherford, Dom, the whole crew. I walked over in front of them and raised the Cup again. It was a gesture to let them know how much I appreciated all their support over the years. It was a an emotional moment for me and one I'll never forget, and in some ways it was the best moment of my career because Graeme and the kids were there to share it with me. They'd all missed Moscow. The Cup was for them, too. Wazza had the box next door and the kids were all going crazy together. Watching the kids celebrate was priceless.

Wazza and I went over to the back-room staff standing by the side of the pitch, watching the players celebrate, and we dragged them on so they could share the moment, which they absolutely deserved. We worked next to the kit men, masseurs and all the back-room staff every day for the whole season and we knew the sacrifices they made. I saw the pride and joy in their eyes, and knew what it meant to them. United had suffered some bad times in the past three years but here we were, back again, winning trophies, and they loved it. It didn't cross my mind at the time, but the other winners were Spurs, who received around £400,000 as a final bonus from United which took my fee with add-ons to £18.6m.

I slowly found my way back to the changing room with an old-school United scarf tied round my neck and a bottle of champagne in my hand. More champagne was sprayed around in the changing room until the news started to seep through that Louis was leaving. Let him enjoy the moment, surely? OK, we had a bad season, two seasons really, under Louis but we still managed to get a trophy. I had sympathy for Louis. It was sad for the manager to think he'd just won the FA Cup and was now about to be dismissed. No manager deserved to go through that. Louis was really upset but kept it hidden. He's a very proud man but it must have hurt.

We all went back to the Corinthia where my family was waiting and the first thing I did was give Dad my medal. I knew what the FA Cup meant to him. It was a thank you to Dad for taking me to football and for always being there for me, for being quiet but strong. I choked up as I passed it to him. I knew how much it would mean to him. He eventually gave it back to me to keep in the safe, but I know how proud he is.

I felt different that night. In the past, I would have enjoyed a great night with the lads and would have got well stuck into a sing-song and a drink. For much of that night, I sat on the edge of the dance floor. Louise was on the dance floor with Ashley Young's daughter, throwing shapes with her and wearing a beaming smile. Jacey wouldn't leave me alone and he's not normally like that. I don't know whether he was proud, thinking, *This is my dad*, or whether he sensed my sadness as I thought it was all coming to an end. Kids are intuitive like that. I just sat at this table with Jacey on my knee and a glass of red wine. Marvellous! It's the first party I can properly remember! Sharing it with all the family is what matters most. Eventually, some of the lads headed to this bar next door and I finally came alive. Ashley Young and Wazza were in there and so was Giggsy with his mates. There must have been 60 or 70 of us, and it just exploded into the best sing-song. The kids were on the sofa, dancing around the FA Cup. I was across the room with Wazza, standing on another sofa, singing our hearts out. I looked across and saw Jacey and Lou with the Cup, belting out United songs, and that's a mental snapshot I'll keep forever. It was 2:30am! They're definitely my kids! Security kept an eye on the Cup, which was just as well as it nearly came back to my room. Lou and Jace wanted to sleep with it.

The next day was like a normal one for the squad. We had breakfast with Louis, and then he gave out our fitness programmes for the summer. I thought to myself, *Well, I don't need that, I'm not playing any more*. Louis then said, 'Have a good summer. And thanks for everything.' And that was it. That was Louis' farewell. Very dignified. I'm thankful to Louis for what he gave me, he taught me a lot and I'm glad he left with a winner's medal.

16

JOSÉ

I was excited when José Mourinho strode into Manchester United on 27 May 2016. José brought some swagger back to the club and brought some hope for me, too. I was in limbo, not knowing what was going on as Louis showed me the door, then beat me to it. I was away with Graeme and some mates at the Monaco Grand Prix when José was appointed, and I got pulled for an interview by Sky Sports F1. I said I felt José would 'be a good fit for the club'. Brilliant for United, I knew that. It was strange talking about the situation at United. Was I going to be part of it?

When I got back from Monaco, José phoned, 'I want to keep you on. I want to give you a new contract.' Thank God! I was nowhere near ready to finish. I felt I had so much more to offer Manchester United. When I went into Carrington to meet José, I was immediately struck by his aura. When you're with him, you know you're with somebody who's the boss, and who's got the ability to make the big, bold decisions. It's this sense of presence that sets the best managers apart from the rest. From the first training session, I realised that José's a winner. It's always about the end-game with him, and that's winning trophies. Whenever I look at José, I just think 'trophies'. He hates losing.

José's obsession with trophies shines through. On 7 August, we were back at Wembley for the Community Shield. We'd never really prepared for it in the past, it was still part of pre-season. He was desperate to win

293

it, to get us into the winning habit, and we did by beating Leicester City. We chased another trophy at Wembley on 26 February 2017. The League Cup was massive to José. It doesn't get the build-up or that special glitz that the FA Cup does. But José said, 'It's not the Champions League, but it is the next thing to win.' So, we beat Southampton 3–2, and took home another trophy. José just sees a way to win them. In the Europa League final in Stockholm on 24 May 2017, José planned how to beat Ajax by letting them have possession, playing on the counter, and stretching them over the top with the pace of Marcus Rashford.

It wasn't just about winning this one, though. This time there was much more to it than a getting trophy because Manchester was in mourning after 22 people had died in the terrorist attack at the Ariana Grande concert at Manchester Arena. The tragedy affected everybody. I've walked through that reception many times to collect tickets. That's so close to home, you think that could have been someone close to me. It could have been my kids at a concert there. What do you do to help? You pray, you try to show support. It broke my heart to read all the stories of families desperately searching for loved ones. We tried to show our support for the families and friends of the victims. In the changing room after the game in Stockholm, we held a banner saying, 'MANCHESTER A CITY UNITED #PRAYFORMANCHESTER'.

When I returned to Manchester, I carried on preparing for my testimonial on 4 June, the hardest thing I've ever done in my life. I'm so meticulous I wanted to be involved in everything, making sure it was right. I was honoured that Manchester United granted me a testimonial and I was using it to raise money for the Michael Carrick Foundation. The charity was something I'd been thinking about for some time and this was the perfect opportunity to get it started. We registered as a charity to create opportunities for kids to feel safe, valued and inspired to achieve. I looked at areas in Newcastle and Manchester where there were cases of child poverty. How can we live in a society like this when children are struggling for a future? I wanted to contribute in some small way to tackling this huge problem so we invested in the two cities that mean most to me. The focus of our projects at Trafford Barn, Wallsend, North Shields and Byker is football, and that draws kids in, but we also teach life skills and discipline. I want to steer kids off that pathway of crime and give them a chance in life. They see coaches helping out who've been to college and can follow them, using them as mentors. It gives them a hope of a future. So the testimonial was vital to provide the funds for the Foundation.

I didn't want a throwaway game, players messing about. I wanted a proper event with top players and a real competitive edge so I put together a Manchester United '08 XI and a Michael Carrick All-Stars. Our 2008 team never had a chance as a group to celebrate what we achieved in Moscow so here was that chance.

My heart was set on Sir Alex and Harry as managers. I didn't want to be disrespectful to José, so I asked him whether he wanted to be involved. 'Don't worry about me!' José replied. 'Look, it's your day. One hundred per cent go for Sir Alex.' If the Boss couldn't do it then it wouldn't have worked. So it was a nervous phone call to Sir Alex, but he never asked the date, just said, 'Yes, I'll definitely do it.' That was a relief. Harry also agreed, and I could start getting the team together, the likes of Gary Neville, Wayne Rooney, Pat Evra, Rio Ferdinand, Nemanja Vidić and Paul Scholes, with Robbie Keane, Clarence Seedorf, Jamie Carragher and John Terry for the All-Stars. It was daunting sitting down with a blank piece of paper, trying to get two squads together. What if the '08 lads couldn't make it and we didn't have enough? What if I couldn't get any good players for the All-Stars? I was aware how embarrassed I would feel if we I couldn't make it happen. Slowly I started sending out texts to some of the lads to make a start. Unfortunately, Steven Gerrard and Frank Lampard got injured and had to pull out, and I seriously started worrying whether we'd have enough players. But they came. I was blown away by the lads' response, flying in from all over the place, some on the morning of the game.

I couldn't believe how many meetings there were for one match! One of the very first meetings, I turned up at Old Trafford, expecting to see the testimonial committee of Graeme, Kay, Lisa, David Geiss, Jo Tongue and Dominik Mitsch. I walked into this room and there were 25 people sat around the table from marketing, ticketing, legal, police, security and stadium managers. It was chaos. Eventually, over the months we got it sorted. That committee did so well pulling it all together. I'm totally indebted to them. It was a complex operation that suddenly became even more complicated. The weekend before the game I was in a cottage in the Cotswolds with Richie who had flown over from Australia with Janelle and the kids to stay with us for a few weeks and play for the All-Stars. I was just relaxing when David Geiss called. 'The testimonial is in doubt,' David said. Ariana Grande had announced she was doing a benefit concert at 6pm on Sunday, 4 June. I agreed with the idea of the concert. I knew how important Ariana's gig was for Manchester and the healing process. I also realised what it meant for my testimonial due to kick off at 4pm at Old Trafford, half a mile from where the One Love Manchester concert was being staged at the cricket ground. We couldn't cancel ours, surely? I spoke to Ian Hopkins, the chief constable of Greater Manchester Police. I spoke to Ed Woodward and Richard Arnold, United's managing director. 'It looks like you might have to pull the game,' Richard said. 'How can we do that,' I said, 'we've sold 60,000 tickets.' I rang David, who said

Family matters: Lisa, Louise and Jacey mean the world to me.

Finally: I'd dreamed of winning the FA Cup ever since I was a kid so to lift it with Wazza in 2016 was an amazing feeling. I was also pleased Louis went out on a winning note.

European focus: Winning the Europa League was special in 2017. 2018 brought the 60th anniversary of Munich, and a poignant memorial service at Old Trafford.

© John Peters

© Manchester United/Man Utd/Getty Images

Driving ambition: My F1 dream was fulfilled going around Silverstone in a 2-seater driven by Patrick Friesacher before the British Grand Prix in 2018.

John Peters

Testimonial: Getting many of the old players back together at Old Trafford was special, the kids loved it too, and it was brilliant to share the pitch with Graeme.

Matthew Peters/Man Utd/Getty Images

Reuters

My two families: Manchester United fans have always been good to me, and their reception made my testimonial even more moving for me. Lou and Jacey asked me to dab, and I couldn't let them down! My parents and Lisa have been with me the whole way.

Above: My last game against Watford. I specifically asked Ashley Young not to organise a guard of honour. Thanks Ash!

Below: Saying thanks to José Mourinho as I leave the pitch for the final time.

'Michael, Ian Hopkins says this is coming from upstairs, way upstairs, this is coming from Number 10.' I'm used to being in control, but now government was involved and this was a different level: absolutely nothing could get in the way of the One Love Manchester concert.

'We can't just cancel the testimonial,' I told Ian. 'It's been going on nine, 10 months, people have got tickets, booked trains and hotels. It's not a little fête down the road you can postpone a week.' Ian was unbelievable, so calm.

'We'll try and make things happen,' Ian said. 'I fully support you, we've agreed it, we've cleared it, it's a low-risk football game.' But there was clearly a lot of political pressure being applied. At one point over the weekend, Ian said policing the two events was just impossible because they used the Old Trafford car park for the cricket ground. That was a tough weekend. Is it on? Is it off? The pressure was building, I was getting calls saying that if they have to cancel the concert then it is on my head.

I talked to Ian again, 'We can't cancel but, look, I want to make this happen. We're happy to bring the kick-off forward.' At first, they were talking 11am. 11am! Then 12am. In the end we agreed on 2.30pm. Ian was brilliant through the whole thing. He could have made it so much more difficult as the police were stretched as it was, never mind with two big events in the same place hours apart. Ian is now a trustee for my foundation. Jo and David were both incredible over that incredibly stressful weekend too. They both had done an enormous amount of work over the 10 months to pull the game together. Jo ended up doing all sorts of different things. It could never have happened without her. Jo went over and above what she was meant to do

On 30 May, we announced the kick-off change and I took the opportunity to extend again my condolences to the families and friends of those who'd died. I wanted to show that we are Manchester, we are together, a city united. We invited some of the families and friends of the victims to the testimonial. How do you handle this? It's an unbelievably sensitive situation. I didn't want them thinking this was a footballer saying, 'Oh, come to a football match and everything will be all right.' Some wanted to come, some didn't, and 15 came in the end. An hour and a half before kick-off, I went up to see them in a corporate box. I walked up with Graeme's wife Kay who works at St Cuthbert's Hospice in Durham and she gave me some advice on what to expect.

I stood in front of the 15 and said a few words, it was one of the hardest things I've ever done. What could I say that's going to make any difference to what they were feeling? 'I'm really sorry for your loss, for your suffering. I can't really imagine what you are going through. I just hope today brings you a bit of peace and happiness.' I felt myself breaking down there and then. My voice went and tears filled my eyes. Here was one of the best days I could ever have, celebrating my career, surrounded by family and friends, and they were suffering, having lost family and friends. I felt so helpless. This game of football, my day, suddenly wasn't nearly as important. I couldn't believe how humble and actually grateful they were to me for inviting them. I was the one humbled by them. I signed a few shirts and programmes, and then headed down to the changing room.

Wow, what a change of mood to a room filled with players laughing and joking. A couple of days earlier, I said to Lisa, 'The thing I'm most looking forward to is being in the changing room with the Boss, the lads, and the staff again.' I saw the same old faces, getting strappings and stretches in the medical room. It was weird how normal it felt, just the lads popping straight back into their old routine. The noises coming from Rio as he was getting neural stretches were hilarious. 'Aaaagh!! Ohhh, Jesus!!!!' Obviously, he was a touch stiffer than he used to be! I was crying laughing.

Sir Alex was perched on a table in the corner, and it was like time stood still. We were back in that Moscow era again, the team back together – it was a beautiful feeling, with the great man directing us, a wonderful sight and sound. 'Do not bloody lose,' Sir Alex said. 'Last game was a 5–each draw,' Sir Alex went on, recalling The Hawthorns. 'At 5–2 I thought we were going to win by 10. Then Lukaku comes on and scores a hat-trick against Rio. Has anybody ever scored a hat-trick against you?'

'No,' Rio replied.

'Well, Lukaku did.'

'No, actually, Ronaldo did,' Rio remembered. The Boss knew Rio rarely got bullied.

'Did you not see him at QPR?!' Nev asked the Boss. We all fell about laughing as the years rolled away again, and we were back in 2008.

'Well done, Nev!!' Sir Alex said. 'The best compliment I can give you, apart from being a great team, is you're great guys. You've done really well, all of you. It's not easy being a footballer and then quitting. Ji-sung's education in Switzerland (on a Masters programme). Rio is running television along with Scholesy. Nev owns the city of Manchester, buying everything. Van der Sar runs Ajax. Fantastic. So, get your warm-up. Anybody any comments? This is an interesting thing, how many times did I ever say to you, "Anybody got anything to say?" Not once did anybody have anything to say!'

'We were usually asleep!' Giggsy said. Again the room filled with laughter.

'An arrow to my heart!' the Boss smiled.

I sat there, loving every second. I looked over and there was Graeme doing his boots, getting ready, listening to all the chat. It was a perfect moment. Having my brother there was brilliant, because I knew how much it meant to Graeme, getting to play with the lads he knew but idolised. I also wanted him there because then he'd understand what this team meant to me even more. I knew his back was in a bad way, but Graeme's a decent player and he'd not look out of place. The lads gave me a guard of honour, and I had to make a speech. I spoke about the tragedy at the arena, and said, 'This game has got extra significance over what's happened, I'd just like to welcome some of the families…' and I had to stop because of the deafening applause from 70,000 people for the families. I continued after a bit, adding, 'I'd like to extend my condolences and thoughts … stay together and stay strong.' Manchester was a city in mourning still and we were very conscious of respecting the victims, and the fire services, ambulance and the like. When I mentioned we also invited 300 of the services here, they got a great cheer. I didn't want to miss anyone out, so I kept going, thanking people, and it did go on a bit. I could hear the players shuffling their feet, itching to start. 'Any chance, Carras?!' I heard one of them say! 'What time's kick-off?!' They thought I was milking it! When you're on the pitch it's difficult to hear the sound system so they didn't know what I was saying.

It was a good match when it got going. I knew it was Wayne's last game at Old Trafford, he'd flown back from holiday in Barbados for it, and it was funny seeing him having a right go at the ref, Neil Swarbrick. Some of the foreign lads really went for it, and Seedorf was absolute class. Even Berba had a couple of little sprints.

When Carra flattened Nev in slow motion I laughed my head off. The fans loved it. Nev and Carra get on, they're good mates now, but there is still that fun rivalry. Graeme came on and played really well actually. I just wanted to keep passing to him. It was our little moment and we'd waited long enough for it. I watched him do a turn and could see him almost freeze with the shooting pain up his back, but he kept going and it was nice that the United fans gave him a brilliant reception. I looked up at all the family and friends in the directors' box, and knew how emotional it was for them, having me and Graeme on the pitch. Lisa was there in with the kids during the game. Mam and Dad were surrounded by friends and family and just beamed with pride. Mam's mam, Grandma Towers, had died not long ago, and we were all thinking, 'It would have been nice if she'd seen this.' It also meant a lot that Richie played. Being back together again on the pitch after so long was special. I managed to get the equaliser in a 2–2 draw and after I scored I looked up to the kids in the stand and did the 'Dab'. Their faces were a picture. They were the only two people I would 'Dab' for! They had asked me if I'd do it when we were messing about before the game, never actually thinking I would. Lisa's family were there too. June and Doug, her brother Glen and his wife Jasmine and their son Bodhi as well as Lisa's Grandpa Bill aka 'Gramps'. We have such a close knit family even though we've lived away so long. It was my fault Lisa moved away from home but June and Doug have always been there for us and never intefered. Not once have we had a disagreement or a cross word. That's not bad going for in-laws! They've given up so much and been so supportive and it was great they were there at Old Trafford.

A special day was made even more special when we totted up that we'd made £1.5m for the foundation. I can't thank enough all those who turned up – players, managers and fans. We had a party afterwards, having a beer with old friends, it was brilliant. Wazza left that summer, and I was gutted to see him go. We'd shared so many great moments, and become close friends.

On 11 July 2017, José made me captain, a real privilege, following greats like Sir Bobby, Bryan Robson, Cantona, Keano, Nev and Wazza. Our first game of the season was the Super Cup against Real Madrid in Skopje, I was on the bench and desperate for us to win as the Super Cup was the only club trophy I'd not won.

Jacey had been on my case, going, 'Can you get me a Ronaldo shirt?' I said, 'Oh, I'll see if I can.' I'm not normally one for asking but I saw Ronnie when we warmed up. Neither of us were starting. He came across to me, actually, and we had a hug and a chat. 'Look, do you mind giving a shirt after the game for my little lad?' 'Yes, no problem. See you after the game.' Ronnie was as good as gold. He came into our changing room afterwards to chat to the players and staff. It was nice for Ronnie to go and say 'hello', to the old staff that were there. He gave me his shirt, and I asked him to sign it for Jacey. 'How do you spell that?' he asked. I spelled it out for him. He only went and spelt it wrong!! Didn't matter. Jacey was all over it when I gave it to him anyway. We spoke for about 10 minutes, and he was talking about life in Madrid, asking about Manchester and after the other staff at Carrington. Carrington played such a huge part in our lives. Ronaldo's the best player in the world but strip all that away and it's just lads going to work, day to day, playing football. Ronnie's relentless. The way he developed has to be admired from creator to rangy winger to goal-scoring attacker, almost like an inside forward, and then changing as he got older to be a centre forward.

Back home, you could see the team developing under José, We needed to keep pace with City and their win at Old Trafford on 10 December set us back. City had a fantastic season, credit where it's due. Emotions ran high after that Derby. City celebrated in their changing room and the noise travelled easily along that tight corridor. It doesn't take much in a game of that intensity for it to spill over. City were entitled to celebrate, and make as much noise as they wanted in the changing room. Some of our lads felt the noise was aimed down the corridor, aimed at us, rather than City celebrating with themselves. One of their players celebrated more than we thought he should, so there was a brief exchange of views in the corridor, all pretty harmless really. I wasn't playing as I'd something else going on.

17

HEART

Suddenly it felt like the life drained out of me. My legs went first, then my head went dizzy. I couldn't focus or think straight, I could hardly stand up. *What the hell was happening?* My first game of the season, a routine League Cup tie with Burton Albion at Old Trafford, we were well in control and I was falling apart. I made this run and all the fuses blew inside me. My whole body seemed to be shutting down part by part. I could hardly move or walk, never mind run. A minute later, my body sparked back into life, like somebody sorted the fuse box, and I regained my senses and my control. Fatigue didn't make sense. We were 3–0 up and very comfortable. Then it happened again and again, like somebody switching my power on and off.

Looking back to 20 September 2017, I search for the warning signs during that game but honestly there were none. No sweating, no palpitations, nothing to indicate what I suffered 10 minutes into the second half. I'd had similar symptoms before, against Reading in the FA Cup a year earlier, which lasted only a few minutes and went away as quickly as it came. I never gave it much thought and it was nowhere near as powerful as this. I finished that Reading game and was totally fine, brand new, and when I mentioned it to Doc at half-time he told me to tell him the moment it happened again. But I'd been fine.

Against Burton, this power outage recurred every few minutes, sapping my energy. When Anthony Martial scored our fourth on the hour, I could hardly move to celebrate with the boys, which was not like me at all. The feeling cleared and I was OK again, playing slightly within myself, keeping it simple. The tie was dead and I should have gone off, but that's not in my nature. I was captain of Manchester United so what example would that set? José had used all three subs by 78 minutes, so I could hardly leave the team with 10. I kept saying to myself, 'I don't know what's wrong with me, but I'll be all right.' I wasn't. Feeling faint again, I stood there, hands on hips, and then it worsened, so I bent over with my hands on my knees until the dizziness subsided. I spent the last five minutes pretty much walking around, just getting through the game, determined not to make a scene. Burton had a counterattack and when we won possession back I tried to make an angle to get the ball and the power outed again. I felt so heavy and weary, like my body almost wanted to go to sleep. I wasn't puffing and panting, there was no pain anywhere, yet I was totally lifeless. I should have walked off. Pride kept me on. Stupid, really. In the final minute, I did one little movement, nothing strenuous, to stop a cross and I actually worried I'd collapse. I bent over and closed my eyes, trying to pull myself together. I was stood on the edge of our box as Burton scored and I hardly even turned around. I knew I had to see Doc but as I walked off I felt fine again.

In the medical room, I said to Doc, 'I had the same feeling as Reading but longer and a hell of a lot worse.' By this time, I felt back to normal again. Doc checked my heart rate. It was slowing as I recovered from the exertion but Doc noted the rhythm was irregular so he wired me up to the ECG machine and took some readings. 'It's not quite right that. I need the better machine.' This was getting serious, I realised. Paramedics dashed over to another part of Old Trafford to get this other machine and I was wired up to that. I lay on the bed, and the lads came in to see if I was OK until Doc stopped them. The doc looked at the second printout. The trace showed a condition called Atrial Flutter/Fibrillation. Listening to the medical people over the next few months I learned this essentially meant the priming chambers at the top of the heart contracted in an unco-ordinated fashion. This made my heart inefficient during the high demands placed on it by exercise and that's why I felt very leggy at times against Burton.

'We're going to run you in to hospital to do a few more tests and observation,' Doc said.

What? Hospital? I didn't want a fuss.

'I feel fine now, Doc. Can't I just go home?'

'No, you can't.'

'Well, I'll drive to the hospital.'

'No, you can't drive.' Doc ordered an ambulance round.

'Leave it out, Doc. Ambulance? I'm fine.' All a bit of drama about nothing, I thought. I just wanted to have a shower and go home. The ambulance reversed into the tunnel, right in. 'We don't want to make a scene,' Doc said. He knew hundreds of United fans were outside, waiting behind barriers for autographs. I climbed into the back of the ambulance, a rackety old banged-out number so at least nobody would give it a second glance. José popped his head in and went, 'Everything all right, Michael?'

'Yes, I'm fine. They've just got to do a check.'

'Can you play again?'

I laughed. 'Yes, yes, I'll be fine!'

'Doc said something about your heart. Are you all right?'

'Yes, I'm all right!' Once José said it, though, I did start thinking maybe this was a little more serious.

'OK. Good luck.'

When the ambulance was away from the fans at Old Trafford, it was a blue light job all the way to the hospital. More tests, more doctors. I caught snatches of their discussion. 'Is it fibrillation?' 'Is it a flutter? 'Was he dehydrated?' 'It might never happen again.' My heart's rhythm soon reverted to normal without needing specific treatment. I stayed for a couple of hours to rehydrate then went home feeling pretty good again. I could train and play. José was understandably cautious but as I was told by the specialists to carry on, I was happy to do that. The medical view was that an otherwise young, fit and healthy person was allowed to have one of these episodes during their life without any real need for concern or intervention but if it happened again then further investigations and treatments might be needed. I also learned that this was something athletes are more prone to as their hearts get really pushed over long periods. I'd had a thorough heart assessment by United's cardiologist pre-season that proved completely normal. The medical people still felt it wise to monitor me further. Doc stuck a small device on me to record ECG traces continuously for four days. The medical experts agreed I should go back to training, with this heart monitor on, and prepare as normal for Southampton away on the Saturday. There was no point taking things easy as that wouldn't allow me to maintain the fitness needed to play top-level football. If it was going to happen again then rest wouldn't stop it or help. I felt normal again.

'Might as well just crack on,' I said.

'Are you all right for the bench?' José asked the next day. He was cautious and very caring, saying, 'You can't just rush back, Michael.'

'I'm fine. I'm back to normal.'

I know it sounds stupid after a heart scare, but I reasoned, 'If Doc's said I can play, then I can play.' José was still very concerned so he asked doc, 'What if this happens again when Michael's playing?'

'Well, he'll just have to come off but it might never happen again,' Doc replied. José put me on the bench at St Mary's, I warmed up a little and felt lethargic. At Carrington the next day, I trained with the subs from the Southampton game, it was a normal day after training for the lads that didn't play, small intense possessions in short bursts. After four minutes high intensity, suddenly I was drained again and I felt the energy flick off. I had no life in me. I went straight over to Doc who was pitch-side.

'Doc, it's no good. I'm feeling it again.' It's unusual for the specialists to have a trace of someone's heart when they suffer the reaction. People usually don't walk round with the sophisticated monitor I wore. After confirming my irregular pulse, we walked in but by the time we got to Doc's room the rhythm was back to normal. I was calm, accepting that something further needed done. I had more investigations including CT scans and they all confirmed the structure and general function of my heart was good. We all knew some intervention was needed.

First thing the next day, I was on my way to this consultant cardiologist Dr Neil Davidson at the Alex in Cheadle. More tests, more discussions. 'Leave it?' 'Cardiac ablation?' *What the hell was cardiac ablation?* Neil's a specialist in electrical conduction problems and he advised that I undergo tests whereby he stimulated the heart muscle to see what rhythms could be provoked. From that, he could decide how to deal with the problem by freezing the areas of heart muscle that were over-excitable and causing the 'short-circuit' into the irregular rhythm. He explained the procedure of zapping the bits sending out faulty electrical signals. I sounded like an old radio with fading batteries. Many patients with the same condition take Beta-blockers to control symptoms but that wasn't an option if I wanted to continue training and playing. 'Do it,' I said. 'The sooner the better.'

The night before Neil operated, the results of the monitor I was wearing came back from the lab. Dr Guido Pieles, a German cardiologist at the University of Bristol who does our heart scans every year at United, called Doc straight away. He saw something that sent my heartrate to 280 beats a minute. I thought my maximum was 200, so that got my attention. Guido, Neil and Doc discussed the best course of action. They spelled it out to me in basic terms – if it was the top half of my heart where I was getting the irregular heartbeat, the 'fibrillation', well that was just a nuisance and not something to fear. If it was in the bottom half of the heart, well that could be dangerous and lead to bigger problems.

'I'll go in tomorrow,' Neil said. 'I'll do the ablation, and test everything while I'm in there.'

Turning to me, he said, 'There are two possibilities. One we go in and sort it.'

'And if it's the other one?' I asked.

'Well it's pretty much you can't play any more.' I was very calm all the way through, probably too blasé now I look back. I never worried or panicked, I just trusted Doc and Neil to do the right thing and that I'd be fine.

Not playing any more didn't bother me really, if I'm totally honest. What could I do? I was 36. 'Go ahead with it. It needs doing,' I said.

The following day, I went on my own to the Alex. I said to Lisa, 'Don't worry about it.' She had the kids at school, and what could she do? I wasn't nervous about going. When I got there, Neil said, 'OK. You can stay awake or be put to sleep?'

'You put me to sleep! All day long! No chance I'm staying awake.' Hospitals and needles get to me. When Louise was born she was breech so we had to have a C-section. They started putting the iodine on Lisa and put the screen up so Lisa couldn't see anything. I was sat on a stool really low with a screen so I could see what was going on. The next thing I know I'm on the floor. I'd fainted. I came round, lying on my back and just started laughing. The doctor was shaking my legs saying, 'Are you all right?' All the doctors and nurses were round me. Lisa was lying there, going, 'Hello?!' I can't do anything about it. It's weird. I'm not scared, something just goes, *boom*. Still now, sometimes I'll get a blood test and I'll be fine and other times I'll say to them 'I have to lie down' because I go funny. I went to get a blood test once as a kid and they put a needle in my arm and couldn't get the blood out. They moved the needle around that much the needle came out bent, no exaggeration.

The players know about the fainting. Wayne Rooney brings it up all the time. He finds it funny. Any time we're around the table and someone else has had a baby, Wazza says something to lead the conversation on to my fainting. He's sitting there giggling, so then I've just got to say, 'Yes, I fainted!' I don't mind! I can't do anything about it. It's weird.

I'd always had anaesthetics done in the little room at the side of the theatre, and once you're knocked out, you get wheeled in. This time, I walked into the theatre, and the anaesthetist put one needle in the back of my hand and one in my arm. They started inserting all the wires and setting up the TV for the scanner, I'd never been awake for this stuff before. I'd never seen so many wires in my life, and then *bang* – I went under. When I came round, Neil explained he didn't find a specific area of abnormal electrical activity. He kept prodding the bottom of the heart for a reaction. Neil felt it was triggered solely by the widening of the four main veins coming into the heart from my lungs during exercise so he froze muscle around all of them. He zapped four bits instead of one. He explained very calmly that the process could have led to a cardiac arrest, which would be in a controlled environment so they could deal with it. My heart took a real hammering as Neil zapped it. I was getting fired up to breaking point really, and my heart was fighting it off.

'You'll be fine,' Neil said. 'I've had athletes back in three weeks after a standard ablation. This was slightly more complicated so it might take longer.' I was keen to leave hospital, and get back to the comfort and familiarity of home.

'Go on. Let me out, please,' I kept saying to the nurse. It got to 11pm and the nurse finally relented.

'You can go home now.'

Lisa was with me by then, but we'd only just reached reception when I felt something running down my leg like I'd peed myself. Lifting the top of my tracksuit bottoms, I saw blood flowing down my leg which made me queasy, as usual. 'Oh, here we go again,' I thought. I'm going to faint. During the procedure, the nurse made a tiny nick in my groin, to feed the wire in and up into my heart, and left it to heal on its own because the incision was too small to stitch. I'd also had blood-thinning tablets as part of the procedure. Well, mine clearly hadn't healed and when I stood up and put pressure on my legs, the bleeding started.

'Lisa, whoa. Wait a sec. I need to sit down. We're not going anywhere.' Blood kept gushing out, so I collapsed into a chair and put my foot up on the table to staunch the flow.

'You've gone totally white,' Lisa said.

'Lisa, you're going to have to get someone.'

Reception was dead quiet but Lisa eventually found a porter. The staff were pretty slow getting to me. They finally located a wheelchair and propelled me back to my old room.

I got home the next day, and all I had in my head was the surgeon telling me 'three weeks'. I was happy to be home and start the recovery. My main thought was the carrot of three weeks out. Then, *How am I going to get fit? What's the plan? First step, walking round the house. Next step, When can I get to Carrington and get the ball rolling? When can I jog? When can I run outside with fitness coaches? When will I be back training? How many sessions before I'm ready to be back involved in games?* I couldn't wait to get back to Carrington, to the lads and the job I love. I like routine and was desperate not to miss anything. Listening to myself say this now seems madness as my body still needed to recover. First day at home, all this planning ran through my mind and my heart wasn't really in my thoughts. I was very fortunate to be in such good hands with Neil and Doc.

My body began telling me, three weeks? No chance. Far too ambitious. For a good few days I was light-headed every time I stood up from sitting the couch. My heart was prodded so much it wiped me out. 'It's just the anaesthetic, I'm fine,' I told Mam and Dad, who were down helping out, as always they were there for us in an emergency. I could see from the look in Mam's eyes and the way she and Dad whispered to each other that they knew I wasn't OK. I knew Mam, Dad and Lisa were worried but I kept just laughing saying I was fine. 'I'll be back in three weeks.' There was no chance I'd be back. I just wanted to reassure them. I'm not sure it worked.

To be back in three weeks, the original plan was to jog after a week. I was on the couch for two, dizzy and weak. I got out briefly to play golf.

'As long as your heartrate doesn't get up, you're fine,' Doc said.

'No chance of that with my golf!' I replied. Louise and Jacey kept coming to see me on the couch, asking how I was and when I'd be playing again. 'I'll be playing soon, it's only a groin problem,' I told them, not wanting to scare them.

I went to Louise's football session one night and at half-time she asked me for her drinks bottle from the car.

'Two seconds, I'll go and get it.'

I jogged there, 100 yards at most, and when I got back, my chest didn't feel right. I didn't say anything, just smiled and wished Louise luck for the second half. It really affected me. I was no closer to recovering. I went into Carrington the next day, and tried to jog across the pitches but couldn't even do that and my heartrate went through the roof. Doc and the sports scientists got me on the running machine, and I was only going 60% capacity, and Doc said, 'Right, you have to stop.' My heartrate was only allowed to reach a certain level, which could gradually increase over time. If it went above I had to stop.

'It's pointless,' I said to Doc. I'd do 10 press-ups and crash out, my fuse box blown again.

I owe José so much. He gave me space and I appreciated him not putting pressure on me to come back. He probably thought I might suddenly go, 'I've had enough. There's no point. I'm packing up.' I knew he supported me, which was so important and reassuring as I returned to my private ordeal.

Slowly, I got out more, and on 7 October I took Dad to the Anthony Crolla fight with Ricky Burns at the Manchester Arena. I like Ant, he's a big Red. He'd just visited Carrington and we had a chat, and as I'd started my rehab I didn't think twice about going to the fight. I was nervous for Ant, wanting him to win and the atmosphere's intense watching boxing, especially being ringside. After three or four rounds, my heart started beating strongly. I first thought I was being over-sensitive. Probably happens all the time but I don't normally notice. In between rounds five and six I was getting hot so I stood up to cool off and went a bit dizzy. Quickly sitting down, I tried to stay calm so Dad didn't realise what was happening. I didn't want him panicking. Between the seventh and eighth rounds my heart beat out of my chest so I looked at my watch to count the beats, again on the sly so Dad wouldn't notice. I didn't have a second timer so it wasn't exact. I kept looking at my watch counting my pulse. The TV camera must have gone on me as I started getting texts from friends asking, 'Is your watch broken?!' My pulse calmed down a bit over the next few rounds and by the end I was OK. I forgot by the end of the fight and bounced out of my chair after the twelfth round when Ant won on points. I was so pleased for Ant but in jumping up I went all dizzy again. I took a few deep breaths, pulled myself together, sorted it. By the time I went in to see Ant in his changing room I was back to normal.

It made me think. I told Doc and Neil, who did more tests and reassured me it was just a reaction to the procedure and not to worry. I waited until a week after the fight to tell Dad. Then I knew everything was OK. He couldn't worry then.

By the end of October, I was thinking, *Those 'three weeks' have long gone and I'm not even close.* I tried doing a few runs with Rich Hawkins, one of the sports science lads assigned to look after me. I'd start off fine, and then *boom* – it just hit. No power.

'Rich, I can't do it.' It was so depressing. It was like hammering away at the accelerator and being stuck in neutral. One day at Carrington, Rich and Doc observed me doing some runs, not crazy runs, but Rich had been at the club for years and knew my capabilities inside out. 'Rich, I'm going to have to leave it. I can't do it.' I never surrender but I had to here, I couldn't summon the strength. I was so far away.

I drove home, thinking, *What am I really doing here? Am I just being stupid?* My plan was always to end in May 2018, so I thought, *I've got six months to go, I've just had a heart scare, I'm miles away from it, shall I just jack it in?* This was a freedom I'd never had. My time was my own and a life without playing opened up to me. I spoke with Lisa. 'This is how it will be if football isn't here.' I could watch Louise and Jacey play sports. I loved being around the house, with Lisa and the kids, just being a family. For all the years Lisa and I had been together, I was a footballer in a routine. I thought about my relationship with Lisa. Being together with time on our hands showed us both that, actually, yes, we're great together. Neither of us felt, bloody hell, a month in the house with you and we're tearing each other's hair out. It was the complete opposite. Family life couldn't have been any better. Louise and Jacey were buzzing that I was around all the time. We could plan things, and actually do them. I wasn't waiting for the squad, going, 'Am I travelling tomorrow? Am I not?' I went and watched games at Old Trafford, and I was totally fine with that which helped me come to a really serious conclusion. I just told myself, 'It's time. I've had my football. I've had a great time. I've loved it. It's just how life goes.'

It's really only now, looking back, that I fully appreciate and accept how bad I was. I was fortunate to be surrounded by the best medical people, and I can't thank Doc, Neil, Guido and all their staff enough. But I didn't want my career to end like this, lying unconscious on the operating table. I wanted to go out on my terms. My decision. Nobody can understand the frustration and pain a footballer endures when deprived of doing what he loves. I hated the inactivity. Let me be fit, let me play – that was how I lived my career. But I found it easier to deal with as it wasn't an injury. It was a bigger health issue, not a pulled calf or hamstring. This was a different level. The heart scare put life and my career into perspective.

By now, I wasn't missing playing and training that much and that's when I knew it was time to stop. I just wanted to get back to the final few months to finish in a positive way. My teammates were supportive, just asking how I was, and some knew I'd had a heart problem but the club kept it quiet which I wanted. News didn't leak out except on some

Norwegian website. There were a few crazy rumours that I had stents put in my heart, and at one stage that I'd had open-heart surgery, so it was easy for United to bat those away. But I wasn't training so the questions persisted.

I worked alone with our fitness coaches under medical supervision wearing the heartrate and ECG monitors throughout then returned to team training on 29 October. I didn't feel great initially but got over that and the important thing was I had no recurrence of the original symptoms and the ECG monitor reports came back clear each time. By mid-November, the medics agreed I was fit from a cardiac viewpoint and I just needed to get my football sharpness back by continuing to train. There were more and more questions about me being put to José, so I went public on 24 November, and released a statement.

I received so many kind messages. Even the trolls took a day off! I was touched by the support. People just assumed I was injured so when the statement mentioned a heart issue, I was aware it sounded dramatic. That's why I delayed the statement until I was back fully training. I was basically saying, 'Look, it's not such a big deal. I've had it done, and now I'm back.' With the statement coming out, I felt it important to tell Louise and Jacey but even then I glossed over it. I just said, 'I had this heart thing.'

It was great to be training with the lads again but then, frustratingly, another setback, this time terrible nerve pain in my calf. 'Old man's calf', as they say. I again started thinking, *I feel like a charity case. Who am I kidding?* I couldn't get through one session without breaking down. I really thought about walking away. Six months left of my career and I was miles away. What was the point?

It was a tough time but it did clarify completely that I was ready to stop playing. Time was up and I was ready to accept the end. I was at peace with myself. I'd only want to be a player at United if I could contribute. I wasn't going to hang around as long as I could just because José allowed it. I've too much respect for him, the club and my team-mates to do that. I said to myself, 'Give it one more go.'

After two or three goes at coming back, the calf cleared up, thank God, and I worked hard to get myself battle-ready. Then on 22 January 2018, José very calmly told me, 'You're playing on Friday.' Yeovil Town in the FA Cup! I was back playing after 128 days out and after so many doubts! José completely caught me out as I'd never expected to play.

'Oh, right! OK!' It was nice when José told me I was playing again but do you know what was best? Hearing Louise and Jacey running around the house, yelling, 'Yes!! Daddy's back!! Daddy's back!!' My kids were even more excited than me! Seeing their little faces made all the suffering worthwhile.

As we arrived at Huish Park, I saw all our brilliant fans behind one goal and I felt at peace. I felt if this was the end of my career, at least I'd be finishing with me in control, and not with the memory of my last time on a football pitch struggling against Burton Albion. Yeovil was made even more special for me because of the fans' welcome back, singing my song. You know when something bad happens to somebody at a club, everyone rallies round, and supports you more than usual and the fans' backing for me that night was unbelievable. After we won, I went over and clapped them. There was a little kid behind the goal, and I gave him my shirt. I've never taken the United fans' support for granted, but coming towards the end, I wanted to show my gratitude even more. I was aware that could be the last time I played in front of them.

I was quickly back in the flow, and even had a go at the ref early on because I wasn't given a free kick. I got told off by Mam for arguing with the ref, 'You were swearing again, Michael. I saw you swearing.' I was back.

18

THE NEXT
CHALLENGE

Eleven days after my return at Yeovil I had the solemn duty of laying a wreath at the Munich memorial service at Old Trafford on the sixtieth anniversary of the disaster. The whole event was so humbling, particularly when I realised I had the honour of sitting next to Sir Bobby. This meant more than football, much more. Harry Gregg was sat behind, his first time back in a long time. Our Under-23s and Under-18s were there as well as the senior squad. The Under-19s were in Belgrade and attended a service at Partizan Stadium where the Babes played their last game. It is so important that the young lads understand the significance of Munich in the history of Manchester United. Talking to some of them afterwards I know how emotional they found the service. It is vital this understanding is passed on from generation to generation. As the service got underway, some of the fans broke into 'We'll Never Die'. The ceremony was so moving. When it started snowing, we sat there in the freezing cold, but the weather just added to the poignancy of the occasion. I joined José as we both laid wreaths and then everyone sang 'Abide With Me'. Dignity shone through the whole occasion. I looked around at the 4,500 people who came to Old Trafford to pay their respects to the Busby Babes, and I thought of all the memorials going on around Europe, and it reminded me again what a special club this is.

I knew my time as a player at this great club was drawing to a close. For the rest of my life I'll watch big Champions League games on the telly, and memories will come back and there will be that feeling of, 'Oh, I'd love to be playing.' But I was past it. My head would tell me one thing but my legs couldn't quite do it any more. It might not have been obvious looking on, but to me it was. My body was telling me it was time to retire.

But what next? The golf course looks brilliant for a couple of months, a couple of holidays and then reality kicks in, and it's like – what are you actually going to get out of bed for? I've seen what retirement can do to some footballers' relationships. It's scary how many footballers' marriages come under incredible strain in the year after they retire. Something like 40 per cent divorce in the first couple of years. Lisa and I've talked about it quite a lot. Lisa and I are a strong couple. We enjoy each other's company. Lisa and I never argue, we've had maybe three or four arguments in the 20 years we've been together. If there's something wrong, then I just go quiet and probably then it's worse for her because she just needs to let off some steam. It is difficult living with a single-minded sportsman. I'll be honest, my life has been harsh on her. But it wouldn't escalate to being a strain on the marriage. Our relationship is rock solid. Some lads keep nicking a night out here, a round of golf there. I've always been quite stubborn, probably over stubborn. Lisa looks at me and gives off this vibe of 'Any chance of you cheering up and having a bit of fun? There's more to life.' I know wives who kick up a fuss at all the commitment to football and still don't grasp what a player has to do. Lisa's always been understanding of my obsession with football. She's never questioned me. She's just allowed me to be the best I can be, and sacrificed a lot for me. I've always felt guilty that Lisa's not been able to have the career she wanted. She went to uni, developed her Pilates practice, and then had it all whipped away by my moving to United. Lisa's an amazing woman and so supportive. She suffers the ups and down with me and has been there the whole way. I'm a very lucky man. She's made it so much easier for me even though I'm a pain at times and drive her mad. A bit like Mam, Lisa gets sick of football from time to time.

I'm a lucky man. Behind every strong man there's a strong woman and Lisa's always there to give advice and thoughts. She just knows me inside out and even knows when I'm in a bad mood before I actually am. She has that sense. The level of love and support Lisa has given me is incredible. We're a team and she's allowed me to devote myself to football. Even if I'd been away with England and then had a game with United, she'd never hand the kids over and say, 'It's your turn, I've had them for 10 days' or 'Let's go out tonight because I've not seen you.' She totally understands what I need to do to perform. She's so unselfish and patient. We're best mates, having the best time when we're in each other's company and it's nice to be like this still after 20-odd years together.

I always wanted children. I wanted my life to revolve around them. Fortunately, Lisa fell pregnant very quickly after we got married. With two weeks until the due date we found out she was breech, so Lisa had no choice but to have a C-section. We packed a bag and left the house at 7am. Seeing the baby in the nurse's arms and hearing her first cry was an amazing moment. I was that caught up in the emotion and so concerned with checking they were both OK it took a couple of minutes to realise the baby was a girl. We had our own little princess. I cut the cord, not realising how tough it was to cut through. We spent the whole day just staring at Lou, a beautiful bundle of joy.

It was much harder for Lisa with Jacey. Her back problems started after five months of pregnancy, she couldn't walk and ended up in bed.

She suffered so much. Again, Lisa had a C-section because the doctors were concerned her back wouldn't withstand a natural birth. Again we didn't find out the sex of the baby. When Jacey arrived, my life was really complete. One girl, one boy, what more could I ask for? More importantly, they were healthy. Lou had just turned two and came in to meet Jacey wearing her nurse's uniform and carrying her little first aid kit.

Lou's passionate about horse-riding. After a few years, we got Lou a little pony called 'Rio'. The lady we bought it off is a massive United fan and named him after Rio. It's Louise's life now. Every time she jumps on a horse, she's Gemma Tattersall. She's blossomed with it. Lisa amazes me. The first time Lou had a riding lesson, Lisa wouldn't go near a horse but she learned from scratch, grooming, tacking up, feeding, everything to help Lou. Lou's even got me mucking out! She was desperate for me to ride and kept nagging me to have a lesson. I'd always had the excuse of playing football, and not wanting to take a risk. After I retired, I went to the yard when Lisa and the kids were away on summer holidays. I got taught to ride by Angela, who owns the yard and gives lessons. I kept it a secret to surprise them. I wanted to do it for Lou. I squeezed in five lessons. Seeing her shock when she turned up and I was cantering around brought a tear to my eye. I'm a softie deep down when it comes to things like that. Being up at the stables with Lou is now one of my favourite places to be. It's so peaceful and totally switches my mind off everything else. I never imagined it would have that calming effect on me. Looking at the relationship Lou has with Rio is amazing. She's so content at the yard, so happy.

As a parent, seeing your children grow and develop is beautiful. Louise's dedication to horse-riding makes me so proud. She has such a fun, easy-going personality as well as the kindest heart I could ever imagine but alongside all that I see a steely determination to succeed.

I could never have hoped to have had such a beautiful daughter inside and out.

My kids are everything to me. They are my inspiration. They are both very different, but equally as loving and caring. Taking Jacey to football, tennis and golf, sharing those moments, is priceless. Being with the kids is my release, my escape.

Jacey has a twinkle in his eye. He gets away with things by winning people over. He's not naughty, just full of beans, and he just loves all sports. He'll sit down and watch golf all night, cricket, rugby, F1, taking it all in and he remembers all the small detail. He's just like me in that respect. I follow almost every sport.

Golf and Formula 1 are my main interests. I'm pretty obsessed with both. I've always loved cars. In 2014, I bought a Ferrari 599GTO. What a beautiful car that was, with the racing livery, a white circle where the racing number would go. I adored it, and it was a buzz to drive, angry and aggressive, more a racing car than a road car, but I felt self-conscious behind the wheel. The Ferrari stood out too much. I pulled into a garage with Lisa one day, and said, 'You're getting out to put the petrol in it, I'm not getting out. I feel so uncomfortable.' So Lisa put the petrol in. I didn't drive it much, maybe three times to training when it was the lads' day off, and eventually I sold it.

A friend at United knows Mark Webber, who used to drive in Formula 1 for Red Bull. He invited us to watch when he was still driving with the team. I've also got to know Daniel Ricciardo, another Australian who drives for Red Bull now. The attention to detail in F1 is incredible. The whole process of building the car appeals to me, the meticulousness of the engineers, the cleanliness of the garage and the efficiency of the mechanics. I'm like that. F1 shares my love of organisation and neatness.

I did a track day once with Dad and Graeme at Croft in the north-east. I got into a Formula Ford, a little two-seater with the old gear-stick, rather than the paddle shifters, so it was a bit of a squeeze. I packed too much on the circuit, and crashed into a wall. Fortunately I didn't massively damage anything. If I'd injured myself I'd have got into a bit of trouble with United. It hadn't occurred to me that I might run into a problem – or a wall!

After I retired I received a call from Mark Webber. 'Do you fancy a drive at Silverstone?' YES! F1! Two-seater! Grand Prix weekend! I'd been desperate to do it. Mark knows how much I love F1, so he had organised for me to have the ride at 10am on race-day. I honestly could not contain myself. I arrived early, 9am, with Dad, Lisa, Jacey and my friend Dominik Mitsch, who used to be head of marketing at Red Bull Racing. They gave me the full kit, race-suit and undersuit for protection, helmet, even racing boots. I looked the part. I had to have a quick medical check and was cleared to go. Patrick Friesacher was the driver and I sat behind him. I had to squeeze into the car. It would have been tight anyway, but with my long legs it was a struggle to get in, never mind comfortable. 'Just get me in. I'll sit with my knees round my ears if I have to!' The engineer tightened the belts over my shoulders and one between my legs, all connecting together, holding me in place. Wow, that's tight. Then the engineer spoke into my visor, 'I've tightened them about 75 per cent. When we get the green light, I'll do the rest.'

'Oh, right!'

There was a panel with a padded cushion between me and Patrick. 'That's to stop your neck from flying forward, when we're braking,' Patrick said. 'Rest against it if you want.' I was adamant I wasn't going to crumble. I'm doing this properly. I don't need that, I thought. My legs went down the side of Patrick's and every time he tested how far he

322

could turn the wheel his elbows banged my knees. I didn't care, though. Just get me out there! I was more excited about this than anything I'd ever done. Football is my job. This was something else. I felt like a fan at Old Trafford getting kitted out to go on the bench. We got the green light, the engineer knocked down my visor, tightened the belts so much I almost couldn't breathe. I gave Jacey the thumbs-up and then felt the revs, boom, here we go. The noise of the engine was incredible. I was in heaven. We left the pits behind Jenson Button, who was driving the motorcycle racer and presenter Guy Martin. As soon as we passed the end of the pit straight, Patrick put his foot down and the noise, the forces, and the pure adrenalin rush was like nothing I'd ever felt before. Patrick was warming up the tyres, twisting the wheel this way and that. My body was a wreck and we hadn't yet reached the first corner. I was out of control, I couldn't anticipate the next move, extreme acceleration, sudden braking, sweeping sharply left and right. *I can't even last a lap like this,* I thought.

We slipped down the inside of Jenson on the second corner, and then the real experience kicked in. I braced myself for the braking into Brooklands. Mark warned me about the forces. Oh, wow, it was brutal. I still can't get my head around how the car can stop so fast. I was watching for the boards to help me gauge when it was going to kick in: 200, 150, 100, then BOOM! Fortunately, I know the track very well, so I could anticipate the next force coming. As we braked, I planted my feet with everything I had to brace my body and stop my head banging into the panel. I spent most of the ride laughing out loud. Flying through Copse, Maggotts and Becketts was surreal. Patrick opened up down the Wellington Straight and the buzz was incredible. As we swept through Brooklands, Luffield and Woodcote, I saw grandstands packed for race day and I couldn't have got any closer to experiencing the real thing. By the time our two laps were done I was really feeling it phys-ically, the constant bracing to fight the different G forces. I wanted to do it all over again. It was the best thing I've ever done. It's ridiculous to think what the drivers go through in a race weekend. My respect for them went up ten-fold. I have to say a massive thank you to Mark Webber, F1 Experiences and the Pirelli Hot Laps Programme as being that close to the action was a privilege.

As I faced retirement, Lisa and I talked deeply about the future. I always thought I'd come out of the game for a bit after retiring, just for family reasons, but the world was turning and I'd always thought about moving into coaching. An important moment in making me believe coaching was my future happened at Carrington on 8 November 2015, when Tony Strudwick showed me this massive questionnaire that revealed your true character.

'Do you want to do this Predictive Index report?' Strudders asked. 'It'll be interesting for you, when you're coaching or managing.'

'Yes, go on, I'll have a go.'

I filled in all these sections like 'words to describe yourself' and random things like 'thoughts'. It gave me a printout of results on my personality, and it was scarily bang on. 'Michael is a helpful, patient, stable person who works steadily and consistently,' the report began. 'He prefers having, and following, a well thought-out process to ensure success. If Michael is responsible for establishing the process, he will do so in a thoughtful, methodical manner, paying close attention to details and time-honoured successes. Once established, he will expect that the process be followed consistently, as he will do himself.' It all sounded so me, so very meticulous. 'He derives satisfaction from helping others and likes to feel part of a secure team,' the report went on. That really struck a chord with me, needing to feel part of a secure team was completely me. It went on, 'In making decisions, Michael is careful, and will take the time required to follow the established process, examine different angles, and explore enough to ensure few, if any, surprises afterward.' I couldn't believe how they had got me so well!

Reading that report helped me realise my future lay in coaching. So late in 2017, I was bowled over when José asked me to join his coaching staff. Being offered the chance to learn off José was unbelievable. It's a privilege that not many players get moving into coaching. José's a winner who reacts quickly and decisively in games and to see that close up is an education.

It was still a strange two or three months at the start of 2018, making that transition from playing into coaching, being still involved but not involved. I was watching games now from a totally different perspective, training differently, looking at different players in the team, thinking, *How can I help him?* I enjoy working with players, trying to help them become better on the pitch and off. This is the challenge I now have, getting my thoughts and ideas across in a way that works for them. It's not about me any more.

On 1 May, we had our Player of the Year awards. 'Lisa don't bother coming, pointless getting a babysitter, just stay,' I said.

'Yeah, yeah, no point,' she said at first. Then shortly before the awards, Lisa said, 'Do you know what?! I think I will come.' That slightly surprised me as the previous couple of years, Lisa hadn't bothered. We went through all the awards, and right at the end of the night, José called me on stage and presented me with a whistle and I immediately started laughing. The biggest issue in training is ref'ing games because the lads moan, and none of the staff want to ref because they get their heads bitten off. 'There's your role next year!' José laughed. 'You have to referee!' José also gave me a coaching top with MC on it, the whistle, and some headache tablets. 'You're going to need them next year!' I wasn't really expecting anything more in terms of a farewell from playing but the video messages started on the screen. Wazza was first and he spoke of me as 'a calming influence on the team', which was nice. Lads like Jonny Evans, Sheasy, Fletch, Scholesy and Rio sent messages, then Sir Alex and then the kids just popped up on the screen. I couldn't believe it! Jacey, big smile on his face, said, 'Hi Dad, you're my hero, you're great at passing.' That was lovely. Louise said something that got me, 'You showed me to follow my dreams. When I feel down you help me get up again.' That was quite strong for her to say that. Kids can surprise you at times. My heart melted. I was emotional but I didn't choke up, I was more filled with pride in the both of them. I looked at Lisa, drying her eyes. We got home at 12.30 and they were tucked up in bed, and I couldn't wait to thank them in the morning.

A couple of days later, José said, 'West Ham or Watford?' I knew immediately what he meant and I really appreciated the gesture. West Ham away on 10 May would be an emotional way to end my playing career against the club where I started. But I wanted the last time I wore a Manchester United shirt to be at Old Trafford, so that meant Watford on the last day of the Premier League season on 13 May. Instinctively, I started doing extra training as I knew I was miles away. I worked and worked as I wanted to do myself justice in my last appearance. I sorted out for all my close friends and family to be there, for Lou and Jacey to be mascots, and the club kindly gave me three places as mascots for the foundation.

'I don't want any fuss, no guard of honour, none of that,' I told the players. I pulled Ashley Young to one side, because he's one of the senior lads, and said, 'Ash, if you hear anything, just tell them, no chance, I'm not interested.'

'Yes, I know, I know,' Ash replied.

Jackie Kay is the team's PA, and I stressed to her, 'Jackie, can you just speak to Ed, and tell him, please don't worry about presentation. I had my testimonial. I had the Player of the Year evening. Don't drag it on. People will be sick of me! Leave it.' Jackie brought back the message from Ed: 'No problem.' As I was about to walk out of the changing room to line up in the tunnel before the Watford game, Ash whispered, 'You've got to wait at the back.' Oh, here we go then!

'What do you mean, Ash?'

'It's a guard of honour!' he said and ran off down the corridor, pissing himself laughing.

'You are kidding me?!' I quickly pushed my way through the players to the front.

'No! You're at the back!' they shouted.

'No chance, I'm staying here.' Then the linesman came up to check us for jewellery and I still had my wedding ring on.

'Shows how long since I played!' I said and had to make my way back through the laughing players to the changing room. I'd already taken my watch off and stuck it in my shoe. I always put my ring and my watch in my shoe. I shoved my ring in there and hurried back out. Ash said afterwards it was the best thing that could have happened as I couldn't get to the front.

I came out the tunnel last, the kids were waiting, the family and friends were watching, and I just wanted to soak it up and enjoy it as much as I could. I was so much more relaxed than I normally would be for a game. It was fine, satisfying in a way that I could set up Juan Mata for the goal. Juan came running to me and we celebrated. At the end, I took the microphone and thanked everyone. 'I've got a lot of memories to cherish. This is the greatest club in the world.' I mentioned what had happened to the Boss with his brain haemorrhage. 'Sir Alex has had a tough week,' I said. And Old Trafford saluted him. When I came back into the changing room for the last time as a player, I saw the lads had placed a signed shirt on my peg with '464', the number of games I played for United. I hung my boots up, took the picture and posted it on social media. The end. I turned my phone off, went out with the family. It was nice to see the reaction and appreciation when I posted that tweet but the first text I saw the next morning was from José, talking through plans for the week. That retirement didn't last very long!

The playing side is gone, but the drive to be successful at coaching and managing is taking over now. My playing days definitely prepared me for coaching. Playing in deep midfield, I had to think about the other positions and understand what a winger or forward wanted, and working with a defender, protecting him and taking the ball from him. I think a lot about the game.

Working with players really excites me as I make the move into coaching. I loved coaching the Under-14s at United. For younger players it's about taking responsibility for their lives and their careers. I was always quite independent as a player and never needed too many people around. It's very easy to live in a bubble. They get so much help these days and, yes, they do need expert assistance, particularly to help them manage the money properly. My concern is that we should give them all the help they need from an early age, rather than doing everything for them, then gradually wean them off, so they start to understand what they need to do to live. There's an awful lot of money in the game these days, especially at the top level. Talented players are the reason for the size of the broadcast deals. I know average players get above-average money but that's the industry's fault, not the players'. I agree the money has definitely softened some players. You set out from school to make a living, to survive through the world, and if by the time you're 20/21 you're a multi-millionaire then depending on your character, you can lose that edge, even if you don't realise. Wages should really be more performance-related for kids. I know it's never going to happen because of the competition for talent, someone else will always top what's being offered because they want the best players. Still, I do believe it would make the game better and actually help the players.

Now José has me working with the first team. I've done my A-licence, and I start on the Pro Licence course at St George's Park in January 2019. I'm enjoying the coaching. It's a long journey towards management, which will take time, dedication and opportunity. I have to put in the same hard work I did as a player. A decent player doesn't automatically make a decent manager, I know that. But I will do everything I possibly can. I'm off to climb the next mountain.

APPENDIX I
CONVERSATIONS WITH MY WIFE

Lisa: I remember that very first phone call with Michael and how I kept him hanging when he wanted to ask me out. When I put down the phone, my mam said, 'You can't do that. You can't keep the lad waiting. That's terrible that.' I didn't want to hurt his feelings. He was already such a good mate. So, I rang Michael back and I said, 'I've got my GCSEs starting in a few weeks and I want to revise and I haven't got time for a boyfriend. I want to concentrate on the exams. Sorry.'

But we used to speak on the phone all the time, just general chat. My girls all said they knew I liked him. A few weeks later, I changed my mind. So that was on 9 May after GCSEs. And then he left in the July to go down to West Ham. It used to break my heart all the time. He said, 'I can't wait until I make it and I'll fly you down.' He was on £42.50 a week, saved up, and flew me down on EasyJet. I was buzzing. We didn't have mobiles. I used to lie on my mam's bed, near the phone, and he'd ring once a week from his digs. We used to write letters to each other. Loads. I've got them all and Michael's got all mine. He used to write me poems. When Michael came home, we'd have a party at his house or my house.

I stayed at school, did my A-levels, and then I thought, *Well, I'll stay in Newcastle and do my degree in Business Administration.* I always wanted to wear a gorgeous suit to work or be on the stage! When I moved down south I tried doing some accounting, and danced quite a bit in shows and pantomimes. But I knew that, being with a footballer, might mean having to move and I needed to find a skill that I could use wherever we went. I got into Pilates after learning about it from Michael who had been doing it to recover from an injury. I loved using the flexibility I learned through dance to help people, whatever their age. In the end, we converted the garage into a studio. All the little old ladies loved it and it was dead nice to feel you've achieved something. I did have to sacrifice pretty much everything, all my dreams, but I never resented it, not at all. Michael always made me feel like we're a team. Our parents always say, 'It's not just about Michael. It's about you as well. Michael couldn't do a lot of the things he does if you weren't here to hold the fort.'

Michael: I'm aware of the sacrifices that Lisa's made for me. Before I came to United in 2006, I felt bad saying to Lisa, 'We're going up north.' She'd built up a good little Pilates practice, made loads of friends and a life away from her family who she's extremely close to. It wasn't that I took her for granted at all, it was a case of, what else do you do? We headed up in convoy, Lisa in her car and me in my tiny Aston Martin with the smallest boot in the world filled with all my clothes. I never went back to our house. Lisa came up for a few days and then went back to Theydon Bois to organise selling the house, packing it up and moving our life to Manchester. It's things like that I appreciate her doing no end.

Lisa: Just before we moved to Manchester, I went to the World Cup in 2006, and when I got to Baden-Baden, I went to the hotel all the families were staying in.

Michael: The families of the players stayed in Brenners Park and it was madness. When the players had days off, and popped down there for the afternoon, it was carnage. There were photographers outside, reporters inside. There was one bar in the town, Garibaldi's, where a lot of families met up.

Lisa: Oh God! I rang home and said, 'Mum! Bring some clothes! All the girls have dead nice clothes. I haven't got anything.' I only really knew Carly Zucker, Joe Cole's girlfriend from West Ham. I also sort of knew Cheryl Tweedy, because I used to dance with her when I was younger. I didn't know Coleen Rooney, but I'd say hello to her and the others. I got on well with everyone. At the time it was, like, 'I'm nipping to H&M. Does anyone want to come?' That was why there'd then be a group of us, just going out. It was either that or sit in the hotel and eat off the asparagus menu. We'd go to that bar Garibaldi's. But, oh God, the next thing I knew I was on the front page of *The Sun*, lifting up the World Cup with Neville Neville in Garibaldi's! We weren't doing anything wrong. We were fans and were excited like any other England fan at a World Cup. Somebody passed the World Cup to us, set us up, so it seems. There were these guys who said they were from the hotel. But they took a picture of us. I didn't know people would take pictures. Somebody rang from home, and said, 'There's something in the papers.' I was, like, 'What do you mean there's something in the papers?' It just would never have occurred to me that someone would even want to take a picture. Still, even now, I'm, like, 'Why would you take a picture?' The girls had never been photographed like that before, and what's wrong with dancing on tables anyway? I was obviously worried when I saw it, and thought that Michael and all the England lads would be really annoyed. So, I'm ringing Michael and I'm, like, 'Are you annoyed?' He said, 'No, not really, you've done nothing.' To think that someone would believe I'd do anything to spoil the lads' chances. I was mortified. We're there to support them.

Michael: It was quite sad, really, because for Mam and Dad, Graeme and Lisa, they were simply there to enjoy going to the World Cup and watch me play. It's not their fault someone wanted to take a photo. Lisa got passed the World Cup, they take a picture. When you look at it from the way it's portrayed, I could see why people thought it was a circus. It looked like a circus, didn't it? But it was the press who made it a circus.

Lisa: It totally wasn't like that at all. All of a sudden, we couldn't leave the hotel. It was horrible. We were frightened to enjoy ourselves. There were pictures every time we did anything. I honestly didn't think that cameras would be hiding everywhere we went but they were. I went to play tennis one day, and there were photos of that. In the end, they had to put screens up around the hotel.

Michael: After the World Cup…

Lisa: We went to Barcelona for my hen do. Loads of us, the girls, my mum, Michael's mum. We stayed in Sitges and danced all night, it was amazing.

When we started organising the wedding we lived in London, so we chose Stapleford Park in Leicestershire because it was halfway between London and Newcastle and because it's beautiful.

Michael: I was in one of the cottages with the lads, had a meal in the golf club, a couple of beers and got back to the cottage about 11.45pm. I was so sensible. I thought I'd get myself to bed and be fresh and ready for the big day. A lot of the others carried on to the hotel bar. The next day I heard it was the best sing-song ever.

Lisa: I heard it! My room was above the bar. I actually went down and said, 'Right, seriously, I'm getting married tomorrow, can you go to bed?'

Michael: Apparently, Lisa snapped! A lot of the lads were dying the next day!

Lisa: Everything went to plan on the day. Michael turned up! I was on time at the church, St Peter's, in Wymondham village nearby. I'm always on time. I was so excited, I couldn't wait to get down there to St Peter's. Michael's speech was amazing. He doesn't speak much, but when he does, he does it well.

Michael: I just wanted to talk about Lisa, and thank her. I wanted to talk about Mam and Dad, and thank them for all the sacrifices and advice, and all of a sudden it was quite a long speech.

Lisa: We hadn't practised our first dance. It was Bryan Adams' 'I'll Always Be Right There', the live version. It was just the song that summed up how we felt. We didn't leave each other's side all night. Actually, we didn't leave the dance floor. We finished up about 3am, and had a sing-song back in the bar. My brother serenaded us with Elton John's 'Your Song'. Then Sunday we had a BBQ, so we could chat more with everyone then. It was the perfect weekend.

Michael: I went back to Stapleford for the first time in 2017 before going to Burghley for the horse trials with Louise. We've got a picture of Lisa on the stairs at Stapleford in her dress, and Louise re-enacted it. The only bad thing about the wedding was a picture someone had taken on their mobile phone from the side of the bar, of Robbie Keane with his tie round his head, ended up in the paper. Our families were mortified, 'Who's done that?' There was no chance of us selling our wedding. Not for us that. I'm quite private. So that's why our families felt so disrespected that someone had sold that picture. It was a family do. I wasn't that fussed but my parents, and Lisa's, are old school. It was the only picture that got out, apart from the ones at the front of St Peter's.

Lisa: The weekend that we got married, Steven Gerrard got married and Gary Neville got married, so the papers and TV made a big thing of it. There was loads of press outside St Peter's. We agreed to do one quick picture as we were walking out the church to the car.

Michael: On the Monday, we went on our honeymoon. A week in Bora Bora in the Leeward Islands, then four days in Vegas. Wayne and Colleen were there at the time, so we met up with them.

Lisa: We got a call in the hotel room in Bora Bora from *The Mirror*. I don't know how they found us. The only way must be checking flight plans. 'Can we have a comment on the wedding?' they asked. I put the phone down, then panicked in case we were being watched. It was a horrible feeling. We've made a conscious decision to keep a low profile. A lot of people might think Michael's quite anti-social at times, because we say 'no' to so many events or parties. We have our family and school friends, too, that's more than enough for us. We go out in couples with the older United lads. That's our gang, having a good craic, a sing-song, and nobody's coming in. Michael doesn't get girls coming up to him, really. I don't worry, anyway. I'm way more fun, so it's fine. Michael's my best mate, and the best husband. I don't really go on holiday without Michael, especially now with having the children – I want us to share amazing experiences together, making memories. I know and understand how committed Michael is to Manchester United. Like everything he does, he gives it 100 per cent dedication. He's a complete professional.

Michael: Lisa calls me cold. If we win, I'm not coming and bouncing around the house. Inside I'm proud of playing well, winning a big game but I'm not one to then be going to Lisa, 'How good was that?!!' I like to keep the feeling inside, and there was no better feeling than winning with Manchester United.

Lisa: Louise and Jacey loved it when they took Michael's FA Cup medal in for Show and Tell at school.

Michael: I said to Lisa, 'I don't think they should take it in, because it's, like, showing off.'

Lisa: I was, 'Let them take it in, man. You're not showing off.'

Michael: I was worried that everyone else would be thinking, 'Who does he think he is?' In the end they took it in, and it was harmless.

Lisa: Louise and Jacey went round all the classrooms. They stood up and spoke about it. They love football.

Michael: Louise and Jacey came on the pitch and have looked back at pictures but were maybe too young to remember the League wins. The FA Cup meant so much to me and the family, and they came in the changing room after we won the League Cup in 2017. The kit men were in there packing up the stuff.

Lisa: They love the kit men. They just love singing with them, all the United songs. Jacey's a bit of a lunatic. They sing Michael's song. The three of us were singing it at Wembley at the top of our voices, and then the kit men joined in. We were waiting for Michael.

Michael: I had a drugs test, that's why. They were waiting outside the doping room, dancing around and singing. And then the kit men came, and we had the trophy, and just carried on singing 'Woke up this morning, feeling fine; Got Man United on my mind...!' There's only so many of the lads that really know United songs now. So, when you're having a big sing-song now, it's all the staff. The kids love it. It was like after we won the FA Cup, when, at 2.30am in the Corinthia hotel in London, Jacey, Louise and Ashley Young's kid were singing United songs, and dancing around the bar with the Cup. They're proper die-hard fans. Louise was standing on a chair and they were singing, 'We're the famous Man United and we're going to Wembley'. They never swear, do they?!

Lisa: Jacey's going on 'the pitch' with Georgie Best!

Michael: Jacey comes into training with me at times. He goes off to see the kit men and chef. Jacey loves them. They're all proper Reds. He gets high fives. He respects where he is but he's comfortable there.

Lisa: Louise wanted Jonny Evans' boots. She used to love him. Louise has DADDY on the back of her shirt.

Michael: Jacey just loves Rashford. He got his boots. He's got RASHFORD, MARTIAL and POGBA shirts. Jacey loves his players and I'd never discourage him to play if that's what he wants. It would be a lot easier for him not to be a footballer because to be judged all the time is hard. There's pressure. It can be difficult to go out with the kids. It can be relentless with people asking for autographs. If I'm with the kids or we're eating, I want some peace.

Lisa: Michael did practise his autograph! When we do go out, people come up all the time. I almost get pushed out of the way as they come up and ask for a picture with Michael. So I say, 'Do you want me to take the picture?' I've taken loads of pictures.

Michael: I tell her not to but she always does. She's there going, 'Smile!' If sometimes I'm not in the happiest mood, Lisa will go, 'For God's sake, will you just cheer up and smile.'

Lisa: I wouldn't want to go to the Trafford Centre with Michael. He rings up, like, 'Oh, my God. I hate shopping on my own. I've just been playing hide and seek in Selfridges. I'm actually hiding behind a clothes rail!' I just said, 'Get out now!'

Michael: I hate going into shops on my own. I feel so uncomfortable. People stare. Some follow me. I just say, 'Ask for an autograph and then let it be.' Whereas some people will walk round behind me. I hate it. I tell you what I really don't like is when someone shoves their phone at me and says, 'Speak to my mate' or 'Speak to my son'. Before my testimonial, Louise actually said, 'Dad, I don't want you to retire really.' When I was in hospital in October 2017, Louise wrote me this card, 'Dad, keep working so we don't have to get jobs off Mummy.'

Lisa: Michael's focus is totally football. Michael's the same whether he's won or lost. Quiet. He's already preparing mentally for the next game especially in the Fergie era. If United lost, we wouldn't go out after the game. Michael doesn't think it's right. If people see him out, Michael feels they might be thinking, 'You're not taking it seriously'. I do get upset. I was watching the game against Olympiacos in 2014, and they'd lost. Michael's such a role model and so respected that he always gets sent out for those difficult interviews after defeats because he does them well. I was getting really annoyed. Roy Keane was in the television studio and was critical of Michael's interview, and that upset me.

Michael: I'm fine doing those interviews. Speaking after we've lost doesn't bother me. We'd just been beaten by Olympiacos away, 2–0, in the Champions League last 16. There's nothing I could say, really. Roy said something about the interview being flat and criticised the performance, which was fine. Lisa took it to heart. So, she reacted, and tweeted. I didn't even know what Lisa tweeted about Roy.

Lisa: That he was such a knob. But I didn't put that. I put ****. That's what I was thinking. Although, I don't think he is, really. I don't even know the guy. I was just dead upset that Michael had done the interview, and it was a decent interview. 'Fair play to him,' I was thinking. 'It must have been really hard doing that.' I fired off a tweet. I was really upset. Oh, my God, the reaction! I can't believe people were so nasty.

Michael: You felt the power of social media. It can be brutal. I get that all the time! I was on the coach, and Lisa was on the phone, crying her eyes out, 'I'm so sorry. I can't believe I've done this, and put you in this position.' It didn't bother me one bit.

Lisa: So, I deleted it. I did another tweet. It just said, 'Sorry. Tweet deleted. Emotions got the better of me.' I don't think I slept for three nights. I couldn't do Michael's job because I'm a worrier. I'd hate to be famous. I'd hate to say the wrong thing. I'd hate anyone to think that I'd genuinely meant anything bad. I like to think I'm quite nice. I haven't really got any enemies. And then someone buzzed on the gate. It was a reporter from the *Daily Mail*, wanting Michael. 'Oh, sorry, he's not home.' I hate that.

Michael: Lisa's a great wife, not materialistic at all. If it was all gone tomorrow I really don't think that would affect her that much.

Lisa: Not at all. I'm here for Michael and the family.

Michael: She's amazing and so supportive. She suffers the ups and down with me and has been there the whole way. I'm a very lucky man. We never argue but Lisa is competitive, badly competitive. She says to me, 'I couldn't play football. I couldn't keep my head.' She'd get sent off! She's not fiery, aggressive or loud, but if we're playing a game of snooker or pool, she's devastated if I beat her. I'd never let her win, no chance! Lisa says, 'I wish I was as calm as you!' I've always felt guilty that Lisa's not been able to have the career she wanted. Even now, Lisa gets irritated as she wants to feel like she's doing something. Lisa's not one of those people who's happy just sitting around the house, doing nothing. She's doing more and more with the foundation and she's brilliant at that. She's given up an awful lot to let me have the career I have had. Lisa's a great mum too.

Lisa: Michael's the best dad ever. Everyone says it. He's brilliant with everybody else's kids, too. He gets on with all the kids in the family. He loves my brother's.

Michael: I love kids. I had such a nice upbringing and I just want my kids to be as happy. My career has dominated the family house for all these years, but we never let it get in the way of the kids. With the kids' stuff, it's madness sometimes, rushing here and there, which is just what parents do for their kids. If Louise is doing a horse show and I've been out with Jacey and I can still get to the horse show for half an hour, I'll make sure I get there. I'll drive however long. I'd 100 per cent sacrifice myself to get there. I learned that from my parents. My mam taking us on three or four buses and Dad driving from anywhere to see me play. We are conscious of the bubble they can live in. We'll choose the best school for Louise that suits her. I don't want to destroy her by pushing her. We want her to be where there's less pressure. She blossoms when she's comfortable and happy.

Lisa: My mam was out with Louise on her bike in Wallsend and she said, 'Mummy and Daddy were so lucky they grew up round here and they could do all this.' Living on a country road here with no paths, she can't walk here because of safety. We always talk about what we had, or didn't have, growing up. We try every day to keep the kids grounded. I've taken them to CenterParcs, been in a caravan – the kids love it. We're lucky we can have nice holidays at some amazing places. But the kids' best holidays are in a tent or a caravan. Brilliant! We always try to take one two-week holiday for the four of us in June. That's the only time we can all be together and Michael can come. These times are very precious to us. We're having room service nearly every night, because Michael's up training early every morning. He goes to the gym and is back for breakfast by 7am, and we're all together as a family.

I'm so proud of Louise and Jacey, because the first thing the teachers say to us at parents' evening, is they're both really kind and really polite. I'm, like, 'Right, great. We've done our job right.' Manners is a big thing for us. Pleases and thank yous. It shows respect. We're quite strict. Kids have far too much these days. Louise has only just got my old phone. We won't let her near Instagram. Jacey hasn't got a phone.

Michael: If Louise and Jacey don't say 'thank you' or 'please' in a restaurant that really gets to me. 'What do you say then?' 'Oh, thank you!' Good. If the kids go on their own, I'll ask the waiter, 'Did they say 'please' and 'thank you'?' And he'll go, 'Yes, yes, they were good.' 'All right, brilliant.'

The kids can wind me up. They press a button that tips me over. I try hard to stop myself most of the time because they're only kids. I'll say something to Jacey, and he doesn't answer me, and then I say it again, and all of a sudden I just snap. It's like his shoes. Jacey comes in from school and dumps his shoes, and I'm like, 'Any chance of you taking your shoes off and putting them in the cupboard?'

The kids are in a small village school. There's a great mix of kids from different backgrounds. It can be difficult for them, especially a couple of years ago when United weren't playing so well and I felt for the kids, especially Louise. She'd never come home crying or whingeing about it, but she'd mention someone said something. Like, 'Your dad's rubbish. He shouldn't play.' It hit me. She shouldn't have to go through that. She's the front for our family. I speak to Louise and Jacey now about things that go on in the schoolyard. The teachers can't keep hold of everything and some kids get picked on. But getting through those tough few days, or weeks will help them in the long run.

I can deal with it no problem. Criticism and attention is what I'm used to. But I didn't give much thought to my kids having to suffer it too – until it happened. It's a lot for them to have to deal with. I feel guilty about putting them in that position. It's not really fair on them but they handle it great. I'm sure they give a bit back!

Lisa and I talk about the future. I always thought I'd come out of the game for a bit after retiring, just for family reasons. But José asked us to go on his staff. It's a helluva opportunity.

Lisa: I think Michael will be an amazing coach. I never thought he'd take time out after stopping as he loves football too much. We love having Michael around, but it's work. He needs it, really. Michael's got so much to give.

APPENDIX II

CONVERSATIONS WITH MY PARENTS

Lynn: When Michael was about 20 months old a health visitor said to me, 'I think Michael has a problem with his legs.' I could see he was a bit knock-kneed but he was walking OK and thought once his nappies came off he'd walk a lot better. Michael was sent through the proper channels to the hospital by the health visitor and we went to see a consultant and he confirmed that he thought Michael had a problem. Nothing had prepared me for what the consultant then said to me. He said, 'If we go ahead and have corrective surgery it carries a very high risk and Michael could end up in a wheelchair.' Wow, that came as a shock. I said, 'There's no way that Michael needs to be considered for surgery.' As far as I was concerned, he was walking and running around like a normal toddler and he had started walking at 10 months old. Michael would never have been to see this consultant if I'd not been referred by the baby health clinic. All these years later when we look at his career and what he has achieved, we think how it could have been all so different. Where would Michael be now if he'd had that operation? He would not have had the career. Yes, he was knock-kneed. But nobody's perfect.

Vince: Michael never knew he could end up in a wheelchair until we told him much later on. I said, 'Hey son, is that how you bend a ball because of your knees?! When you take a free kick, son, is that how you get more bend on it?!' Michael always had a ball at his feet or was watching games as a kid. We used to watch videos of the great players all the time at home. George Best was my hero. I'd seen him in the flesh when Manchester United came to St James' Park. I was in the Gallowgate end. I looked at Best playing and went, 'How did you do that?! How did you get past four players?!'

Lynn: One day when Michael was in first school, he came out of school asking, 'Mammy, all the boys have sports bags, can I have a Liverpool one?' I replied, 'You have your "A-team" bag but when Daddy gets paid we'll see what we can do.' The next morning he went happily to school. When Michael came out of school later on that day it was, 'Hi, Mam.' He threw his 'A-team' bag on to the shopping tray of Graeme's pram. Michael seemed a bit flat and quiet. We chatted as we walked home from school, then the bombshell hit. When I went to take Michael's bag from the pram, the handles were pulled away from the stitching at both sides. Michael looked at me when I asked what had happened to his bag. He said, 'There was an accident with it at school.' So I kept calm and said, 'You mean you and your friends pulled the handles very hard until they came away from the stitching.' 'All right, yes Mam, that's what happened. Does that mean I'll get my new sports bag?' 'No. You'll now have to wait a lot longer for your new bag.' I never got angry or annoyed with Michael, we just carried on as though nothing had happened. He went out into the garden and played with his friends. Dad came in from work, we had our tea and I mentioned about Michael's sports bag and that he was sorry. Michael went to bed as normal then I took his bag, got a needle, thimble and thread and stitched the handles back on. I had sore fingers, but his bag was as good as new. The next morning Michael and I were walking to school and he said, 'Mammy, are you going to buy me a new sports bag today?' 'Not today, son.' I gave him his mended bag from under the pram and said, 'Maybe when Dad gets paid.' I was surprised as Michael made no fuss, took his bag and ran into the schoolyard. Later that week he did get his Liverpool sports bag but on our terms, not his. When we talk and laugh at this story, I cringe with embarrassment. Did I really do that to learn Michael a lesson? Yes I did and when he received his new bag it meant so much more to him.

You know when boys get to middle school and all they want to do is wear their football strip, it sends you crazy. So, after morning upon morning of having the same discussion about wearing the footy shirt under the school uniform, one morning I snapped. I calmly went to the bedroom window, opened it wide and threw Michael's full football strip out into the garden. Michael was shouting, 'No, no that's my favourite strip.' He ran down the stairs to pick up his scattered shorts, socks and shirt that were lying on the grass. After picking up his strip I said to him, 'It has to stop. There's a dress code for school.' I would not give in but Michael could always have a football shirt in his bag and after PE in the afternoon he could keep it on. You could say we met halfway on this one!

Michael started getting well known and when he was 13 we were asked by the BBC about Michael doing the TV show *Live & Kicking*. We were hesitant because we didn't want to push Michael into anything. He did it and said, 'That was all right!' Michael never made a fuss. In the show, Michael has a go at me for not doing his boots well enough. 'You've missed a bit!' he said. Cheeky monkey! It was only because Michael used to make a mess of cleaning his boots. It was a standing joke at home. If Vince wasn't there, it was me that did them. Michael did have a trick with his boots. He used to put Dubbin or Vaseline on the bottom of the boots so the dirt would drop off after he'd played.

Vince: Michael didn't really have any other interests. He enjoyed hanging around with his mates and just loved playing football, whether at the Boys Club for the school, county or whoever.

Lynn: As Michael got older, there were different little things in the paper about him but he never tried to be better than the other kids. Some talented kids go, 'I can do this and I can do that', and make children from the other schools look inferior. Michael never did that.

Vince: If Michael's school or Wallsend Boys Club were winning 5–0, Michael would deliberately try not to score or he would pass to a mate.

Lynn: That's the way we brought Michael up. We told him, 'You show respect, you get respect.' Manners are very important to him. Oh, but Michael swearing on the pitch, that's a pet hate of mine. We don't use language in the house, never have done. That's my upbringing, and that's from church. I'm in the Salvation Army and in the Salvation Army, you don't use foul language and you don't gamble. I wear uniform, so I've chosen not to drink alcohol. Vince isn't wearing uniform, so he goes out for his pint, which is totally acceptable. Everyone swears at games and I just hate it. Michael's two children are pretty good. If Louise or Jacey say, 'Oh, for God's sake', I'll turn and say, 'Pardon me?' And they say, 'I know, Grandma, sorry. Oh, gosh.' Michael went to the Salvation Army when he was young. He didn't choose to wear the uniform and that was absolutely fine, but I took it a step further because that's the way of the founder William Booth. Michael read the Bible and said his prayers before bed. He did the nativity in his shepherd's outfit, with a dressing gown and a tea towel around his head. Michael looked after Graeme on stage and held his hand. Michael nurtured Graeme from day one.

Michael and Graeme have got the basics of how to live their life, they know right from wrong. They aren't perfect, but hopefully they have good values. Footballers are role models on the pitch, and children watch them from an early age. Michael watched *Match of the Day* with Vince. He stayed up too late to watch it. Our Jacey tried to spit once or twice. I said, 'Well, you don't really see your daddy spitting,' but he could mention the players that did.

Vince: Whatever you do on the pitch, kids are going to copy. What was said at the Boys Club was that, 'Managers manage, parents are just spectators.' If anybody gets out of line using foul language, they'd be asked to leave or go back 100 yards. Off you go. One night, at the Wallsend Schools Football Presentation, the Wallsend Town manager, Mr Graham, said to Michael, 'Was your granddad called Owen?' 'Yes.' 'Well, my dad was in the same class as your granddad.' 'Never!' 'Oh yeah, they won loads of things. Your granddad was a good footballer.' Michael and I talked about it afterwards. I knew my dad had been a decent player but he never spoke about it. About a week later, I got a letter from the Wallsend manager's dad, and he said, 'By the way, Michael's granddad had trials for England in 1938.' I said to Lynn, 'Get my dad's birth certificate.' We looked at the date. 1920. It tied in. Then the war broke out in '39, so it went kaput. Michael's granddad was on HMS *Rodney*, the ship that helped sink the *Bismarck* in 1941. I've got a photograph of me dad in his shorts right next to the big 16-inch guns. When I captained Gateshead Boys and played for Durham County Boys, my dad would come and stand on the touchline, just watching, and he'd say nothing until afterwards. He'd then say, 'When you get the ball, switch it. Put it just inside the full back so the winger can run on to it. Get a bit of pace on it. The full back is turned.' It's funny because Michael does just that.

Lynn: Vince's dad loved nothing better than going to see Michael play at the Boys Club. He died when Michael was eight. That was the one wish we'd had, to have him see Michael play. Football's always been in the family. Michael's great uncle John played for Millwall.

Vince: Right up until we got married, I played. I broke my leg in 1979, a double fracture, and one of the lads goes, 'Run it off.'

Lynn: They dumped Vince at the front door. He wouldn't go to the hospital.

Vince: I thought it was just another knock. The next morning, Lynn calls the ambulance, I'm lying in the ambulance and this paramedic goes, 'What size football boots do you take?' 'Why?' 'If they're size nine can I have them? Because you'll not be using them again this season.' I still play now, at 66, at the Boys Club. I still show them one or two tricks! Michael loved the Boys Club. He played there from five to 16. But he struggled with growing pains, especially aged 13, 14, when there were scouts at the door all the time. Then for about six months, a year, when he was 14, 15, everyone outgrew him, he wasn't playing well and the scouts stopped knocking at the door. Michael had always been the best and then, at that stage, he wasn't. He also had a late birthday, being born in July, and so was always playing catch-up. Then Michael grew, and it came back to him again. And the scouts returned. One club offered to clear our mortgage if Michael signed for them. I said, 'No.'

Lynn: I told the scout, 'I wouldn't sell my son.' We didn't tell Michael until later. 'Mam, Dad, why didn't you tell me? I would have gone to that club if you got your mortgage paid.' And we said, 'No, because you wouldn't have been comfortable or happy there.' We know a lot of boys who got offered different things at different clubs, and none of them are playing football. Michael went round many clubs. 'I don't like Arsenal because of the dormitories,' he said. He didn't like Chelsea because he got his watch pinched. Newcastle were offering him different things. 'We can put something in the drawer for later,' one scout said when he visited the house. I said, 'No way, you can go out now because that's not the way we work.'

Vince: But we liked West Ham and trusted them. We'd take Michael to Central Station. He had to go down every six weeks.

Lynn: Harry Redknapp was good, wasn't he? He used to write when Michael first started, saying, 'Michael's so grounded. He comes from a nice family.' Vince and I were going, 'Well, you don't normally read things like that.' Harry told us that Tony Carr and Peter Brabrook, who looked after the kids, would tell him, 'Michael doesn't have to show any aggression. He just gets on with it and takes it to the next level.'

Vince: Michael liked West Ham so much he ended up signing. When he signed his first pro contract at 17, Michael didn't have an agent. We talked to their director of youth development Jimmy Hampson, who goes out of the blue, 'What signing-on fee do you want?' I looked at Lynn. 'Signing-on fee?' Jimmy said, 'Yes, what signing-on fee do you want?' I had all of five seconds to think. I went, '£30,000.' Top of my head. Jimmy goes, 'Hang on a minute.' And he went outside. I was thinking, 'Have we done the right thing here? £30,000, man!' Jimmy came back in after about 10 minutes on the phone, walking up and down the outside of the house. He goes, 'Right. Michael's got his £30,000. £10,000 a year for the first three years at the beginning of the season.' And I went, 'Oh, all right!' If you don't ask you don't get. I hadn't a clue to be honest.

Lynn: When Michael got to 16, he was going away to West Ham, and I wasn't ready. It was tough, losing him. The comfort was he was actually being looked after. He went to Pam and Danny's at first, going into a nice home, being fed and watered. It stopped him eating rubbish. Not that he ate loads of rubbish, but dinner time at high school, they'd go out down the main street. When it came to diet for Michael, he knew he had to look after his body.

Vince: Michael could have gone away earlier, to Lilleshall. But he just didn't feel comfortable there, and didn't try in the trial match. I can fully appreciate why some lads can't be away from home. I trained with Middlesbrough for six weeks when I was 15 and they put us in the reserves instead of the youth team. I was playing up against Willie Maddren, a really good central defender who should have played for England, and Eric McMordie, who came over from Northern Ireland with George Best. They were class players and I struggled. I was in digs in Middlesbrough but I couldn't hack it so I came back.

Lynn: Vince worked hard. When people say, 'Oh, well, it's all right for you and Vince because you've got Michael,' I go, 'Whoa, one minute. Don't underestimate what Vince has done for his family. He worked all those hours.'

Vince: I couldn't get a job locally, so to look after Lynn, Michael and Graeme, I worked on the nuclear power stations all over, starting in Hinkley Point, Somerset – seven days a week without a break, 90 hours. I used to bring plastic containers of Scrumpy back! Then it was Sellafield. It was dangerous, aye. I had a Gamma com and if you collected too much radiation, they stopped you working in the reactor. Working away, I missed out with Michael and Graeme when they were little. One day, I was working 180 miles away at Hunterston B power station, near Largs in Ayrshire, and Michael had a Boys Club Presentation Night at the Grand Hotel at 7pm. Usually they put the younger ones on first, so I left at 4pm and got there at 7.30pm, but they put Michael on first, so I missed him. I got back in the car and went back to Largs. A few times, I left work, drove to West Ham, watched Michael then drove back through the night.

Lynn: Often on a Saturday, Vince would be working even just at Torness, up the coast, and he'd come down, pick me up at 5am and we'd go down to West Ham. We'd have our breakfast in a café in Barking at 9am.

Vince: The chap used to know me by my first name. 'Hi Vince, full English?' 'Yes, go on!'

Lynn: Then we used to go to Chadwell Heath for 11am and watch Graeme when he joined West Ham. Loads of clubs wanted Graeme, again offering cash and contracts, but he chose West Ham. 'They treat us as Graeme, not Michael's brother,' he told us. Everywhere else he went, they were, 'Oh, this is Michael Carrick's brother.' After watching Graeme, we'd go on to see Michael at Upton Park, then drive back, get home at 2am, so that Vince was ready to go to work first thing. And we left knowing Michael was loving it down south at West Ham.

Vince: When we went to penalties in Moscow, everybody was standing up. I stayed sitting on the groove on the flipside of the seat. There was this little chap in front of me, and there was a gap, and the only gap I could see was the 18-yard box. It was like tunnel vision to that goal. And it just happened to be the goal where they were taking the penalties. Lynn goes, 'Michael's taking a penalty.' And I went, 'No, Michael doesn't take penalties. You've got that wrong. It'll be Giggsy or somebody.' 'No, no, Michael's taking a penalty. Vince, calm down.' Then, I could see Michael go to the penalty spot. 'Michael, hit the target,' I was telling myself. 'Don't shoot wide, don't pull past the post, don't pull it over the crossbar. Hit the target. If Petr Čech saves it, good save, but just hit the target.' And he scored. I went, 'Right, thank goodness for that.' The first thing that came into my mind was the papers cannae slate him off for missing a penalty. They can slate someone else off.

At the dinner afterwards, all the players from the different tables were getting up, one by one, and Scholesy's just sitting there. And they stood round Scholesy and started singing, 'Paul Scholes – he scores goals.' And Scholesy's going, 'Shush.' Scholesy gets embarrassed. So they started singing louder. Then who got up for the first dance? Sir Alex was waving at Sir Bobby Charlton. They both went on the dance floor with Lady Cathy and Lady Norma. It was a special moment: the fortieth anniversary of winning the European Cup and fiftieth anniversary of Munich. There were fish and chips at 3am in these little cones. The party really started at 4am in Moscow. We had to be at the airport for dead on 12.

I do get nervous watching Michael. It doesn't bother us if they lose. I tell him, 'Well, Michael, as long as you do your job, you play your best 100 per cent, it's fine. If you get beat 1-0, you get beat. Simple as. Play better.'

Lynn: We're always here for Michael, but since he went away from home, he's become quite an independent person. When football's really affected family time, I turned around a couple of years ago and said, 'I'm sick of football now, I wish it would just all finish.' Michael misses birthdays and family get-togethers because of the football. It's just taking too much of family life away. We'll go down a lot to see them, FaceTime them, they come up here and we can have holidays together but we miss everyday things. People have far worse-off jobs than Michael, like the Forces, and I appreciate that. It's just it was my mum's eightieth birthday, and she had dementia so she was in the care home near Sunderland where Michael was playing. Sir Alex told Michael and the players that they were going to a Champions League game on the Tuesday, so they were taking them straight back down after the match. 'We're having a little tea for her,' I told Michael. 'Try and come.' Michael would have only been there an hour because it was only on until 7.30. By the time he got from Sunderland it would be 6.30. But he had to go back with the team. Everybody in the family was there. The only person that wasn't was Michael. He was so near.

Vince: It's a job of work. Same as a fitter, a turner, a welder. Michael used to say, 'All right, Dad, come to the training ground, at Carrington.' 'Yes, right, OK.' Michael parked his car always facing the training area and I'd just sit in the car and watch. Sir Alex and the players would come out and all the cones would be set out ready for the first session. Sir Alex would be walking around. I thought, 'I'm not getting out.' If I went up and started speaking, I'd feel as though I'd be intruding. It wasn't my business, it's their training session. I wouldn't want Sir Alex to say, 'Well, who are you?' It's Michael's job of work.

Lynn: I can go into Wallsend, people might know who I am, but I don't tell anybody. We just keep ourselves to ourselves. We're not people who want to live our lives through Michael. Everybody knows we're proud of him, but it's his life.

Vince: He's pulled from pillar to post.

Lynn: It's not very often that Michael ever, even on holiday, lets his hair down. They go away with Lisa's brother and his wife and Graeme and Kay to Ibiza for a few days and let their hair down. If we're in the house at New Year, Michael will have a couple of drinks, but he still doesn't let his hair down.

Sometimes we'd like to go and see them, but if Michael's been away, I won't go. I'll say, 'No, this is your family time. You need that family time.' I know how precious it was when Vince worked away. So, I relate to Lisa in that respect. Jacey would come into Michael and Lisa's bedroom, lift the covers to see if Daddy's toes were there. Jacey was saying, 'Oh, my dad's away again,' and he would cry. Louise is at school where a lot of them support, naturally, Man City and Manchester United. When she must have just been about six, these boys were going on about Manchester City, and she turns around and goes, 'That's OK, you can support them, and I can support Man United, but we can still be friends.' But it is hard for the children. There's so much interest in Michael. Michael and Lisa's wedding at Stapleford Park wasn't a celebrity-staged event, they didn't want to sell themselves to the magazines. Michael said, 'I'm not doing that.'

Vince: It was ridiculous in Baden-Baden at the World Cup. Some of the reporters were actually hiring local lads to cycle round on bikes, and if they saw anybody to come back and tell the photographer and then he'd run and take a photograph. It's a job, I guess. I was talking to one photographer and he goes, 'Hi, Vince. When I get back I'm going to buy myself a Porsche.' 'Buy yourself a Porsche?' He said, 'I've got a photograph of Victoria Beckham, and it's on the front page of the papers.'

Lynn: Everywhere Lisa went in Baden-Baden she felt as if everybody expected her to be all made up. 'All I want to do is go out and have a little jog,' she said. One day she was so upset because across from the hotel there was a beautiful park but the photographers were up the trees. So she felt as if they were looking in the room so she always closed her curtains. One day it got so much for Lisa that she was in tears. There was nothing else for the reporters to write home about because all the England supporters were so well behaved. So the papers focused on the players' families. We were out quite often with Lisa, having food, and the younger ones would stay on and have a party, but would they not do that if they were on holiday anyway? There was just too much scrutiny of them. One day we went off to where the players were staying, up on the castle on the hill, and it was all beautiful and green, but the papers made it so bad that we felt as if we couldn't breathe. We're just Lynn and Vince walking down the street. They followed us round the shops. There was a time when Neville Neville said, 'Be careful when you come back to the hotel.

There's somebody in disguise.' It was a woman, and she came into the hotel, and was trying to pick up on the conversations. She shouldn't have been there.

Vince: Nev warned us. 'I've just come out because I've been sitting with Sandra Beckham and having a chat, and there were two settees back to back, and this girl came and sat and pretended to read a magazine but she was trying to listen in, aye.' So Nev moved and he said, 'Sandra's going to move to another seat and I'm going to go back in and sit beside Sandra, right? We're going to see if this person moves. Just watch.'

Lynn: So we sat beside Nev and then this woman went out, got changed and came in with a baby in a pram. A doll or something, aye. She got thrown out.

Vince: The next day, we were sitting with Paul McGrattan, Steven Gerrard's best mate, in a fairground. Paul goes, 'Hey Vince, what's that over your shoulder?' 'What?' 'You see that lady over there?' 'Aye.' 'That's the person who got thrown out the hotel yesterday.' I went, 'It's not, man. Different hair.' He goes, 'Go like that.' And Paul puts his fingers in a square so we'd just look at her face. 'It's the same face.' It was her again, aye. Another day, we were in a theme park, and Victoria Beckham asked park security to stop the photographers following her. 'No, we've checked and they've bought their ticket, so they've got the right to walk around,' the park people said. Everywhere we went there was a crowd just following us.

Lynn: Michael found the next World Cup in South Africa difficult because he wasn't playing, and Jacey had just been born. I'd had rods put in my back in February, and I shouldn't have really gone, and I said to Vince at the last minute, 'We've got to go because Michael might just need us.' Normally Lisa would have been there as well, but she was at home with Jacey and Louise. Michael was really disappointed about not playing. Michael doesn't really show emotion a lot, but this time he said, 'I don't know what I'm doing here. I've got a family back at home, and happiness, being with Lisa, getting bonded with the baby.' So that was a bit of a low one when he was there. It was a difficult time for Michael.

Lynn: We were on holiday in Spain when Michael had his heart problem. We watched the game against Burton and then Michael rang to tell us, 'I'm in the ambulance going to the hospital with the club doctor.' 'What?!' 'Don't panic, Mam, don't panic. I'm all right.' His heart! He was 289 over 300. 'We'll come back now,' I told him. 'Mam, nothing's happening until after you're back anyway.' Michael's very independent but you want to be there to support him, don't you? He said, 'No, I'm fine. I'm with Lisa.' We went and looked after Louise and Jacey and let Lisa go and see Michael. They knew Daddy was a bit poorly but they've not mentioned the operation. They try to protect the kids because there's enough going on in their little lives.

Vince: Michael told us, 'At the beginning of the season, everybody, the apprentices, everyone gets tested. First half I was fine, second half I felt a bit tired and I went to see the club doctor.'

Lynn: It's frightening just how quickly something like that can come on. After that, I wouldn't watch the game. I just watched Michael all the time.

Vince: He's had a great career. People asked me, 'Will Michael come up to Newcastle United?' I'd love to have seen him pull on that black-and-white shirt once, aye. But what he did at Manchester United was incredible, really. The good thing was when we won the FA Cup in 2016. People say, 'Well, the FA Cup's not what it was.' You ask any footballer, seriously, and they want to win the FA Cup, because they're brought up that way since they were kids. We used to put the television on at 9am on FA Cup final day and it didn't go off until 9pm. So winning the FA Cup was special. Lynn and I were just standing in the hotel afterwards, and Michael and Lisa and the kids came in. 'Here you are, Dad, that's yours,' Michael said. 'What?' 'That's yours.' He actually gave us his FA Cup medal. And the strip as well, aye. Away from Michael, I was actually crying, and I don't cry. Well, I try to be the hard man, which I'm not. But that was a touching moment. I've given it back to Michael to put in the safe. Deep down, I wouldn't take that from him, no way. But that was a beautiful thing for Michael to do.

Lynn: When we went to Michael's testimonial in 2017, I took a picture of me mam, because she'd just died the previous year, and a photo of Vince's mam and dad. 'I've taken the grandparents with us,' I said. They'd have been so proud. I've got to say I let myself really enjoy the testimonial. You could see us jumping up and down on the television. Jacey was sitting behind us, and he was so excited when his daddy scored and I turned around and said, 'Do a Dab, do a Dab!'

Vince: I was very proud, listening to Michael's little speech, thanking people. It was off the cuff. He never wrote anything down, it just came from the heart.

Lynn: People told us, people who don't normally do football, said, 'I'm putting Michael's game on because it's on Tyne Tees.' They said, 'Aah, Michael's speech at the beginning, it was lovely.'

Vince: It was special when Graeme came on. At West Ham, they'd trained together but never played a competitive game in the same team.

Lynn: Graeme was so proud. He'd been trying to train to do it. His back was killing him but he was that determined. It was a special day, and showed how well thought of Michael is.

Vince: Michael gets fan mail from China, Poland, all over the world. It goes to Carrington, and Michael gets carrier bags, and goes, 'Dad, Mam can you sort through it?' I've come back with four large carrier bags, about 1,000 letters, but that's over a period of six weeks. It's usually, 'Can I have a signed autograph?' Yes, yes, yes. There was one letter from Beirut: 'Dear Michael, I would like you to come to my wedding. I will keep a seat for you next to my best man.' It was a proper invitation! With the address in Beirut! Once I came to this brown envelope, bubble wrapped, put my hand in, and couldn't believe what I pulled out. My mam's prayer book. There was a letter that read, 'Dear Michael, your grandma gave me this prayer-book and I've had it 40 years. I think it should go back to the family.'

Lynn: Fans write 'best footballer ever' and 'we love you' to Michael. We get a lot of Chinese fans writing to Michael. The girls always send presents for him, little gifts, mini-loaves, good luck charms. There's a lot of people who don't put a stamped addressed envelope with their letter, which is fine, especially if it's a child that's written it. So many send strips for signing without an address to send it to. Somebody has spent £70 on a strip, to put CARRICK on the back, Michael signs it but there's no address. I said to Vince, 'This looks bad on Michael, because they think "well, we've sent him the shirt".'

Vince: Michael's played with some great players. Me and Lynn were there at West Ham when Paolo Di Canio did that scissors kick on the edge of the box against Wimbledon! Trevor Sinclair put the ball in and Paolo scissor kicked it into the far corner. I just stood up and went, 'How did he do that!?' There are some great characters, Paolo at West Ham, Robbie Keane at Tottenham. Robbie got the players to go out for a Christmas party and they had to get dressed up. Michael went as Superman. You've got Scholes, Ronaldo and Wayne Rooney – all at the top of the game when Michael played with them, all class players. I tell Michael, 'That's one thing you can say, Michael, you've played with the best, aye.'

APPENDIX III

CONVERSATIONS WITH MY BROTHER

Graeme: We need to place value on developing intelligent players, players who out-think as well as out-do, playing with their brains as well as their feet. We need players who are curious in their game, asking questions of their opponents, searching for an edge, dictating attacking and defending situations through skill and wit and craft, not just physicality. We need to develop players like Michael who have the courage to take the ball under any circumstance, and are full of imagination. That's the way the very best play. That all stems from kids having loads of opportunities to play, being encouraged to take risks, expressing themselves, thinking for themselves to come up with their own solutions, with the right type of guidance. You don't get that from just picking the biggest kids or by shouting at kids from the sidelines to 'get rid of it', 'hoof it', 'not in there' and 'don't pass to them if they're marked'. Why, if that's all we do, would we then think our future players could be comfortable and exciting on the ball, being able to craftily play out of, or even into and through pressure? Where I work in coaching at the FA we've been trying really hard for a long time to shift our youth footballing culture positively, but it's everyone's responsibility – parents, coaches, teachers, policy makers. Michael and I were so lucky to grow up at Wallsend Boys Club and West Ham playing creative, attacking football where a great environment was the norm.

I've always looked up to Michael. He's always been my role model. I'm four years younger, but we were always close, as we are now. We didn't fight as kids much. Michael's not aggressive. He's single-minded, competitive, really stubborn and has a strong moral compass of right and wrong. When we played in the garden, Michael would always win. He was the skinniest kid with long, gangly legs, but playing off both feet in his little Beardsley way, the way he'd twist his hips and drag the ball. From as early as I remember, Michael moved naturally, floating across the grass or the wood floor at the Boyza, always effortlessly comfortable with the ball.

I don't think people know how much Michael struggled with growth spurts and loss of coordination that came with that. It was really hard for him, especially as football was all he wanted to do.

Michael: I was all right at school, passed all my GCSEs, but Graeme was the one with the brains. He's like the Nutty Professor. I see his work and think, *What the hell is that?* But the detail is really good. I can see why he's such a good coach with the FA.

Graeme: Michael's neater, more organised.

Michael: I take pride in presenting things. I tidy. When Lisa's cooking, I'm washing the pans, so I know when I sit down to dinner, there's nothing else to wash. I'm like Dad. He'd have your cup away before you finished drinking! Lisa says to me all the time, 'You're turning into your dad!'

Graeme: You're more OCD than Dad.

Michael: If I go into a hotel room before a game and you know all the brochures they leave out? I'll shuffle them to one side. If I'm on my laptop or iPad, and I'm sitting at the desk and there's a little hotel notepad, I just shove it in the drawer so the desk's tidy. It's the little things that bother me. When I leave a hotel room, I put the covers on the bed, turn the telly off, turn the lights off and make sure the towel's in the bath not just on the floor.

Graeme: Your game's like that – tidy. You need to tidy stuff up. Everything must be in order.

Michael: If I'm watching the game, something really small would get on my nerves. 'What's he doing that for?' If I send a text, I make sure the spelling's right and that I've used capitals at the right time. If it's not quite right, it bugs me. I've just done my coaching A licence, and I kept thinking my presentation is not great.

Graeme: It is, though. You have an obsession with the colours on your chart!

Michael: Yes! I did my eight-week training plan – Premier League games, Champions League games, all in a different colour. That had to be spot-on right. At school, sometimes, the actual content was crap but the writing was neat. Do you know what I love doing, and Lisa takes the piss out of me? Do you know the symmetry thing where you draw the line down through the picture, and copy that side? It was so neat that I used to really enjoy doing that. I am neat. Sometimes, I can't leave a book on a table if it's at an angle. I need to straighten it. Sometimes, I'm tidying up and thinking, *What am I doing here?* But I can't stop. With kit, some of the lads in the changing room just chuck it on the floor. I throw it on the bench or put it next to the big bins for the kit, so the kit man doesn't have pick it up off the floor. I try and help them. I turn it the right way, I can't leave it inside out. That's me being tidy and showing respect for the kit men.

Graeme: I didn't truly realise how good Michael was until I trained with him at West Ham. One particular day stands out during pre-season 2004, shortly before he left for Spurs. I was 19, he was 23, and we were training in sweltering heat. Michael and I were on the same team, Michael in midfield and me up front, when Michael played this ridiculously impossible disguised pass with spin over 40 yards while facing the wrong direction, which landed perfectly on my chest on the wrong side of Tomás Repka, the opposing defender, putting me clean through on goal. Outrageous! All the lads just stopped and clapped! It frustrated me massively that Michael was underused by England. There were a couple of spells specifically, from 2006–09 when Michael was right at the top of European football and not getting a sniff with England, and again from 2011–14. Typically, Michael would say maybe he could've done more when he played but there were plenty of times when he played well and didn't stay in the team. I don't think he ever truly felt trusted by any of his England managers. It just seems a shame, really. Michael's properly appreciated by the lads at Manchester United, yes. By the wider game, maybe not. Michael has a uniqueness in his game. Even if two or three people are coming to press him, he's not fazed. Michael has the technique, composure and imagination to get out of it. He can play around corners off either foot. He deals with the pressure, controls the situation and not many British players typically do that well. He brings control and balance to a team. Michael just does what's right for the team. One of his biggest strengths was he could play with any midfield partner. Being with Scholesy was the best partnership he's played in, it was telepathic. Sharing the ball so much with Scholesy wasn't imposed on him, but they were on a wave length, and he loved. To Michael, feeding Scholesy when and where he wanted it, was best for the team.

Michael: I've got a genius next to me! I'd be mad not to give it to Scholesy!

Graeme: There might be times when Michael was playing with Scholesy that he wouldn't try and get the first pass. Scholesy could get that, so Michael would just move away to create space, reading the next passage of play. If he was playing with someone different, Michael would tend to get the first ball.

Michael: I'm really conscious of who I'm playing with, and how I can play to make the best of us playing together.

Graeme: Michael would just be thinking, *This is what the game needs.* I could see it from the stands. Fans often love eye-catching actions. But the way Michael plays – shifting position by five yards, making an angled supporting movement to entice an opponent out of position and opening up better possibilities for teammates or creating more possibilities and time if he receives it himself – is key stuff at the top end of the game. Culturally, we haven't valued the craft, creativity and tactical insight required to find solutions on the pitch, compared to say Spain or Germany. Michael subtly finds solutions. Michael plays passes others don't play because he doesn't finalise his decision until late. He's so comfortable with pressure, and having the technical range he's got, he'll wait until the last moment before executing. If the defender moves, he can intuitively change and go elsewhere. We speak about it loads, it must drive our wives mad. We've had the culture in English football of 'move the ball with tempo' but it can be more effective to stay on the ball that split-second longer.

Michael thinks ahead. As well as the rhythm and tempo, he'll control the opposition sometimes with a soft or fast pass. Instead of passing fast directly into a player's feet, Michael might pass it softly on an angle, forcing the receiving player to come off sideways for the ball, posing a question for the defender, whether or not to follow? If the defender doesn't follow then the receiver can turn. If the defender is attracted to the receiver, Michael can get it back with the passing line he originally wanted now open as the defender's been moved out of position. The key isn't only in executing the technique but in the thinking. He also has a rare ability to play a fast pass smoothly.

Passing forwards between opponents' defensive lines has always been Michael's biggest skill. A lot of it is down to timing and disguise.

Michael: It's not a highlight and it's not glamorous. People won't necessarily think, 'What a pass that was!' But it's the right pass, the most effective pass. I've never played a pass for applause.

Graeme: The Hollywood pass might look nice but what's the intention behind it? It might be that's the best pass at that time, and players need to have it in their armoury to unpick the lock of a packed defence, but there needs to be a reason for it and it should be for the benefit of the team.

Michael: Graeme's the first person I call after a game to talk football. Actually, he's the only one. He's sees the game the same as me. We've been through so much together, living apart for so long but staying close, always best mates. Graeme's my go-to man. He's always had my back. It wasn't easy for Graeme when his career was cut short by injury in his early twenties, but he pulled himself together when it could have gone downhill. To have him play alongside me at my testimonial was worth every single sacrifice I'd made my whole life. I was happier for him that day than for myself. He's carved out a successful career with the FA, where he's been for more than ten years now and I'm so proud of him. We have a special bond that will never be broken.

When Graeme married Kay I was best man and it was just as emotional as my own wedding. They're made for each other. He's my little brother (even though he looks older) and seeing him so happy was just perfect. I take my hat off to Kay for putting up with him. Graeme and Kay arranged their wedding for June as it was the only time I could guarantee being there. They've always put me first, but I feel incredibly guilty that the whole family has to revolve around my timetable. It's the same with birthdays. They must have been thinking, 'For Christ sake, any chance of you retiring or what?!'

APPENDIX IV
CONVERSATIONS WITH MY FRIENDS

Steven: When Mick won the Champions League a good few years ago, he called me up the following day. Given he'd just won the biggest club competition in the world, apart from a quick 'congratulations' at the start of the call it wasn't really mentioned after that. All we talked about was me catching a flight out to meet him in Majorca in a few days' time. I went out there for a week and the fact that he'd just won the Champions League again wasn't really mentioned. That's Mick. I know Mick's won nearly everything there is to win, he's captained one of the biggest clubs in the world, he's recognised wherever he goes, but he's normal. He hasn't changed. The most common comment I hear when someone finds out we're mates is, 'It's good that he's stayed friends with you.' I can never really understand where they're coming from because to me he's just Mick.

Sometimes it's a bit like he has a separate life. On one hand he's The Footballer, who does his football thing with all the circus that surrounds it, and on the other he's Mick, the bloke I've been good friends with for 25 years. Whenever I speak to Mick it's no different to speaking to Stephen, Hoody or Graeme. There's always a bit of a conversation about work, what we've been up to and general craic. He doesn't go into the football that much unless you really push him. That might just be because he knows me and Stephen aren't really massive football fans. We love an afternoon in a hospitality box though!

Mick always plays down what he does. There'll be times when Mick tells you he's been doing a 'football thing' and he'll be all over the TV or in the papers the next day because it was some big event. Football's a massive part of his life, but there's a lot more to Mick than the game. You see pictures of trophy rooms that players have built for themselves and fair play to them, they're rightly proud of what they've achieved and want to show it off. But that's not Mick. I can't remember seeing any trophies or medals on display in his house. There are some football-related photos, but you'll find far more photos of friends and family.

One thing that doesn't come across in the football world is that Mick is actually a good laugh. We've had some great times over the years and when we all get together everything goes out the window and it's like we're all 15 again! We went with Mick to the Montreal Grand Prix. It was pretty surreal, to be honest. One day I'm sat at my desk at work, the next I'm flying to Montreal where for the next few days we're guests of Red Bull, walking down the pit lane, meeting some of the drivers and watching a lot of the race from the garage. To top it off at the end of the race we're stood below the podium getting sprayed with champagne. We were then taken around part of the track in a minibus which nearly toppled over taking a corner too quickly! I half-wished it did go over – would have made a great story! On the last night everyone ended up in a club covered in Grey Goose vodka and dancing on tables. A fight broke out in the club and the manager wanted to hide Mick in the walk-in fridge for safe keeping!!

It was a pretty amazing experience and the Red Bull guys were fantastic with us. I wasn't sure how they'd take to us at first as they're probably used to entertaining the rich and famous and they ended up getting the cast of *Auf Wiedersehen, Pet*! We had the same craic as normal, just in a much better setting! It was certainly a 'money can't buy' weekend, and we're just really fortunate that Mick had been able to make those contacts. Sometimes it doesn't seem real.

Hoody: Mick's always had commitment to his mates, the people he grew up with. He's lived away from home for longer than he lived in Wallsend while we haven't moved. Yes, he was a great footballer but he was Mick first and foremost. Even though his football, and the playing demands that went with it, grew more as we grew older, Mick was still Mick. He still wanted to play football with us on the school field at the top of the street. He still wanted to knock about with us or come around to our house to play on the Sega Mega Drive or the Nintendo 64. He still wanted to be one of us – because that's who he is when you get down to it.

I look at it like this: back in the days before 24-hour sports news, sponsorship for shaving products and Twitter handles, footballers were normal, working-class people. They were put on a pedestal by those around them because they were just the same as us, except they could do something extraordinary, something we can't do. That's what made them special. I'm talking about Jackie Milburn, Malcolm Macdonald, Paul Gascoigne and Alan Shearer. We don't have footballers of that ilk any more because you can't – the world's a different place. However, to those who know Mick, know of him or support Manchester United, they do put him in that category. Me and the lads are even luckier that he's our friend. I can honestly say that I know he's a great footballer but he's an even better person. Both Mick and Graeme, plus Stephen and Steven, are all godfathers to my two kids and they're the only people I would have picked. Cheesy I know, but like five fingers in a glove, it just fits when we get together – always have and always will. I'd love to say Mick can be a bit of a shit or has fucked up here and there, but I can't because he never has been and he's never fucked up. Mick's generous and caring, loves a laugh and is always there whether you need him or not.

Nothing seems to faze Mick and also nothing seems to change him and that's a combination of a few things. Firstly, his family. Lynn and Vince are down to earth, so both Mick and Graeme were always going to be like that. They gave love, encouragement and a humility to both their lads, so they could achieve whatever they wanted but also always remember what made them and where they've came from.

Secondly, the teams Mick played for. At school, we were all surrounded by good teachers and coaches, especially our PE teacher at Western, Mr Colin Mackay, whose enthusiasm and competitiveness were infectious. He made you want to be a better person and a better player – I still thank him and I know Mick and hundreds of other lads also do to this day.

Thirdly, Wallsend Boys Club – and specifically the five-a-side leagues we played in. This place was the catalyst that made Mick into the player he became. It was a small-sided game, which meant you got more touches and had to be smart. You were performing on a stage because so many people were watching you. You wanted to win because no one discussed simply 'taking part'. No one got slated if you lost, but you certainly didn't want to lose! It was your life, what all your mates and family talked about and all you thought about. This place made you want to be the best you could be but never knocked you if you didn't quite make it. And it made Mick.

Stephen: Most of the time I forget that Mick's a world-famous football player as he's always remained the same Mick I grew up with. Football and the fame that it attracts have never changed Mick's personality.

He'll quite happily sit and have a good catch-up over a cup of tea. Sometimes you have to remember what a great career he's had.

Mick, in my eyes, is an 'exactly what it says on the tin' type of friend and that's how our group of mates who've grown up together from Wallsend like it. When we all get together it just feels like we've never been apart. Unless you ask Mick about football and the life that surrounds it he'll not even talk about it. He asks about how we are and what's going on in our lives, like work and family, or we just talk about old times and funny events we all experienced together.

From the countless hours playing football in Wallsend to winning every trophy in the professional game at the biggest club in the world – it's all a story worth writing about, but this one thought of who Mick is keeps coming back to me: Mick's a bloody good friend and person, grounded in his roots and in his very good upbringing and the ethics instilled in him by his parents. These are the things that have stayed with him through his career and family life.

We've partied in some great places in different countries and big events over the years, but it was always about his friends and family for Mick. And never the shitty sparklers on the champagne bottles and 'look at us' types in the busy club. That's just not Mick. He's our normal mate.

Michael: Bradley, Hoody and Rutherford are true friends. We live different day-to-day lives and don't see each other much at all but when we do there's no big fuss, it's like we've seen each other the day before. That level of support and friendship is very hard to come by. We're a tight-knit group and Graeme is also a big part of that. We just laugh so much when we are together. They never hassle or want things. There's no agenda. They're just mates. We can sit for hours and have a great time, talking, laughing, singing. The boys adapt to different environments but are always themselves, whether it's the Montreal Grand Prix paddock or the local pub. I love them for that. I made friends for life at school.

ACKNOWLEDGEMENTS

I'd like to thank Mam and Dad, my brother Graeme and his wife Kay for their unwavering love and support, and Louise and Jacey for being the best children I could ever have dreamed of. The support of June, Doug, Glen, Jaz and Gramps means so much to me. My friends have always been there for me. I'm indebted to all at Wallsend Boys Club and to all my managers, especially Harry Redknapp for giving me my chance, Sir Alex Ferguson for believing in me and for his huge influence over my life and career, and José Mourinho for his help and support on his coaching staff. I'd like to thank the Manchester United fans for their constant support and my adviser Dave Giess.

In putting together this book, I'd like to thank Henry Winter of *The Times* for recording my thoughts. I'd like to thank my literary agent David Luxton of David Luxton Associates and my editor Matt Phillips at Blink Publishing. I'd also like to thank the rest of the team at Blink including Charlotte Atyeo, Joanna de Vries, Katie Greenaway and Emily Rough.

Lisa has been with me the whole way. Every step of the journey. We could never have expected to be in this position as innocent fifteen-year-old school kids. I've leaned on her for help at times in a way she probably didn't even realise. Her mood and the way she sees things rub off on me and have shaped me over the last twenty years. Wow, when I say twenty years it seems like ages but in truth it doesn't feel that long. It's flown by and we've grown even closer on our little adventure. I feel so incredibly lucky to have Lisa as my wife and mother to my kids.

In memory of my grandparents, Owen and Winifred Carrick and Alma Towers.

INDEX

(the initials MC indicate Michael Carrick)

Round, Steve 256
Rutherford, Stephen 24–5, 27,
  57, 290

Saha, Louis 111, 129, 136, 209
Santini, Jacques 94–5, 96–8
Schalke FC 206–7, 208
Scholes, Paul 76, 111, 112, 117,
  121, 122, 124–6, 130, 132,
  136, 137, 145, 160, 167,
  178–9, 180, 202–3, 204–5,
  214, 221, 222, 223, 224, 234,
  246, 250, 253, 257, 261, 264,
  295, 299, 326, 351, 362
  leaves Man U 264
  sent off 136, 141
Schweinsteiger, Bastian 195–6,
  279
Scudamore, Richard 102
Sealey, Les 287
Seaman, David 73
Seedorf, Clarence 145, 295, 300
Senna, Marcos 108
Shaw, Luke 279–80
Shearer, Alan 12, 47, 70, 229,
  367
Sheringham, Teddy 75, 224,
  229
Silvestre, Mikaël 75, 111
Sinclair, Trevor 35, 63, 77, 358
Slone, Bob 9, 10, 11–12
Smalling, Chris 200, 276

Smith, Alan 'Smudger' 29, 30,
  137, 143, 232
Solskjaer, Ole Gunnar 75, 111,
  112, 137, 180–1, 251
Southgate, Gareth 219
Speed, Gary 70, 123
Stam, Jaap 75
Steele, Eric 176, 205, 256
Stephenson, Gail 134
Stoke City FC 28
Storrie, Peter 89–90
Strudwick, Tony 35, 132, 151,
  157, 172, 205, 264, 324
Suárez, Louis 245, 256
Sullivan, David 286
Swindon FC, MC on loan to
  66–9

Taddei, Rodrigo 141
Taylor, Sam 61
Taylor, Steven 12
Terry, John 44, 161, 163–4, 295
Tévez, Carlos 137, 152, 156,
  167, 174, 185
Thompson, Alan 12
Thompson, David 59
Thorman, Chris 25, 26
Tongue, Jo 296, 297
Tottenham Hotspur FC 79, 93,
  206, 291
  Champions League missed by
  103